the short story in midcentury america

the short story in midcentury america

Countercultural Form in the Work of Bowles, McCarthy, Welty, and Williams

Sam V. H. Reese

Louisiana State University Press Baton Rouge

Published by Louisiana State University Press
Copyright © 2017 by Louisiana State University Press
All rights reserved
Manufactured in the United States of America
First printing

Designer: Barbara Neely Bourgoyne
Typefaces: Berthold Akzidenz Grotesk (display) and Whitman (text)
Printer and binder: McNaughton & Gunn, Inc.

Library of Congress Cataloging-in-Publication Data

Names: Reese, Sam V. H., author.
Title: The short story in midcentury America : countercultural form in the
  work of Bowles, McCarthy, Welty, and Williams / Sam V. H. Reese.
Description: Baton Rouge : Louisiana State University Press, 2017. | Includes
  bibliographical references and index.
Identifiers: LCCN 2016027044| ISBN 978-0-8071-6576-8 (cloth : alk. paper) |
  ISBN 978-0-8071-6577-5 (pdf) | ISBN 978-0-8071-6578-2 (epub) | ISBN 978-
  0-8071-6579-9 (mobi)
Subjects: LCSH: Short stories, American—History and criticism. | Counterculture
  in literature. | American fiction—20th century—History and criticism.
Classification: LCC PS374.S5 R45 2017 | DDC 813/.0109—dc23
LC record available at https://lccn.loc.gov/2016027044

To Alexandra—my stars, my ocean

Contents

Acknowledgments ix

Introduction: "A Snail of Language" 1

1 Writing Counterculturally in Midcentury America 6

2 Mary McCarthy and the Containing Mask 53

3 Tennessee Williams and the New School of Decadence 88

4 Paul Bowles's Verbal Violence and Patterns of Words 119

5 Eudora Welty and the Photographic Capture 153

Conclusion 177

Notes 187

Bibliography 199

Index 207

Acknowledgments

This work began with a nerve-wracking phone call across the Tasman, and I owe a great deal of gratitude to Paul Giles for seeing potential in the first hesitant steps of my research. He has proven to be a patient and insightful mentor, and I am grateful for his friendship and advice. I am equally grateful to my colleagues at the University of Sydney—particularly Mark Byron and Peter Marks—for their encouragement as I developed this study. Parts of my chapter on Bowles were published, in different configurations, in the journals *Poe Studies* and *Papers of Surrealism*; I am very thankful to my respective editors, Jana Argersinger and Joanna Pawlik, for their advice on this material.

I finished this study across the world from where it began, and I appreciate all the support that my new colleagues at the University of Northampton have provided, especially Richard Canning and Janet Wilson, who have been a source of constant encouragement. I am particularly grateful to Margaret Lovecraft at Louisiana State University Press, who saw enough in this work to take it on, and to James Long, who has helped me through its final stages. I was also lucky enough to have a generous external reader, whose astute suggestions led to a more focused and effective study.

Throughout my work on this volume, I have had the help of a few other very attentive and generous readers. Thank you to Mark, Kent, and Rafe—as much for your patience as your thoughtful advice! Thank you, too, to Jo, Kathy, Jessy, Linda, Rebekah, and Kaitlyn for your support, friendship, and laughter.

This book has always been a project of love, and I owe an enormous debt to the short story writers I consider here (and to all those I don't) for daring to write in a minor key. More than anyone, though, I want to thank Alexandra Kingston-Reese, for your constant, unconditional support, and for always seeing things from your unique perspective—you give me clarity, coherence, and calm.

the short story in midcentury america

Introduction
"A Snail of Language"

As a form of expression, literature has always offered writers a way of speaking out. But as an involuted and introspective form, the short story embodies the silent, unspoken quality that also characterizes literary writing. Describing it as a "snail of language," the Argentinian author Julio Cortázar noted that the short story had earned "a place of special importance" in Latin America "that it had never enjoyed" elsewhere.[1] In the case of the United States, however, the status of the short story is more of a paradox than Cortázar may have recognized. For the short story has proven commercially and popularly successful in the United States to the point where it is acknowledged as a kind of national art form. But from the mid-twentieth century onward, it has also been increasingly neglected, even marginalized, by critics and scholars, to the point where Robert Lamb characterized it in 2010 as "something of a bastard step-child" in the world of American letters.[2]

In critical terms, the American short story reached crisis point in 1950, at precisely the moment that more volumes of short fiction were being published than ever. The political narratives of the early Cold War pushed critics toward a celebration of novelistic prose, where they endorsed expansive, open-ended fiction as representative of democratic freedom, in opposition to the formal and thematic limitations associated with Soviet totalitarianism. This led, in turn, to a broad devaluing of the short story; critics insistently misread the aesthetics of its compressed, contained form in terms of limitation and disempowerment. At the same time, however, writers increasingly turned to the short story as a way to resist political coercion and conformity in ways that few critics were able to appreciate. Interrogating this contradiction, this book is concerned with the short story as both introspective and expressive. It looks at how American writers used the confined, unspoken aesthetics of the form as a way of speaking out about freedom and open expression.

1

In unpacking their stories, through close analysis of both their prose and its conceptualization, I trace the origins of the short story's critical exile, and its relationship to the kinds of political narratives that these authors sought to critique.

I focus on four particular writers, all of whom developed a public profile through publishing short fiction during the 1940s and 1950s. Born between 1909 and 1912, Mary McCarthy, Tennessee Williams, Paul Bowles, and Eudora Welty all chose to work within the specific confines of the short story at the start of their respective careers, using it to develop a kind of fiction that was immediately recognized as countercultural, running against the grain of contemporary expectations of literary and cultural narratives. While other writers certainly inflected their stories with an air of insurgency, the short stories of these authors stand out because of their relationship to highly developed aesthetic practices outside of written literature: Bowles's career as a composer, McCarthy's criticism and memoirs, Williams's theatrical work, and Welty's photography. This book would look quite different if its subjects were, say, Vladimir Nabokov, John Cheever, and Bernard Malamud, and it makes no claims toward totality. Instead, I hope to shift the critical discourse around midcentury American fiction and provide an alternative perspective on the silent eloquence of the short story.

Unlike the other authors on whom this study focuses, Mary McCarthy did not position herself outside the critical mainstream of midcentury America, whether through exile like Bowles or regionalist focus like Welty. Best known today for her 1963 *New York Times* best-selling novel, *The Group*, which served as the inspiration for the essays and television series *Sex and the City*, she was an active member of the politicized and critically influential *Partisan Review* circle and achieved as high a profile as critic and reviewer as she did as writer of fiction. Indeed, her marriage to Edmund Wilson and work for the *New Yorker* might suggest something of the conventional, and she maintained personal relationships with many of the critics who were responsible for the limited scope of the midcentury literary mainstream. Her fiction, however, insistently undermined the critical narratives that her milieu and publication venues would suggest—driven in part by the Irish-Catholic heritage which marked her as outsider, and her own deliberate deconstruction of the boundaries between fiction and autobiography, novel and short story. It is this formal disruption, until now neglected by critics, with which I am initially concerned. Like the other authors in this study, her style is generically hybrid, moving sometimes uneasily between the formal tropes of fiction and nonfiction. Taking up McCarthy's claim that her novels were constructed as short stories but that her stories needed to be understood in the context of the larger works they inspired or were drawn from, I provide a reading of her work based on ideas of scale and representation. This needs to be measured against her own suggestion that her fictional works were divorced from the facts of her biography (but at the same time developed directly from her own experiences and beliefs). It is my contention that her writing used deliberately destabilizing formal structures as a way to critique culturally enforced normative identities and articulate an opposition to the social and political forces that demanded a rigid, nationally oriented set of beliefs. In a broader sense, with a focus on her short fiction and its relationship to her novels and criticism, I establish a way of considering her as a public intellectual, whose work is valuable beyond its biographical appeal, as an exemplar of countercultural writing.

In contrast, thanks to his critically and commercially lauded theatrical works, Tennessee Williams has occupied a central place within the American literary canon for decades. In much the same way that any critical attention on McCarthy's short stories has been subordinated to her novelistic works and memoirs, however, Williams's impressive body of short fiction has been either willfully ignored or read with constraint as a prototype for his plays. With the rise of queer studies, moreover, critics have increasingly expressed disquiet at the lack of explicit cultural critique in his stage pieces, given his profile as one of the most notoriously unorthodox and insurrectionary figures in midcentury America. By looking at his first collection of short fiction, *One Arm and Other Stories* (1948), I show how it was through his short stories, rather than plays, that Williams engaged in a structural and thematic attack on the normalizing politics of conformity and consensus. Taking up his own contention that his short fiction offered a private literary space in which he could openly articulate his own opposition to cultural narratives he saw as constraining, this chapter reads his short fiction as oppositional in terms of its compressed aesthetics and often lurid or sensational content. I also draw on Williams's abortive concept of starting a literary movement, the "New School of Decadence," reading his countercultural approach in terms of collapse and decay. In doing so, I reposition an author traditionally understood as working within a national, or sometimes regionalist, tradition, within an expanded, transnational context, suggesting links to both Oscar Wilde and the French symbolist poets. Its critical contribution is to map out the destabilizing orbit these short stories occupy around Williams's plays, as well as the heteronormative values implicit within postwar cultural criticism.

As a writer who clearly prioritized his short fiction and who consciously drew on aesthetic traditions from outside American literature in order to shape an alternative model of writing, the composer and longtime exile Paul Bowles offers the best test-case for this book's concept of countercultural fiction. Despite a popular belief that he was reticent to comment on his own work, across letters and interviews Bowles succinctly articulated the unsettling and deliberately destabilizing effect that he hoped his writing would have. I begin by sketching the terms in which Bowles's short fiction was originally received, reading this against the much more positive reception of his debut novel, *The Sheltering Sky* (1949). Departing from the traditional readings of his work, which have framed him in terms of his residence in Tangier and involvement in North African culture, I instead turn to his largely neglected involvement with the French surrealists, exploring the influence of surreal aesthetics on his first volume of stories, *The Delicate Prey* (1950). I consider this in conjunction with Bowles's prominent career as a classical composer, in order to account for the uniquely patterned aesthetic of his short stories. Bowles's short fiction explicitly sought to undermine political narratives of progress and freedom through a model of writing that drew on alternative aesthetic traditions to offer an oppositional perspective, guided by closure and claustrophobia. By sidestepping his novels and later reputation as a reclusive guru and instead considering the stylistic and political nexus that underpinned his early work with short fiction, I hope to recuperate the earlier, aggressively countercultural writer.

Where Bowles, Williams, and McCarthy were all attacked for their use of the short story and encouraged by critics to turn to longer, more socially responsible genres of writing, Eudora Welty was celebrated for cultivating a crisp and contained style. Her success as a dedicated short story writer provides an intriguing counterpoint to the politically motivated critiques of works like *One Arm* and *The Delicate Prey,* particularly given that Welty's fiction relies on a compression that is commensurate with the most tightly controlled prose of these other authors. As a reclusive southern woman, Welty has tended to be read as a regionalist writer, whose work, while precise or even beautiful, is predicated upon a fundamentally conservative southern ideology. Certainly texts like Mark McGurl's *Program Era* have read her work as a cipher for literary conservatism, within a larger configuration that understands the short story as inherently static. Welty's fiction, however, draws on a cultural and aesthetic register that extends far beyond the limitations that such a characterization suggests. Reading her short fiction through her photographic practice, I close this study by arguing that her approach to the short story approximates the process of the photographic crop, unsettling macronarratives by focusing on small details. In general terms, the contemporary critical discourse around midcentury fiction in the United States tended to align the novel with plot, movement, development, and growth, and the short story with description, stasis, and stagnation. By moving beyond such a reductive dichotomy, I suggest that Welty's decision to work within the structure of the photograph is part of an aesthetic program that uses order and compression to interrogate totalizing narratives that, on the one hand, reduce individual moments to part of a sequence, and on the other, smooth out difference while valorizing the individual. Welty's success at using the short story, despite its critical disfavor, reveals the cultural logic that led critics to ignore the social and political implications of McCarthy's, Williams's, and Bowles's attempts to speak out.

chapter one

Writing Counterculturally in Midcentury America

In his 1971 monograph on American fiction between 1950 and 1970, *City of Words*, Tony Tanner described the "abiding dream in American literature that an unpatterned, unconditioned life is possible, in which your movements and stillness, choices and repudiations are all your own."[1] Having established a model in which the desire for freedom is the underlying principle in American literature, Tanner conceived of the dream for "a genuine freedom from all cultural patterning" as the defining feature of the postwar novel.[2] While his argument could seem naïve in hindsight, oversimplifying some of the complications that the period presents, it does capture something particularly compelling about America's imaginations of itself. Indeed, it builds upon solid ground: almost from its inception, America has defined itself by its unique brand of freedom and by its progress toward greater liberty. John Dewey, writing on the cusp of war in 1939, declared that "the attainment of freedom is the goal of [America's] political history"—in a crucial sense, Tanner was capturing what was essential to America's understanding of its own history and future.[3] The idea of freedom, moreover, was to become radically charged after the Second World War, as America took on an international burden as democratic superpower, and "the American novel itself took on a new world role."[4] Previously a detached configuration, the narratives of democratic freedom and the specific literary form of the novel were drawn together systematically by critics and writers in order to explain America's past and project its future global significance.

The fate of the short story, on the other hand, was to prove paradoxical. Practitioners used the form to work subtle but incisive changes, both aesthetically and culturally, on the fabric of U.S. society; however, the critical regard for short fiction was colored by these same political concerns that saw it maligned and neglected in a way that has had lasting repercussions. But if, from a critical standpoint, the decade after the Second World War marked a decline in the fortunes of the short story, from a publishing perspective the midcentury seemed, for a moment, to be its zenith. Indeed, reflecting back on the previous year in an article from 1951, the prominent critic Leslie Fiedler noted in wonder that there had "never been so favourable a moment for the short story."[5] Despite his substantial reservations about the value of these works, he drew attention to the fact that "after years of assuring us and themselves that the publication of such books is the surest way to bankruptcy," publishing houses had nonetheless "given us a more imposing list of short fiction than we have ever seen in a comparable period" ("Style" 156, 155). Many of the collections to which he refers, moreover, bear names readily recognizable for later readers. Among the thirteen different volumes that his extended review encompasses, collections stand out by high-profile figures like William Faulkner, William Carlos Williams, Mary McCarthy, and Irwin Shaw. This roll call was further expanded by the annual anthologies of *The Best American Short Stories* and *The O. Henry Awards,* which between them featured works by Kay Boyle, John Cheever, J. D. Salinger, Saul Bellow, and Fiedler himself.[6] Tellingly, however, none of these authors, save Cheever, remain primarily recognized for their work in the form of the short story, and even in the face of this wealth of publication, Fiedler's review acknowledges the tenuous position that the short story had in his own contemporary culture. Stressing the "paucity of new writers and their quick turning away to the novel under pressure from agents and publisher," Fiedler captured the cultural and economic factors which signaled a change in fortunes for the short story; his more pointed criticism that the short story had "fallen heir to various alien obligations" gestures to the larger political concerns which formed the background to this shift ("Style" 156, 158). In many ways, his criticism replicates the cultural logic of writers like Dewey, who associated American identity with freedom and a sense of cultural expansiveness.

Indeed, Dewey's declaration on freedom ultimately proved prophetic: postwar political rhetoric conceptualized the new role of America as one of "protector of freedom." While the kind of freedom that had engaged politicians—and writers—before the war had been an individual, or at least local, one, in the power vacuum after the Second World War, America "had to assume a world role."[7] Moreover, as it found itself competing for hegemony against the Soviet Union, the concept of freedom was increasingly co-opted as part of the rhetoric of American dominance—"the claim to global authority" that "cold war American asserted . . . in a narrative that permeated most aspects of American culture."[8] This narrative relied upon a competition between two modes of existence—one free, one restricted—and the explicit equation of freedom with democracy. Turning to a speech delivered in July 1950, the same year that produced the unexpectedly (and unrepeatably) high yield of short story collections, in which President Harry S. Truman addressed the American people on the subject of the Korean War, it is clear the extent to which concepts of freedom and democracy were conflated with an ideal of America as global superpower. They were a nation "determined to preserve . . . freedom—no matter what the cost . . . for all people"; Truman's stress on America's exemplary brand of democracy, "how free men, under God, can build a community of neighbors, working together for the good of all," suggests the universal benefits of freedom and the necessity of American involvement in its expansion.[9] But perhaps most importantly, his pronouncement that "the American people are unified in their belief in democratic freedom [and] are united in detesting Communist slavery" established a polar difference between America and the Soviet Union, where America's democratic freedom rendered it an exemplary world power. America's image abroad and its own conceptualization of itself were now intrinsically tied to an identity of freedom—a freedom that was at once individual and contingent upon a democratic society.

Of course, this ideal of a shared American passion for freedom did not simply exist as an empty term in the realm of political rhetoric. Profoundly influential, it was argued for with equal force and conviction by a large body of literary critics in the postwar period who, from a liberal bastion in New York, developed a model of "ethical fiction" whose goals accorded with those expressed by Truman to an extraordinary degree. Indeed, to understand the position from which American readers approached short stories, it is important to understand the priorities associated with liberalism in postwar America. Liberalism has often been considered as a unifying feature of the American political scene in the mid-twentieth century. To this effect, Louis Hartz, in his 1955 text *The Liberal Tradition in America*, offered a narrative of American history that was characteristic of the position held more widely by a loosely associated group of

New York Intellectuals, in that it placed the concept of liberalism at the center of American culture and history.[10] Basing his argument on what he described as "the storybook truth about American history"—where the country was founded by men escaping the oppression of Europe to find freedom in a "New World"—Hartz considered the most salient feature of American society to be that "the American community is a liberal community."[11] Rather than liberalism sitting at one end of an ideological spectrum, in opposition to a conservative alternative, Hartz argued that there had "never been a 'liberal movement' or a real 'liberal party' in America" and that, instead, the belief in the primacy of individual freedom constituted the foundation for national identity: American society "only had the American Way of Life."[12] His characterization of this transpartisan ideology, where "'Americanism' brings McCarthy together with Wilson," suggests the particular importance that liberalism had taken on with the onset of the Cold War.[13] It had become the defining feature around which Americans could orient themselves against the totalitarianism of the Soviet Union, whether one aligned oneself with red-baiting McCarthyism or Wilsonian politics. Ironically, this position was itself defined through a totalizing narrative, which made authors and readers who engaged with it complicit in its logic.

The position that American critics adopted was naturally related to the larger political narratives of the period, so it should not be surprising that critics like Hartz sought to conceptualize American history in terms that reinforced this dominant ideology. Alan Nadel has noted the seductive logic of this postwar position, where "the narrative called *democracy* placed Americans in the roles of reader and viewer of a series of adventures, in which the heroes and villains were clear, the desirable outcomes known, and the undesirable outcomes contextualized as episodes in a larger narrative that promised a happy ending."[14] What is more surprising is the extent to which such critics promoted programs of novel writing that dictated the stylistic and formal characteristics of works that could be considered American. Nadel, however, astutely contends that "the boundaries between narratives of personal policy and narratives of national policy are, in fact, hard to maintain, because if our narrative of national hegemony contained both the free world and the Communist world, it also contained the readers who consumed this narrative, making them participants in the narrative by virtue merely of the fact that they had consumed it. At the same time, it also protected them by containing them within that narrative in the privileged position of readers, implicated only vicariously in the narratives with which they identified."[15] As such, the totalizing embrace of the American narrative of democracy necessarily co-opted future cultural production and implicated authors within an aesthetic program contingent upon America's hegemonic position within an international sphere.

From this perspective, it is easier to understand why American critics of this era, particularly other New York Intellectuals like Lionel Trilling and Richard Chase, positioned themselves deliberately along liberal lines and conceptualized the role of criticism in the postwar period as particularly concerned with promoting novels (as opposed to short stories) that emphasized personal responsibility and bore a close relationship to the lived experience of the American people. This emerging strain of "modern" literary criticism was designed, in Trilling's words, "to construct people whose quality of intelligence, derived from literary study or refined by it, would ultimately affect the condition of society in certain good ways."[16] Underpinning their desire for a new paradigm of fiction and criticism was a belief that, in the wake of the inexplicable violence that characterized the Second World War, contemporary society was uniquely in need of such a change. The ethical dimensions of their program were impelled by the sense that "perhaps at no other time has the enterprise of moral realism been so much needed."[17] Their perspective, however, just like the broader currents of liberalism, was further inflected by the shadow of the Cold War and the demonization of the Soviet Union as coercive and totalitarian. Geraldine Murphy has demonstrated how "formerly radical intellectuals like Trilling . . . felt it incumbent on them to deplore the 'totalitarianism' of the Soviet Union and embrace the 'freedom' of the West."[18] The concern that Fiedler expresses regarding the "alien influences" upon contemporary short fiction is reflective of this broader concerns to shape a literature that could oppose a Soviet culture characterized as restrictive and oppressive through a democratic, *American* aesthetic.

As Trilling proposed, in one of the clearest enunciations of the ambitions of this liberal criticism, society needs "books that raise questions in our minds not only about conditions but about ourselves, that lead us to refine our motives and ask what might lie behind our good impulses."[19] Literature could be a powerful tool in bettering individuals and helping to develop them into more sophisticated citizens. Trilling was not endorsing a program of self-help, however, but one of literature that could communicate something that made the individual freer. After all, as Dewey argued, in America "the idea of freedom has been connected with the idea of individuality of the individual"; fiction that could offer its readers a greater level of self-awareness would necessarily give them a greater degree of liberty.[20] Just as Truman's speech suggested that the freedom of the individual could be co-opted as part of a strategy to win greater freedom for mankind, however, Trilling and fellow liberal critics argued that literature should be leveraged to engender a greater level of freedom for society as a whole. As such, the postwar author had an obligation to engage with contemporary issues and communicate a vision for a better world, as literature needed "people who are specifically and passionately concerned with social injustice."[21] Of course, fiction could not exist in a critical vacuum or enact its social benefit without the help of a secondary apparatus. The vision of freedom that fiction could offer would be refined by the emerging strain of modern literary criticism: designed "to construct people whose quality of intelligence, derived from literary study or refined by it, would ultimately affect the condition of society in certain good ways."[22] Underpinning the desire for this new paradigm of fiction and criticism in the late 1940s and early 1950s was a belief that contemporary society was uniquely in need of such a change. The urgency of their program was impelled by a sense that at "perhaps at no other time has the enterprise of moral realism been so much needed."[23] In this light, it seems hardly surprising that critics like Fiedler should place so much emphasis on the lack of freedom displayed by the characters of the contemporary short story—the issue of freedom formed the heart of contemporary criticism's concerns.

Trilling's assertion that society was in need of moral realism, moreover, suggests a particular aspect to this model of so-called ethical literature. Ideally, it would espouse a specific kind of engagement with reality. On a superficial level, this could manifest in works that were in touch with the reality of contemporary America and the particulars of contemporary life. Such an understanding certainly reflects critics' insistence that authors turn their attention to peculiarly American subjects and turn away from the bizarre and frequently international premises that had characterized the short fiction of the previous decades. As Trilling argued, "the novel, then, is a perpetual quest for reality, the field of its research being always the social world, the material of its analysis being always manners as the indication of the direction of a man's soul."[24] Moreover, the sense that writers should be dealing with specifically American themes, presented in an idiom and with an energy that was peculiarly *American*, was charged with the ideals of William Carlos Williams, whose concept of writing "in the American grain" had, by the 1940s, gained traction. Like Benjamin Franklin, one of Carlos Williams's central American figures, the midcentury author ought to be "borrow[ing] . . . from the primitive profusion of his surroundings."[25] But critics were also demanding a more particular model of engaging with "reality." Trilling and his fellow liberal critics were deeply concerned with how the individual reacted to, received, and processed the "real world" around them, arguing that fiction ought to provide a similarly nuanced interaction. In part, this could be engendered by a return to realism in fiction; certainly, critics prioritized realistic prose, and as Malcolm Bradbury notes, after the Second World War there was a tendency of writers "moving back towards realism."[26] But this neorealism was inflected by a new sense of complexity, suggested by the experiences of war. As Thomas Schaub has argued, "the novel's relationship to social history—to 'reality'—was the central preoccupation of the critics who wrote about narrative fiction in the years after World War II." It was no longer possible to consider "reality" as a straightforward, or self-evident, monolithic concept.[27] Instead, they prescribed an attitude to reality that was at once realistic and nuanced with an awareness of the uncertainty of experience and the nebulousness of morality. They, and many of the prominent authors of the era, were "much concerned with moral uncertainty and metaphysical complexity."[28] In fact, because the novel was such a "perfect vehicle for the ironies and paradoxes of the moral life and the social history it produces," authors had an *obligation* to acknowledge the uncertainty of modern experience, to produce "a fiction deeply conscious of alienation and anomie, often voiced in the despairing intonations of modernism, yet also turned towards society."[29]

So far, my argument has focused on the liberal critics based largely in

New York and has overlooked the dissenting voices of the southern New Critics and their emphasis on technique and style. Instead, it has followed a model that understands Trilling and his peers to be unconcerned with the finer points of prose styling and attuned instead to the ideas and meaning of a text. But as Schaub so neatly emphasizes, the New York critics and New Critics were surprisingly "in accord" that "how literature achieved [relevance] relied . . . on form."[30] The presentation of the kind of reality that the liberal critics advocated relied upon extended, novelistic prose that was sophisticated and attuned to doubleness, uncertainty, and indeterminacy; their "moral realism" was as much a concept of style as it was of intent. The most prominent victim of this stylist ethos was naturalism—increasingly eschewed by authors and condemned by critics, it presented a view of the world that was labeled simplistic and, in light of the newly complex understanding of the world, actively misleading. As Schaub explicates: "During this time, 'naturalistic' methods seemed to provide too little access to how things really are or might be. In its materialism, its assumption of determinate behavior, and its documentary methods [naturalism] relied too much for its truths upon surface detail and failed to provide an adequate portrait of the inner life."[31] Because naturalistic prose was too concerned with the superficial appearance of the world and was not sufficiently attuned to the complexities of interiority or able to register deeper layers of meaning, it was seen as completely unsuited for the modern enterprise of literature. Moreover, it was unable to reflect a particular point of view and "seemed bereft of moral conviction or ideological consciousness."[32] From this position, short fiction was never going to be able to generate a perspective sufficiently nuanced to confer a sense of meaning to its reader. Given that it is predicated upon the close observation of a select number of pivotal moments, the short story form is unable to ever escape the specific, except in an allegorical register. Even then, it must necessarily elude the reflexive self-awareness that critics expected of novelistic fiction, only ever able to offer a glimpse of the possibility of interiority.

Fiedler's extended review shows the extent to which this attitude governed midcentury responses to the short story. His approach to the disparate writers he had chosen as emblematic of the wealth of short fiction published in 1950 is commensurately wide-ranging; however, his observations are drawn together through a simple coda: "we have no common agreement about what a short story is" ("Style" 156). This conceptual confusion, he argues, has led to "the over-all poverty of performance in the actual short story" by American writers, whose efforts in the form will necessarily be clumsy and abortive, given the absence of a clear understanding of the social and artistic function of the form. He does not dismiss the short story outright, then, but rather relegates it to a secondary form, juxtaposed against the clarity of purpose and style associated with the novel. The form's lack of purpose was tied, in Fiedler's mind, to its increased association with foreign traditions of writing—the "alien obligation" I noted earlier. On the one hand, he contends, such traditions have "thrust upon" the short story "certain functions of the lyric poem, most importantly the symbolic realization of an immediate emotional response," while on the other, "it has had to come to terms with various obligations of the essay, learning to take in its stride discursive and witty commentary" ("Style" 158). These demands are not only alien in the sense of being foreign but also in the sense of being false or manufactured; Fiedler notes the "impulse toward a high artificial diction, whether the result be the DeQuincyish elaboration of an Aiken, or an Oscar Wildish play of ornamental wit as in Mary McCarthy" ("Style" 159). Where the social and moral obligations of the novel were clear (at least to critics), therefore, the short story was caught between a purely aesthetic function—"the Romantic tradition of High Rhetoric, the stance of self-conscious virtuosity"—and a polemical role, completely detached from contemporary society ("Style" 159).

But Fiedler was not alone in viewing 1950 as an exceptional year for the short story—there was a wide consensus regarding both the breadth of published material and the scarcity of quality. With an ambit similarly wide to Fiedler's, Nolan Miller concluded in the *Antioch Review* that "we read, not with pity, but with embarrassment."[33] Unlike Fiedler, however, Miller emphasized the homogeneity of that era's short story writers. Noting the "the surfeit of sameness" across the volumes he considered, he found it "clear that not only characters but stories, too, come 'preshrunk' these days." Crucially, he attributed this to the emphasis on form over content in these works, whereby the "technical sureness of the stories, however remarkable, achieves a mechanical and stylish monotony."[34] The implicit contrast in Miller's analysis is with the novel, which was lionized for its ability to articulate freedom formally, by breaking free from the writer's control. The well-known critic, biographer, and social activist Irving Howe teased out this comparison explicitly in a 1949 review of several "Best of" short story anthologies. Arguing that, "unlike the novelist, the short story writer can seldom enjoy a sense of distance from his materials; he must always intrude on them," Howe explains that "the novelist, if he has any command of his craft, can count on major advantages unavailable to the story writer: the accumulated, unpredictable effects of prolonged characterization." This "advantage" meant that "a good novel" could seem to "start writing itself, breaking out of the author's clasp of intention and spinning off on its own course." From this perspective, the ideal short story was always going to fail to live up to critics' demands for formal and conceptual openness, for it was "precisely this [novelistic] freedom for his materials and this intermittent withdrawal of his creative self from the forefront of his writing that the story writer cannot risk."[35] Fiedler echoes this analysis, concluding that "the general inadequacy of the actual short story is the failure of style," both in terms of writers' "inability to achieve a critical justification of style and of a more deeply underlying inability to make enough of essential contemporary experience amenable to the control of language ("Style" 161). As Howe and Fiedler saw it, literary freedom came from a withdrawal of authorial presence; the short story's success was contingent on a formal care and patterning that precluded such openness.

　　Not all critics were so fatalistic about the possibilities of the short story. Some, like Edith Mirrielees, instead contended that contemporary fiction simply lacked sufficiently good writers. Beginning his article "Short Stories, 1950" with an assertion that mirrors Fiedler's—that "1950 was, in one respect, a banner year for short-story writers," in which "more collections of stories written by one author appeared between cloth covers . . . than in any previous twelve months in a very long time"—Mirrielees contrasts the batch of writers of 1950 with their illustrious predecessors of the modernist era, whom he identifies as Rudyard Kipling, Katherine Mansfield, and O. Henry. He notes that although, "now and then," a contemporary short story "seems to have been read and, what is more, remembered by almost everybody who reads the shorter forms of fiction," the authors of such stories "have for a considerable time poured most of their energy into novels."[36] Such a claim reiterates the epochal logic of critics like Trilling; the implication of Mirriellees's claim (also explicitly identified by Fiedler) is that there was something peculiar about the postwar years whereby the best writers were being drawn to the novel over the short story. As Granville Hicks noted two years later, moreover, this trend was driven by the broad cultural predisposition toward the novel. Although both Hemingway and Faulkner wrote vast bodies of short fiction, Hicks pointed out that were you to "ask a hundred critics who the two outstanding *novelists* of the period from 1925 to 1950 are . . . ninety-nine will say either 'Hemingway and Faulkner' or 'Faulkner and Hemingway.'"[37] What seemed clear to critical commentators at the time, whatever their view on the inherent value of the short story, was that the swelling body of short fiction culminating in the surge of 1950 was characterized by its overall lack of quality. As Robert Daniel concluded, in his pessimistically titled 1948 article "No Place to Go," "anyone who has the task of reviewing a dozen recent volumes of short stories must face the question of what is wrong with fiction in this decade."[38]

The ideological pressure on contemporary fiction in the postwar period directed writers increasingly toward open, expansive works, articulating freedom in terms that were both structural and stylistic. The corollary to this is borne out by the critiques leveled at midcentury short story writers, whose work critics dismissed precisely because of its diminishing, minor aesthetics. Looking at the dominant form of characterization in short fiction, Miller noted that "labels, often unclear, often tentatively affixed, do persist for the insignificant protagonists of these stories, momentarily caught up by the guilt and embarrassment of being alive"; by reducing the scale of character to that of a type or classification, short story writers were curtailing the very concept of identity.[39] Equally, critics argued that writers were reducing their narratives and plots in both length and importance. In the "The Structure of the Modern Short Story," written for *College English* in 1945, A. L. Balder observed that many of his peers maintained "that the modern short story is plotless, static, fragmentary, amorphous—frequently a mere character sketch or vignette, or a mere reporting of a transient moment, or the capturing of a mood or nuance." Their charge that in such stories "Nothing happens," in fact conflated two positions: sometimes it seemed "to mean that nothing significant happens, but in a great many cases it means that the modern short story is charged with a lack of narrative structure."[40] What exacerbated this problem for critics, given their general impulse toward a nuanced fiction that reflected the complexity of modern culture, was the fact that such diminutive narratives tended to "retreat from an over-complicated world." As Mirrielees explained, although this "retreat may be, and often is, into a world as painful as any known to today's adults," fundamentally it presented "a world simplified."[41]

Overall, critics seemed in agreement that the modern short story was insufficiently complex or nuanced enough to account for the complexities of postwar life and that it was unable to escape from an introspective obsession with technique and engage with the leading aesthetic priorities of openness and freedom. Given his otherwise caustic tone, however, Fiedler *does* put forward a case for the potential viability of the short story in midcentury America. Arguing that the "most interesting writers" of the batch of 1950 "are the excessive ones" (among whom he includes McCarthy and Bowles), he explains that they "share at least the quality of the outrageous which separates them from the glutinous grey mass of the two collections, Shaw, Sykes, etc." ("Style" 162). Just as Trilling and other intellectuals had promoted the need for a reinvestment of morality and complexity into fiction as a response to the violence of the Second World War, so Fiedler suggested that the short story might de-velop into a new kind of form that could respond to violence and terror in meaningful ways. In a surprisingly pleading tone, he asks whether "it is permitted to believe that the form will rise to its terrible obligation as the unforeseen poetry of our perhaps ultimate hour"—making a case for a possible form of short fiction which could reconcile the terrible with the human ("Style" 172). His suspicion, however, that "for terror to be truly redeemed, humanized for use in moving and substantial human fictions, it must be understood as real evil" implies a model of catharsis he is skeptical that the short story can actually manifest; indeed, he sug-gests elsewhere that the short story's length and narrow focus prohibit such a psychic reconciliation. Instead, even when a writer like Paul Bowles "compels from us the shocked, protesting acceptance of terror as an irreducible element of being," the brevity of the individual pieces means that "whole impact of his work is the insistence on the horrible, and his stories seem only literary by accident" ("Style" 170). The problem that Fiedler sets out preoccupied a range of critics during the 1950s and perhaps finds its clearest echo in Ihab Hassan's 1959 essay "The Victim: Images of Evil in Recent American Fiction." Here, Hassan recognized the political implications of arguments like Fiedler's, explaining that the contemporary writer's "vision of evil, his image of the victim, is nothing more than a versatile attempt to reconcile dream and order without recourse to doctrine or ideology," whereby the victim "takes upon himself the unreason of human existence and redeems it by giving it form."[42] For fiction to be able to reconcile the irrationality of modern existence by giving it aesthetic coherence through form, it needed to be divorced from authorial control or the clear presence of formal constraints. It is this demand by critics, regardless of their varying sympathies toward the short story, that precluded it from being taken seriously as a literary form in the midcentury—it was simply too controlled, too patterned, too contained. Howe summarized this most clearly when he concluded that the essential difficulty facing the story writer is that a tone can so easily be wrenched from its necessary context," so that the story becomes dictated by the writer's concern with technique and voice. This is why, as Howe put it, "what should be a means for controlling a story becomes a clamp destroying the writer's individuality."[43]

What troubled critics the most about this conceptualization of the short story was the idea that such constraint could affect people's lives— after all, Trilling's concept of fiction was predicated on its potential social impact. So the disquiet that this containment and terror raised in postwar critics was based not simply on the idea that such stories might shock or adversely affect the individual reader; critics were concerned that this kind of antirealistic fiction could harm society as a whole. As Truman's speech made explicit, American fiction was contingent upon a democratic model. Certainly, the freedom that both the political and critical machines were promoting was one that validated the individual, but as part of a broader program whose ambit always recognized, even favored, the development of society as a whole. If America's democratic identity was founded on the freedom of the individual, then its concept of freedom was just as inextricably linked to the welfare of the nation as a whole. In particular, its identity relied upon an idea of generative debate, and growth through difference; as Dewey maintained, "democracy is expressed in the attitudes of human beings."[44] American society was uniquely free because it allowed for the expression of personal, individual feelings, which, through dialogue with opposing ideas, continually shaped the country for the better. As Trilling suggested, "a culture is not a flow, nor even a confluence; the form of its existence is a struggle, or at least debate—it is nothing if not a dialectic."[45] When, after the Second World War, America came into ideological collision with the Soviet Union, America's image as defender of freedom became even more contingent upon this democratic dialogue. Literary critics in particular seized on this as a powerful expression of what was needed from contemporary literature: Trilling and fellow liberal critics "served to reinforce the dominant Cold War polarities which privileged American democracy, imagined as a fruitful tension of conflicting groups, in contrast with the monolithic repressiveness of the Soviet Union."[46] Because the concentrated prose that characterizes many of the short story writers of this period—but particularly that of McCarthy, Williams, Bowles, and Welty—was only able to present a single, uninflected view of the world and failed completely to register conflicting perspectives or arguments, it was entirely unsuitable for the kind of role fiction ought to be playing. The short story as a form, moreover, was inherently limiting in scope; defined by its brevity, it was an unwieldy way to try to communicate the kind of "fruitful tension" that critics commended, ill-equipped to deal with multiple perspectives or even gesture to their possibility. Indeed, from this perspective, the form's inability to represent a democratic experience implicitly aligned it with an opposition toward America freedom.

In fact, the short story was almost completely unsuitable for achieving the aims of this liberal critical agenda. If we return to Tanner's vision for an "unpatterned, unconditioned life" and a model of fiction that enunciates such a freedom, what is most striking is the extent to which the literature he describes is underpinned by a *formal* freedom: a lack of restriction on style, on representation, on structure or lineage. This parallels the liberal critics' broader conceptualization of fiction, as needing to enunciate in form, as well as meaning, the democratic freedom they envisaged—Tanner and Trilling were surprisingly in agreement that for fiction to deliver a message of freedom, it must communicate it in a prose that is equally open. As a form, the short story is characterized by its compactness and its formal restrictiveness—there is only so much that can be expressed within the confines of such a limited word count and, at the end of the 1940s, before the advent of postmodernism, still only a limited number of accepted ways of communicating it. As I have argued, there was a strong feeling at this juncture, too, that the short story had been hijacked by an alien agenda that was frustrating its ability to communicate anything "worthwhile" to its reader. By contrast, the novel was ideally suited to communicate freedom. Open to experimentation, unburdened (in America) by tradition or by editorial expectations, the novel had become "the central form in which the aspirations and contradictions of the changing American culture was expressed."[47] It allowed the expression of a story that could at once communicate the contingencies of modern life, render conflicting viewpoints (and, in fact, be driven by internal conflict) and enunciate a truly democratic freedom that could better the individual reader. By the 1950s, the novel that dominated American fiction, most valorized by critics, was a kind of sprawling picaresque. Fueled by "romantic anarchism, emphasizing spontaneity, instinct, open style and free expression," it propelled its characters from one adventure to another, creating a storyworld at once open and unpatterned.[48] But at the same time as it allowed for a more original, more open kind of fiction, the novel was also still closely related to the real world and the "reality" that was so important to postwar critics. Unlike the short story, which (as reviews like Fiedler's insistently suggested) seemed to have accumulated layers of stylization and allegory that disconnected it from real life, the novel was still considered to be fundamentally rooted in reality. Trilling argued that its value as literature lay, in part, in its "tell[ing] us about the look and feel of things, how things are done and what things are worth."[49]

The burden that this critical agenda placed on writers was not insubstantial, and it could be suggested that it placed too much responsibility upon writers to produce novels that could communicate a larger, politicized model of individual freedom. From the perspective of the rhetoric surrounding postwar American identity, freedom itself was not simply a right: if Americans were free, then they owed a responsibility to that freedom. This was reflected, on a national scale, in Truman's declaration that freedom was "the goal we seek not only for ourselves, but for all people."[50] Just as America had a responsibility to protect global freedom and ensure that they validated their own position as free; the individual (whether writer, critic, or reader) bore a responsibility to promote freedom in the same way. Truman's speech also clarifies the extent to which the proper use of this responsibility is based upon moral judgment—he envisages freedom as "essential if men are to live as our Creator intended us to live."[51] This development was not specific to the Cold War, however; freedom has traditionally been regarded as an intrinsically moral concept in America. American democracy has been consistently conceived of as "a way of personal life . . . which provides a moral standard for personal conduct."[52] However, the relationship became particularly loaded as America was drawn into opposition with the Soviet Union: democratic freedom had to become even more connotative of morality, as its opposition to the inherently (for America) amoral position of communism increased. There was greater urgency to recognize that "the source of the American democratic tradition is moral,"[53] to give it greater validity against "godless" and "moral-less" communism. A naturalistic prose style, then, with its explicit lack of morality, would naturally be in conflict with the goals of liberal fiction (and the broader responsibilities of America) and seem "bereft of moral conviction."[54]

Containment Culture

Until now, the reader would be forgiven for thinking that the New York Intellectuals, and indeed postwar critics more generally, espoused a version of the novel that was conceptually open, embodying "freedom" in every sense. Although the description "liberal" is not inherently incorrect, or misleading, I have thus far occluded the extent to which such critics were also responsible for a doctrine that was constrictive and conservative. It should be apparent that the kind of fiction they espoused occupied a narrow field and that the parameters for producing such literature were restrictive and demanding—this is evident in their critique of the short story, which was increasingly figured in terms invoking compression and oppression. In a way, they were operating against Tanner's ideal "freedom from all restrictions," as they were arguing for a set of clear restrictions on fictive expression. This is particularly obvious when one places, as Schaub does, the explicitly formalist demands of the New Critics and these more tacit demands of the New York liberals side by side. With their openly demanding set of critiques, "the New Critics help demonstrate the degree of conservatism that liberal criticism embraced."[55] And although contemporary America promoted its unique brand of freedom more vigorously than ever—defining itself by it on an international stage, even justifying its global hegemony on the basis of it—within its own borders, it was much more conservative than this image suggests. The 1950s saw conformity and homogeneity spread through America on an unprecedented level; this process, moreover, was enabled and advanced by the governments that promoted, to the outside world, an image of independence and freedom. In this light, countercultural short stories can be considered to be dealing with a force larger than the liberal agenda of freedom. Williams's short fiction, with its open portrayal of gay relationships, is a particularly clear case of this tendency; in contrast to his less openly oppositional (and higher-profile) dramatic works, his short stories engage in a critique of a broad range of cultural assumptions. Taken together, the short stories of Williams, Welty, Bowles, and McCarthy interrogate the forces of conformity and conservatism within America in surprising and complicated ways.

The popular image of America in the 1950s, continually reinforced by film and television, is one of consumerism and conformity. Oriented around a nuclear family with traditional gender roles and an insistently middle-class identity, the typical conceptualization of postwar America has a strong grounding in reality. Nadel summarizes it as "a period, as many prominent studies indicated, when 'conformity' became a positive value in and of itself."[56] This was not a spontaneous reorganization of society but a move that was directed to a large extent by narratives deployed by the government: "the virtue of conformity . . . became a form of public knowledge through the pervasive performances of and allusions to the containment narrative."[57] The containment narrative proved to be the essential element of the United States' response to the perceived threat of the Soviet Union. Driven by a preeminent concern with "American security," it originally referred to "U.S. foreign policy from 1948 until at least the mid-1960s," where America would attempt to contain the progress of the Soviet Union from a distance rather than through direct engagement.[58] Its original proponent, the diplomat George Kennan, described it as "a sort of long-range fencing match in which the weapons are not only the development of military power but the loyalties and convictions of hundreds of millions of people and the control or influence over their forms of political organization."[59] So, as a strategy, containment was fundamentally concerned with limiting and patterning—as much with regard to its own subjects as any foreign power. America's branding of itself as global defender of freedom was part of a broader deployment of narratives around which American citizens could—or were sometimes forced to—orient themselves. The anticommunist agenda of the House Un-American Activities Committee, for example, provides an example of the way that official organs of state ensured that the general populace conformed to a "democratic" ideal. In a very specific way, this policy of containment affected Bowles; it was fear of reprisals for his membership in the Communist Party that provided the impetus for him to emigrate from America, permanently, to Morocco. But it exerted its influence on him in much less direct ways, too. Nadel makes very clear that "containment was perhaps one of the most powerfully deployed national narratives in recorded history," and the extent to which it shaped the opinions and ambitions of critics and authors alike was of equal magnitude.[60]

The most obvious influence was on the agenda of the New York critics, whose vision of a "greater social liberty" reinforced the orthodox narrative of America as a global defender of freedom.[61] Their model of fiction relied upon the communication of ideas and endowing a text with meaning—literature needed writers "specifically and passionately concerned with social injustice."[62] But their concern with effecting social change necessitated that they prioritize certain modes of communication, which coalesced around the form of the novel, the "medium through which a relation between art (novel as aesthetic form) and politics (novel as social history) might be sustained."[63] This emphasis on a particular aesthetic—on molding a text to shape and reinforce a particular meaning—inherently drew them away from their own ideal of liberty and brought them closer in line with conservative, formalist critics: "In valorizing the literary idea the New York critics effectively endorsed the stylistic priorities of the New Critics."[64] In this way, it is possible to imagine a reasonably coherent

drive in American literary criticism in the postwar period that argued
for a specific kind of form and representation and culminated in an insistently "prescriptive orthodoxy with which young writers after World
War II had to contend."[65] As I have argued, there is a clear pattern to the
relationship with reality that criticism demanded. Taking issue with "the
chronic American belief that there exists an opposition between reality
and mind and that one must enlist oneself in the party of reality," Trilling
instead delineated a type of prose that would engage with reality while
still registering the complications and nuances which "mind" threw in its
way. Henry James's *Princess Casamassima* offered a paradigmatic instance
of this kind of prose and structure: "It is one of the great points that the
novel makes that with each passionate step [the princess] takes towards
what she calls the real, the solid, she in fact moves further away from the
life-giving reality."[66] James could voice the complications of interiority,
manifested in his protagonist's "passionate steps" and her own peculiar
conceptualization of "what *she calls* the real" while still emphasizing the
power and authority of the external world of real life. Transferring "the
quality of 'hardness' from the material world to the emotional complexity of a psychological world engaged in tension with the outer," Trilling
prescribed a model of fiction that was oriented around the relationship
between inside and outside.[67] In this, Trilling and fellow liberal critics
were drawing on a much more traditional pattern of literature: the use
of contradiction and paradox as the central impulse of fiction. With a
paradigm cutting across partisan lines, emphasizing "the aesthetic, or
formal, standard of contradiction as the central quality of great art,"
as well as demarcating a set of parameters within which this standard
could be achieved, it is no wonder that some writers felt hemmed in by
criticism, even when it was ostensibly endorsing liberty and openness.[68]

Faced with such a coherent series of critical demands, which exacted
not only a particular social function from the text but a tight model of how
the text should be formed, writers began to chafe. Fiction during the 1950s
attempted to radically assert its own independence from critical demands,
resisting the conformity demanded by both the general populace and the
criticism of their work. The collusion between critics and the reading
public, in spite of critics' attempts to construct it otherwise, was great:
both parties were equally interested in "social details" that "continued

to assume a world of discrete, atomistic individuals interacting socially through rumor, dialogue, physical action and dress."[69] Furthermore, as Schaub notes, "for the most part," writers in the postwar period "saw themselves in distinct opposition to both their critics and popular audience, rather than engaged with them in a dialogue structured by shared assumptions."[70] The most prominent group of writers who attempted to wrest control of literature from critics were the emergent Beats, who felt controlled by the force of critical expectations to the extent that their fiction "was influenced by an explicit determination to break free of it."[71] With open, often seemingly unformed prose, their fiction (and poetry) seemed to manifest an antithetical model to the prescribed boundaries that liberals and New Critics demanded alike. Moreover, it offered a challenge to the conformity of mainstream America; the Beats were "in growing revolt against the conformity, respectability and materialism of lonely crowd America" and presented an alternative way of interacting with the world, and representing it on the page.[72] So their fiction represented a double challenge, to the conformity expected of them by critics and to the conformity displayed by their audience. The challenge that they posed was explicitly oriented around the prose style which they adopted and reflected in a broader trend among countercultural authors; from those who, like William Burroughs and Jack Kerouac, were integral to the Beats, to more disparate and unaffiliated writers. For dissenting writers, "the logical strategy of choice was a way of telling stories which both reflected their rupture with society and established at the same time a legitimate source of autonomy for describing a redefined 'reality.'"[73] Even though the manner in which they registered these oppositional impulses varied considerably, these disparate writings can be considered as motivated by a fundamentally countercultural impulse.

But, at the same time, the Beats' project of fictive liberation tapped into the same ideology that lay behind the containment narrative they aimed to resist: the ideal of the liberty of the individual and a freedom from external patterning. In attempting to challenge the formal demands of midcentury criticism and the expectations of their homogeneous reading public, the Beats (inadvertently) valorized and reinforced the message of their opponents. Indeed, the language that characterizes the scholarship on these authors emphasizes the extent to which the cultural ambitions of the Beats and liberal critics overlapped: both were attempting to change the ethical experience of the individual, were deeply conscious of America's new place in a global community, and made explicit the extent to which the *modern* condition placed greater demands on the author to promote liberty and shape society. In a crucial way, the Beats were engaged in replicating the very process of containment, elucidating a narrative that strengthened the mainstream American ideal of freedom. While they were advocating for a different set of experiences to those that the critics or administrations might endorse, their vision was still one located within the same structures of liberty and freedom, and it was communicated through a prose that reinforced this, even as it ostensibly challenged critical expectations.

In retrospect, it is easy to see why the containment narrative was able to exert such force on the shaping of American culture of the 1950s and 1960s. With its Orwellian promise of freedom in conformity, it at once aligned citizens around a central—and essentially American ideal—and provided a structure for living their lives. In their model for ethical literature, liberal critics in the postwar period replicated the containment model and applied it to fiction. Their conservative expectations from literary form, which they considered necessary for communicating literary ideas effectively, offered an analogy to the specific roles expected of an American citizen. At its heart, the function of literature was to effect social change, which in the specific context of the postwar period meant advancing the liberty of the individual—just as America's responsibility was to advance the freedom of its citizens and of the global community. But both moved toward greater liberty by enacting a conservative narrative that controlled how individuals existed, whether authors or the general populace. The Beats attempted to resist the impulses of conservatism and conformity by producing deliberately unconfined prose. Their open expression, using "experimental" formal structures, emphasized the autonomy of the individual and validated the freedom of the author to communicate with an unfettered liberty. However, their aspirations bought into precisely those priorities for which their erstwhile opponents were advocating: those of the "abiding dream in American literature that an unpatterned, unconditioned life is possible, in which your movements and stillness, choices and repudiations are all your own."[74] Their fiction enacted yet another narrative of containment, with the same core ideology of individual liberty; the Beats were attempting to shape society through an *unpatterned*, rather than patterned, model of existence. As such, the critical turn away from the short story can be understood as predicated upon the formal demands of the genre: even when they can be read allegorically, because of their limited scope and necessary dependence upon the specific, short stories emphasize the restricted, the confined, and the patterned nature of individual existence. Thus, were a writer to emphasize the compression of their short fiction, it could voice the inversion of the American dream: no matter how unlimited the world might seem, life is necessarily containing and confining.

Inclusion and Omission

The fate of the short story in the postwar period was clearly shaped by the way that critics read the form in contradistinction to the novel. This was exacerbated, moreover, by their tendency to conflate the concept of "fiction" (and indeed "literature") with the specific form of the novel—a tendency that extends to contemporary criticism as well. As I have argued, this slippage in terminology is in part due to the political priorities of critics like the New York Intellectuals, which extended beyond a concern with the details of what literary texts communicated, to the kind of generic structures they were organized around. For a text to contribute toward the kind of social renovation that influential cultural commentators such as Trilling emphasized, it needed to enunciate in its form the same qualities of freedom that its characters and actions expressed. This meant, in general terms, a novelistic mode of expression—to the extent that it became increasingly difficult to discuss the concept of fiction without invoking the formal qualities of the novel. Occasionally, a critic like Fiedler acknowledged this elision—as when he considered the way that "groups of short fictions lacking all novelistic line or coherence, like Mary McCarthy's *The Company She Keeps*" were nonetheless described as novels ("Style" 158). This did not stop him, however, from limiting his interpretation of short stories based on these very qualities of novelistic line and coherence, nor did it stop other critics from transposing novelistic qualities onto the broader generic expectations of fiction at large.

Why did this formal dichotomy extend so pervasively throughout midcentury criticism? On the broadest level, certainly, the ideological imperatives of early Cold War politics inflected the kind of literary values that critics valorized in terms of content and style. But in a much more specific and programmatic way, the midcentury also saw a growing concern for the formation of a distinctly American literary canon. The short story's relegation to a second tier of cultural production was tied to established scholars' attempts to construct a national canon, the works of which articulated (over a broad historical sweep) the open-endedness that was taken as paradigmatically American. In such a configuration, which privileged writers who invoked expansion or inclusiveness, the short story was positioned as the alternative: restricting and reductive. The language with which critics like Fiedler, Howe, or Miller dismissed broad swathes of short story collections is testament to the power of these generic expectations. Ironically, the fact that they associated the short story with an antithetically cold, formal determinism was in no small part a product of the way the foremost practitioners of the short story, particularly Poe and Hemingway, had theorized the form's mechanics.

Today, novels held up as exemplarily American are still characterized by the same formal expansiveness, which is taken as the definitive cultural embodiment of America as a geographic and historical entity. As a firmly entrenched equation, this configuration has largely (although not entirely) usurped and submerged an earlier critical trope—that the short story represented the uniquely democratic and American literary form. This assertion, whether made in earnest or ironically, must be considered endemic to the short story, regardless of its currency outside of short story criticism. My aim is not to provide a new verdict on this potentially vexing question but rather to register this persistent discourse around the short story's Americanness, its competition with claims about the novel as part of postwar criticism's political concerns, and the consequent effect this has had on critical interpretations of the form. One author who has produced an astute consideration of the effects that this underlying theme has had on the development of short story criticism is Andrew Levy, whose study *The Culture and Commerce of the American Short Story* is informed by close analysis of the political and market factors that influenced the trajectory of the short story in the United States. In terms

that echo the tenor of postwar criticism, Levy suggests that "the most interesting aspect of the nationalistic claim is how it has limited short story
criticism to an expressive but strangely restricted debate over whether or
not (and how) the short story has performed the one function for which
it was apparently designed: to advertise American life, and to advertise a
particular set of assumptions about Americans in general."[75] The problem
of critics trying to define what an American literary approach is coincides
with what Levy suggests has been an endemic problem within short story
criticism: because it is considered a uniquely American form, criticism
has been guided by a search for a representative short story form, where
this "nationalist claim has framed and transformed short story criticism
[and] has filled magazine pages in the twentieth century with thoughtful
conjecture on what, exactly, it means for a form of communication to be
structurally American."[76] Just as the problem of representation motivated
detractors of the short story, it has equally animated those authors and
critics who have seen the form as essentially American.

Before the emergence of a containment culture within a larger narrative of democratic identity that encouraged expansive literary endeavors,
the short story was lauded as a national form in the United States, not
only because of the long tradition of authors working in the medium and
the importance of their contribution to shaping expectations of the form
but because the short story was seen as offering a democratic model of
accessibility. In contrast to the novel, which was traditionally associated
with high cultural ideals and characters of high social standing and was
consequently regarded as a "difficult" form of writing, the short story
offered easily digestible entertainment, where enjoyment rather than
social realism was privileged. This long-standing perspective on the short
story culminated in the first decades of the twentieth century, in Martin
Scofield's words, when the short story "was seen as the ideal popular form
because of its easily assimilable length, and its frequent preoccupation . . .
with the sensational, the strange and the dramatic."[77] Given the specific
culture of magazines publishing short fiction that emerged in the United
States, moreover, the status of the form bears strong comparison to that
which television held after the Second World War; indeed, as Scofield
notes, the "heyday of the popular magazine short story in the United
States was probably around the late 1930s just before the widespread

adoption of television."[78] This is not a new observation—William Peden, one of the most prominent critics of the short story in the 1960s, noted that throughout the 1940s and 1950s the "mass entertainment media of big slicks, Hollywood, and television were draining away the lifeblood" of short fiction.[79] Unlike the novel, then, the short story was a socially equitable form of literature, able to be enjoyed equally across society but diluted by its direct competition with other populist forms of entertainment.

The political imperatives of the Cold War shifted emphasis away from mass access to a new set of ethical concerns, tied to individual growth and larger narratives of progress. In a more poetic turn of phrase, Trilling described the novel as ideally suited for generating such growth, as it offered "a perpetual quest for reality" whose material offered an "indication of the direction of man's soul."[80] But the novel was also uniquely suited for such a task because, as Trilling himself would suggest, it was construed as an essentially American form. As Geraldine Murphy has argued, however, it was the conventions of the romance that offered such intellectuals a literary framework around which to orient their identification of the novel as a structurally open form, in direct opposition to the short story. Elucidating the ways in which "American romance remained open-ended, resisting formal resolution," she has demonstrated the extent to which the conventions of the romance—openness, integrity, a play between the real and the imagined—embodied the ideal of freedom that liberal critics used to define their literature against Soviet totalitarianism: the romance "promoted freedom, just as American democracy did."[81] Writers like Saul Bellow or Ralph Ellison were critically valorized for novels that offered sprawling, picaresque tales, whose freedom allowed their characters to develop in a supposedly autonomous manner. Within the conventional expectations of genre, action, and characterization were contingent upon a structure that could emphasize the narrative's imagery of freedom.

As an example of the kind of novelistic work extolled by such critics, it is useful to consider Ralph Ellison's landmark 1952 novel *Invisible Man* and the terms in which critics praised it as an exemplary American form of writing. Indeed, the approach that critics took in reading the novel can be understood as symptomatic of wider intellectual currents in America, which informed the contemporaneous criticism and production of short fiction. Writing in the *Kenyon Review*—the same influential journal in which Fiedler had published his concerned reflections on the spate of short story collections—the prominent critic Richard Chase reviewed *Invisible Man* in contrast to Bowles's second novel, *Let It Come Down*, both of which were published the same year.[82] Chase's evaluation of *Invisible Man* rests on Ellison's ability to express a nuanced version of reality, which is sensitive to "the ultimate contradictions of life" yet can still offer an image of freedom through its "transcendent" vision.[83] His analysis emphasizes the traditional aspects of Ellison's approach, locating it within the specifically "romantic" American framework of "the classic novelistic theme: the search of the innocent hero for knowledge of reality, self, and society."[84] This sits in contrast to the "pallid and futile" attempts of Bowles, whose only "occasional real triumphs" come in the form of "scenery painting."[85] Just as had been seen in the critiques of his short fiction, it is Bowles's "failure of characterization and of dramatic action" that Chase underlines, assessing him on the criteria on which the romance genre, like Ellison's text, is predicated. The priorities of liberal criticism direct his reading of the novel, and Chase concludes by arguing that Bowles fails because of what he considers to be the inherent nihilism of his work—"it doesn't matter what anyone does, since every act is equally valueless and equally without meaningful consequence"—which divests the characters of the responsibility required of a democratic society.[86] Moreover, he reads Bowles's patterning as a parallel to the coercive oppression of the Soviet Union, suggesting that since "the hero cannot go anywhere," there "can be no dramatic action."[87] The reaction against specific aspects of Bowles's writing—his characterization and structure—and the contrasting praise of Ellison's together point to a larger issue: read as an extended short story, with the same formal limitations, writing such as Bowles's was seen as antagonistic toward the democratic, liberal trajectory of American society. Ellison's novel, on the other hand, exhibited a formal openness whose aesthetics could be read in parallel to narratives of political freedom.

The valorization of *Invisible Man*, therefore, enacted on a small scale the critical metanarratives that were guiding American fiction in the postwar period. It is worth noting that Ellison's short fiction, some of which had been written and published in magazines before the war, was not brought together into a published collection until 1997, three years after the author's death; the genre of these stories has precluded any substantial critical discussion. Critics have misread or neglected such short fiction, not simply on the grounds of length but based on their dedication to cultural production that enunciated a democratic model of individual freedom. In the case of *Invisible Man*, the novel was positioned as uniquely American because the romance structure of its protagonist's journey could be read as articulating the democratic freedom so central to the national narrative of postwar America and which, as Murphy has shown, sharply guided the thinking of critics. Ellison was, himself, not unaware of the way that the structure of his text related to the core narratives of American society, noting that in America, "the novel has always been bound up with the idea of nationhood."[88] Given Ellison's understanding of his own work as intimately connected to the question of U.S. identity, therefore, it should not be surprising that critics seized on the text as an exemplary study in the relationship between literary form and political ideology.

Indeed, as Lawrence Buell has suggested, the novel quickly became a contender for the title of Great American Novel. Buell's recent incisive intervention into the history of the American novel has recuperated an often parodied theme—the quest in the world of American letters for what Buell helpfully shortens to the GAN—within a measured and thorough study of the underlying drives behind this quintessentially American form. In accounting for the popularity of *Invisible Man* and its formal influence on later writers, Buell notes that "since colonial times, American audiences have been attracted to coming-of-age stories featuring the extraordinary adventures of ordinary persons."[89] The sense of inclusiveness that Buell attributes to *Invisible Man* is symptomatic of the way that the novel has been construed as a genre by literary critics, and if his study has a weakness, it is that it recapitulates the logic that drove the canon-forming texts of the midcentury. Like Murphy, he identifies the dominant strains of the bildungsroman and the romance as fundamentally connected to the political narratives of the United States, "in correlating the travails of their protagonists' history with national history and values," and although authors "seized upon, ramified and quarreled with this script," they nonetheless "remained bonded to it."[90] *Invisible Man* thus attests to the extent to which these equations of narrative form and national identity influenced the writing and reading of novels in the postwar period.

Reading of Ellison's novel in such a light, moreover, reflects the despecified way in which postwar critical concerns shifted away from the individual text (with the notable exception of the New Critics), toward a larger concern with the trajectory of American writing at large; the impulse behind the search for the Great American Novel was subsumed within the larger project of tracing a whole lineage of "great" texts. As I have argued, the novel was co-opted by postwar critics as a literary expression of the democratic freedom that America embodied on the world stage. By establishing an historical tradition of "classic" American novels concerned with freedom, a series of critics, beginning with F. O. Matthiessen, attempted to provide a narrative that actively reinforced America's authority to speak for the West. Trilling had summarized the program of modern literature as "directed toward moral and spiritual renovation" where the modern author was the one who could offer a vision that could lead to a better (in the context of America's hegemonic agenda, a freer, more democratic) society.[91] Within canon-forming texts like Matthiessen's *American Renaissance*, the American novel was therefore characterized as part of a larger tradition, defined by its ability to articulate a model of individual autonomy.

This is not to say that, across postwar American society, critics articulated a coherent and cohesive argument, uniformly informed by the same political considerations. Indeed, to an extent this chapter has been guilty of overemphasizing the strength of the position held by such ideologically guided critical intercessions into American literary culture. The case of Matthiessen and other canon-conscious critics attests to this neatly; although, from one perspective, Matthiessen's work engages with the same nationalistic principles as Trilling and "emerges as a 1948 New Americanist," Trilling himself nonetheless "found the author of *American Renaissance* [to be a] threat," penning an article for the *Nation* to try to distinguish their respective positions.[92] The work by Donald Pease in this field has been particularly productive, however, in emphasizing the importance of the congruency between the various critical stances adopted in the postwar period. Following the arguments made by the more recent scholars who identify as New Americanists, that "an American literary imagination was in fact an ideological construct that developed out of the consensus politics of liberal anticommunism of the postwar era," Pease has shown that, fundamentally, when these later scholars interrogate the politically inflected cultural criticism associated with Trilling's *Liberal Imagination*, they "articulate the critical difference between themselves and their predecessors in American Studies."[93] This difference is the awareness that "the liberal imagination discloses itself as ideological when it produces an imaginary separation between the cultural and the public sphere [which] enables liberal subjects to experience the otherwise threatening cultural contradictions released by the cold war consensus as the negative capability of a whole self."[94] From this perspective, the exact correspondences between individual critics is less significant than their joint endeavors to promote certain kinds of writing, based on the political exigencies of the Cold War, while maintaining the illusion that these motivations are not a factor. As such, we can align Matthiessen's writing with Trilling's in the same way that Pease suggests that "Trilling used *The Liberal Imagination* as a history-shaping force in an ideological struggle, after the manner in which [Harriet Beecher] Stowe used *Uncle Tom's Cabin*."[95]

Considered within such terms, it is clear that the question of genre and a more broadly construed definition of literary form dictated the terms in which novels and short stories were read, with the former associated with inclusiveness, the other with omission and constraint. Underpinning the work of critics from Matthiessen to Trilling to Fiedler (and it is here that Buell's study is particularly helpful) was the idea of the representative text, the work that could, in and of itself, account for the whole of the American experience. Pease rightly notes that the definitive canon-forming works of this period "presuppose a realm of pure possibility . . . where a whole self . . . can internalize the major contradictions at work in American history . . . in a language and in a set of actions and relations confirmative of the difference between a particular cultural location and the rest of the world." In other words, the kind of literary text they sought to cultivate and promote was one that could express the exceptionalism of the American experience, speaking both longitudinally to its unique history and broadly to its geographically vast cultural makeup.[96] Buell suggests that one factor that has influenced American anxieties about a Great American Novel "may be sheer territorial bulk," where the expansiveness of the country has necessitated a novel of correspondingly vast scope and ambition; "the heady challenge of getting a whale-sized country between covers is almost certainly an incentive to dreaming about a possible great national novel."[97] As such, it is little wonder that critics valorized the long- and wide-ranging forms of the bildungsroman and romance (or, ideally, a confluence of the two); in order to represent the scope of a nation as grand as America, writers needed to adopt an appropriately expansive genre. Understanding the ideological stance behind *The Liberal Imagination* helps account for why critics exerted such stylistic pressure and how contingent that pressure was upon political concerns.

Contributing to this understanding was the tradition of impermanence that Levy attributes to the early periodical culture of the time of Poe, from which point onward the short story tended to be "designed as a culturally disposable artefact—a thing to be read once and enjoyed."[98] In more dismissive terms, Peden suggests that in the postwar period, after the epoch of the first decades of the twentieth century represented by Joyce's *Dubliners* and Sherwood Anderson's *Winesburg, Ohio* (which he described as "towering landmarks"), succeeding work in the genre of the short story had come to constitute "a form of literary garbage."[99] The conditions of production, which in an earlier context reflected the appeal and easy access seen as characteristic of democratic culture, would be viewed differently from the perspective of a culture concerned with effecting social change and for whom democracy entailed growth, individualism, and a firm adherence to the lived experience of the American citizen.

The short story's necessary failure to live up to these new standards of representation is exemplified by an author often considered emblematic of the American tradition of short story writing—Ernest Hemingway. While his prewar popularity survived the rigors of postwar literary priorities, as Hassan suggested in 1959, his reputation came to rest upon his novels (in particular, *The Sun Also Rises*) rather than on his short fiction. As critics emphasized, because it is defined by its limited size, any short story must inherently narrate events limited in scope, detail, or both. Elevating this intrinsic quality to the defining stylistic feature, however, Hemingway's "famous prose style—plain words, simple but artfully structured syntax, the direct presentation of the object"—was coupled with a subject matter that focused insistently on "the fragmentary nature of modern life, with its small local victories and defeats, its focus on the present moment and its prevailing mood of disillusion."[100] Crucially, this aesthetically precise and miniaturist register was deployed within a deliberately isolated and fractured structure, concerned with the episode, the glancing view, or the turning point. Organized around a central narrative of social progress, the political narratives of American identity that emerged in the postwar period led critics to project a commensurate sense of narrative progress onto new writing and recuperate the national literary tradition in line with a model of growth. In contrast, the short story was dependent upon its detachment from precisely such a narrative of progress; unable to develop a story of appropriate scope, the form was incapable of presenting the trajectory of growth critics expected of a truly representative literature.

Indeed, Hemingway was himself responsible, in no small part, for the equation of the short story with overt emphasis on craft, coupled with minimalism of plot and characterization. By the 1950s, his particular model of story had become canonical and fixed postwar critics with a certain image of the short story, as suggested by Fiedler's invocation of "Hemingway and his followers" ("Style" 159). Equally as influential were Hemingway's own observations of the form, which were articulated across a sequence of interviews and essays, the most important of which, "The Art of the Short Story," was not published until after Hemingway's death, when it was featured in an issue of the *Paris Review*; since then, it has been more widely available, reprinted in the 1990 collection *New Critical Approaches to the Short Stories of Ernest Hemingway*. This essay, begun early in the 1950s and completed in 1959, reflects Hemingway's own critical consideration of the form and in many ways synthesizes the relatively coherent way his stories had been understood by his peers and critics. At the heart of this essay was one central piece of advice about writing short fiction: one of the "few things" that he had "found to be true" was that "if you leave out important things or events that you know about, the story is strengthened."[101] This "theory of omission" rehearses the same theme as critics, but from the camp of the writer, that the short story was an inherently constricted genre that operated on the logic not of inclusion but of omission or absence.

Paul Smith has noted the extent to which Hemingway's position not only was treated seriously by his contemporaries but has "been treated seriously in several critical studies."[102] But he also points out that, despite Hemingway's own sense that this theory was profound, in many ways writers and critics regardless of genre "would have seen [Hemingway's theory of omission] as a version of the commonplace that the structures of literature, like the sentences of the language, imply more than they state and make us feel more than we know." What Hemingway was able to do, however, was cement an association between the short story and an allusive, technically adroit style of writing preoccupied with a central, unspoken subject. In his theorization on the short story, this "theory of omission" is "written into law," so that it became "not only the essential feature of his stories" but also the "evaluative standard for his work and others in the genre."[103] Is it any wonder, then, that critics mistook the abbreviated form of the short story for an aesthetic of containment, given Hemingway's neat coupling of brevity with absence?

The way that the prevailing political and cultural ideologies served to limit appreciation of the short story, reading it as a genre aligned with constraint and all that is reductive, is best illustrated by the critical response to the stories of two authors who are now regarded as leading practitioners of the form. In retrospect, 1953 was, like 1950, a propitious year for the short story; it saw the publication, within little more than a month, of John Cheever's *The Enormous Radio* and J. D. Salinger's *Nine Stories*. Reviewing Cheever's collection in the *New York Times,* William Du Bois noted that "John Cheever has always seemed to this review to epitomize the New Yorker Manner." This sentiment, which has continued to govern Cheever's reception, was echoed a week later by James Kelly, who identified the pieces collected in the volume as "New Yorker Stories." While both critics express their admiration for his style of writing—Kelly, for one, argues that "American writer in business today is more on top of his genre than Mr. Cheever"—it was precisely this sense of embodying a particular school of writing that led them to critique to the book. Du Bois argued that the "hallmark" of *New Yorker* stories like Cheever's was "the writer's ability to dissect the carapace of each dweller in Metropolis and to expose and explain the shrinking face of reality beneath"; the problem with such a dissecting style was that "too often the rather puny entity that emerges from its overlay of big-city shell is less interesting than the shell itself"—a "drawback" that Du Bois argued was "much in evidence" in *The Enormous Radio*. In other words, although Cheever had mastered a particular genre of writing, that genre was itself essentially reductive, revealing characters as limited and isolated. Kelly seemed to concur, describing the "subject" of *The Enormous Radio* as "the abrasive loneliness of drifting people," where this focused subject matter was both a strength and a weakness. Crucially, these initial readers tied the formal qualities of Cheever's prose explicitly to his attitude toward society. Du Bois remarks that "listening to this cacophony of hatred and despair, one harassed reader could only wonder if the human race, as Mr. Cheever views it, is worth saving," before concluding that "it's quite possible that this is the very message he intends to convey."[104]

Salinger's first anthology of stories (which, like Cheever's, had at least partially appeared in the pages of the *New Yorker*) was met with similar disapproval, predicated upon his use of the short story form. Although the reviewer, the prolific Charles Poore, admitted that Salinger could "write rings around most of the others in his generation," as in the responses to *The Enormous Radio,* this praise was tempered with a dismissal of the genre of *Nine Stories;* Poore described the collection as an "exploration of disjointed, uneasy little dreams." Like Du Bois, moreover, he connects formal compression and fragmentation to a negative, even dangerous social outlook. Comparing Salinger to the *New Yorker* cartoonist Charles Addams, whose work would later inspire the 1960s television show *The Addams Family,* he described *Nine Stories* as "over-rich" in "small monsters and large shadows of the macabre and the malign," asking whether Salinger was "bucking to be a prose Chas Addams." Most telling, however, is the way that Poore predicates his critique of Salinger, fundamentally, on its divergence from his breakthrough novel, explaining that, on the whole, the collection was "somewhat disappointing, coming from the man who wrote the outstanding first novel of 1951, *The Catcher in the Rye.*" The only story that Poore could award some praise to was "For Esmé—with Love and Squalor," and then only because he could see in it the template for a novel; his review concluded that "now all we ask is that Mr. Salinger put away his Halloween tricks and write as good a novel of World War II."[105] The qualities that the reviewers of Salinger and Cheever prized were precisely those that they argued the short story lacked, so that even recognized masters of the form were condemned for working within a prohibitive genre.

The critical bias that underpinned reviews such as this is all the more obvious when the same volume is reviewed by a fellow short story writer, sympathetic to the expansive possibilities of a form that critics could only construe as constrictive. Also writing in the *New York Times,* Eudora Welty described Salinger's writing in *Nine Stories* as "original, first rate, serious and beautiful," where his stories are "so interesting, and so powerful seen all together" because "they are paradoxes": although "from the outside, they are often very funny, inside, they are about heartbreak." Rather than a limitation, Welty argued that Salinger's concise focus and use of juxtaposition was a strength of the stories; their internal contradiction, Welty suggested, allowed the collection to develop a more poignant aesthetic and reveal, in a way that inclusive, novelistic fiction could not, "the crazy inability to make plain to others what is most transparent and plain to ourselves and nearest our hearts; the lack or loss of a way to offer out passionate feeling, belief, in their full generosity; the ruthless cruelty of conventional social judgments and behavior; the persistent longing—reaching sometimes to fantasy—to return to some state of purity and grace." Inverting the logic of critics like Poore, Welty convincingly suggests that these stories succeed because Salinger writes with "a loving heart."[106] Whether or not exposing such human failings undermined political narratives was irrelevant; Salinger's ability to use the compression of the short story to articulate the claustrophobia of a painful human existence belied his essentially compassionate outlook.

Ultimately, then, the outcome of cumulative critical interventions and pressures, particularly as the national rhetoric around America's Cold War identity intensified, was that the short story began to offer clearer opportunities for countercultural writing than the novel. Even a text like Ellison's, which shone a spotlight on the social and racial inequalities of contemporary American culture, both rural and urban, democratic and Marxist, ultimately reinforced the ideals of contemporary society. The formal freedom and breathtaking geographical and intellectual scope of Ellison's novel replicated in structural terms both the politics of openness and the sense of national grandeur intrinsic to America's oppositional identity adopted against the Soviet Union. By choosing to write, instead, in a form conditioned by its limitation and isolation, midcentury authors created an alternative narrative which opposed the ideals of the representative, the open, and the free. This is not to suggest, for a moment, that all writers approached short fiction from such an interrogative perspective or to concede to a reductive view of Hemingway's short story aesthetics of omission. But, given the political implications of writing novelistic fiction within the context of containment culture, the short story necessarily developed a more subversive tone. This not only led critics to either avoid or denounce the form, but it also led to certain writers cultivating the qualities of the form that would enhance its resistance to totalizing narratives. Focused instead on the particular, the individual and the specific, such short stories denied the possibility of the representative and forced readers to question the cultural narratives around them which insisted on the universal. As reviews such as Fiedler's emphasize, moreover, despite its clearly European roots, the novel was characterized as a domestic form in contrast to the "alien" short story; such a dichotomy encouraged short story writers to deliberately adopt a more transnational aesthetic, further emphasizing their fiction's role as a countercultural voice, articulating an alternative and subversive perspective.

Writing Short Stories against Interpretation

As he attempted to wean himself off the opium which had invigorated his work and debilitated his body, the great French dramatist Jean Cocteau composed a series of sketches, written and visual, which were published in 1930 under the title *Opium: Journal d'une désintoxication*. In these self-reflexive and often hallucinatory meditations, which directly influenced several American authors (most notably Bowles), Cocteau articulated a unique hope for his future work. Perhaps surprising, given the usual Coleridgean association of intoxication and inspiration, is the plea that Cocteau sets down for medicine to provide an opiate that does not harm its user. Indeed, what Cocteau ultimately aspires toward is not romantic sublimity but something at first glance more quotidian and mundane; he writes, "I would rather not be concerned any more about writing well or badly; and achieve the style of numbers."[107] While such a position may not immediately seem to correspond with that of short story writers in postwar America, Cocteau's desire does articulate a resistance to the forces of literary criticism that resonates strongly with the formal opposition many short story writers adopted against the cultural criticism of the Cold War–era United States. The evocatively suggestive phrase "the style of numbers" seems to denote a genre of writing that is compressed, clear, and—most significantly—specific. Read in these terms, Cocteau's ideal suggests a writing that defies the conventional expectations of literary interpretation and could be seen to prefigure Susan Sontag's famous concept of writing "against interpretation" and Deleuze and Guattari's theorization of Kafka's writing as a "minor literature." Taking these disparate theorists together offers a framework for more closely conceptualizing the way authors used the short story to enact a countercultural resistance against the formal and political restraints embodied in the liberal imagination.

So far, my argument has suggested two levels of cultural interaction with literary genre, both of which influenced writers in this period in terms of both style and subject matter. On the broadest political scale, in spite of its emphasis on the ideal of freedom, postwar American policy (and the narratives it promoted) enacted a process of containment on domestic culture. In closer, specifically literary terms, postwar critics moved beyond providing readings of texts, instead engaging in a process of interpretation concerned with actively shaping literary traditions, and more specifically, seeking to reposition and recontextualize the genre of the novel in support of political narratives with global implications. Both of these impulses shaped the production of written texts, regardless of their author's conscious interaction with them, and formed an intrinsic part of the cultural context in which they were composed. Given this framework, the idea of writing counterculturally can be conceptualized as engaging with either or both of these sources of pressure. Some writers, particularly those whose short stories were the overt targets of such criticism, sought explicitly to undermine the model of criticism, which they saw as guiding authors toward a rigidly conceptualized set of subjects and stylistic approaches—a cripplingly prescriptive attitude to genre. Other authors wrote with a less critically inflected perspective, more concerned with challenging the cultural status quo and the ostensibly homogeneous narratives being promoted regarding national identity and cultural values. From either perspective, however, given the formal pressures that yoked style to an ideology of representation and freedom, it should be apparent that the very qualities that caused the short story to be misread also meant it was ideally suited to countercultural resistance.

One way of conceptualizing how authors used the short story as a formal challenge to these increasingly prescriptive critical demands is to turn to Susan Sontag's celebrated collection of essays *Against Interpretation*. Although not published until 1966, two decades after the end of the war, the framework that Sontag established for writing in such a way as to resist the act of critical reappropriation resonates with the strategies many writers adopted when working with short fiction in the immediate postwar years. Several authors, moreover, admitted to the resemblance between Sontag's ideals and their own conceptualization of the formal coherence of their works; Bowles, for one, wrote to Sontag not long after her book was published, noting his admiration for the work, "particularly the first two and the last essays."[108] And whatever tensions may have existed between the two, Mary McCarthy certainly recognized something of her own counterculturalism in Sontag's writing, allegedly describing the young intellectual, on the publication of *Against Interpretation*, as "the imitation me," or "the ersatz me."[109] The congruence between the position staked out by writers like McCarthy and Bowles, and the possibilities that Sontag suggested for a literature that would defy "interpretation," suggests the extent to which all parties were invested in a similar program of writing.

Susan Rubin Suleiman has noted that Sontag is often portrayed "as an intellectual who had moved from the formalism and aestheticism of her early work to the ethically engaged stance of her later essays."[110] I would argue that the idea of writing *Against Interpretation* helps account for the countercultural impetus of postwar short stories precisely because of the formalist stance it took against the "overemphasis on the idea of content" in the interpretation of literature.[111] In the titular essay, Sontag argues that literature has been overtaken by the process of interpretation, and that in both writing and in criticism, "what is needed, first, is more attention to form in art" (12). Indeed, Sontag's main issue with criticism is its "overemphasis of content," where critics ignore the form of a text in favor of explicating its "ideas"; as Sontag explains, most criticism assumes "that a work of art *is* its content" (4). This approach to understanding literature is a product of what Sontag considers a utilitarian attitude to texts, where the critic finds "meaning" in the text by making it "about something" (9). In giving a text a functional role, the critic "makes art into an article for use, for arrangement into a mental scheme of categories" (10). Sontag's resistance to interpretation, therefore, is the resistance to the imposition of a reductive framework that ignores the form of the text, a framework that translates its words into a meaning that exists discretely from the text. As such, it is just as concerned with staking out an opposition to models of literary form that are based upon ideological interpretation as it is to the disregard of formal consideration.

As her general call for "more attention to form in art" suggests, moreover, Sontag sees at least some of the responsibility for the state of affairs she describes as borne by the artists themselves. In fact, she argues that "novels and plays (in America) . . . don't reflect any interesting concern with changes in their form," and her primary criticism of contemporary American writers is their failure to attend to the form of their work—she dismisses the majority as "either journalists or gentleman sociologists and psychologists" who are "writing the literary equivalents of program music" (11). Her solution—a model of writing that would "elude the interpreters"—is reminiscent of Poe's much earlier ideal of unity of effect: Sontag argues for "making works of art whose surface is so unified and clean, whose momentum is so rapid, whose address is so direct that the work can be . . . just what it is" (11). Sontag herself slips into the same vocabulary as those she critiques, often eliding the difference between literary forms even as she emphasizes writers' needs to reinvest their works with renewed formal coherence. Nonetheless, given her emphasis on the formal integrity of the ideal work, it seems natural that writers like McCarthy and Bowles should agree with Sontag's position. With their deliberate resistance to the formal demands of critics and their attendant novelistic expectations, it is fair to suggest that such writers were motivated at least in part by the same considerations as Sontag. Their compositional aesthetics emphasized the formal patterning of a work so that any interpretation of it would have to be predicated on the way in which it was told.

The antipathy toward literary "meaning" that Sontag expresses, however, does not presuppose that literature is functionless. Indeed, for midcentury writers of the short story, the use of a compressed and patterned form was guided by clear, culturally specific aims: to counteract the narrative being articulated by the novel and, more importantly, being reconstituted by critics. Indeed, the success of such short fiction could be measured by the extent to which it provoked its reader to reconsider the expected function of writing. So although working in opposition to the dominant model of the liberal imagination, the countercultural short story writer nonetheless wrote with the same audience in mind as someone like Ellison. But their distinctive approach, which contrasts so viscerally with sprawling texts like *On the Road* or *Invisible Man*, is symptomatic of a wider agenda to contest and disrupt the nationalistic narratives of postwar America. We can consider such countercultural writing, then, as directed toward challenging a specifically American audience, through an aesthetic strategy of disruption.

As appealing as both Sontag's and Cocteau's idealized anti-interpretive texts may appear conceptually, both delineate a model of opposition which fails to fully account for the necessary intersection between writing (even when it undermines contemporary culture) and the culture, language, and forms of that culture upon which it inherently draws. However much authors like McCarthy, Bowles, Williams, and Welty may have styled their short fiction as a counternarrative to the totalizing ideals of postwar America, their fiction nonetheless operated within the parameters of American fiction, couched within the same cultural influences as the writing and criticism they opposed. But if, as I have argued, American literary criticism positioned a certain type of open novelistic prose as the "major" national cultural production, it is logical to extend this terminology and frame the deliberately closed short fiction that was produced in the postwar period as "minor" literature. I appropriate this terminology freely from Deleuze and Guattari's 1975 study of Franz Kafka's fiction, *Kafka: Towards a Minor Literature*, in which the French critics articulated a way of reading Kafka that runs counter to the major trends in literary interpretations of his work—indeed, that was deliberately opposed to the traditional means of engaging with a literary text. In their alternative conceptualization of Kafka's work, Deleuze and Guattari suggest that his work needs to be considered as a minor literature that sits in orbit to, and dependent upon, the major literature from which it has sprung, and argue that this divergent course has an inherently destabilizing effect.

Framing the critical position of the text itself in oppositional terms, Dana Polan, the translator of the University of Minnesota edition of *Towards a Minor Literature,* suggests that Deleuze and Guattari's critical model stands "as a challenge to previous readings of Kafka—especially to that present reading of Kafka as a misanthrope of negativity, a case of Oedipal neurosis, a refuge into the interiority of subjectivity as against the collective enunciation of mass political action."[112] Although Kafka's work may have accumulated a particularly dense matrix of such overtly interpretive models of criticism, Polan suggests that the anti-interpretive stance that Deleuze and Guattari put forward can stand independently from the case study of Kafka; here, the work of Kafka "is really a pretext, no more, or less, than one of the many ways to enter into the field of history, to find oneself . . . carried away on one of history's many, many lines of escape."[113] It seems appropriate, then, to reframe the relative positions of Deleuze and Guattari's concepts of major and minor within the context of American short fiction, given that they themselves return to America as the site of just such dynamics on several occasions. The aspect of their theory that lends itself most readily to this context is the way that they formulate the dependence of minor literatures upon their major counterpart, where the term "minor no longer designates specific literatures but the revolutionary conditions for every literature within the heart of what is called great (or established) literature."[114] In the same way that I have suggested short story writers intended their focus on the specific and isolated incidents as a counter to the way such discrete episodes were taken by romantic American novels and woven into a representative tapestry, Deleuze and Guattari argue that "what interests" Kafka is the opportunity to make "his own language—assuming that it is unique, that it is a major language or has been—a minor utilization." Such a resistance necessarily gains its identity and delineates its parameters in contradistinction to the alternative, so that if we are to conceptualize countercultural short fiction as a minor literature, it needs to be understood as the corollary to the literature envisaged in the terms of the ideologically inflected novel.

Where Deleuze and Guattari's reading of Kafka aligns with the strategies of writing that Sontag suggests is in their consistent attention to the specificity of Kafka's prose. Indeed, while their suggestions of the broader applicability of their reading to other cultures and contexts are apt, it is their analysis of the particulars of these stories that provides the most utility for reappropriations such as mine. Introducing the now famous analogy of "the burrow" as a way to account for the formal compression and claustrophobia that marks Kafka's writing as minor, the critics suggest that this "functions to trick the enemy."[115] This suggestive image—the enclosed trap—provides a metaphorical approach for defining a minor genre against the sprawling openness of a form like the novel, oriented around the ideal of representation. Indeed, it is their desire to circumvent the idea of the representative and totalizing that motivates Deleuze and Guattari's analysis; in establishing their strategy, they propose that they "won't try to find archetypes that would represent Kafka's imaginary" and protest that they "aren't even trying to interpret, to say this means that." Instead, they maintain that they "believe only in a Kafka *politics* that is neither imaginative nor symbolic." This suggests a reading of minor literature oriented around the way that formal and aesthetic strategies, specific to the works, contribute to an overall insurrectionary approach— what they describe as a "Kafka *experimentation* that is without interpretation or significance and rests only on tests of experience."[116] From this perspective, the role of the critic in reading minor literature shifts from interpreting their work to analyzing how their textual strategies actively resist interpretation.

Ultimately, in their analysis of the way Kafka's fiction enacts such a subversive politics, Deleuze and Guattari delineate a process that is bound up with the compressing processes of syntax and structure, arguing that Kafka's literary style drives "language slowly and progressively to the desert" where his use of "syntax" is "in order to cry, to give a syntax to the cry."[117] Their recourse to the language of inarticulate noise, particularly their frequent reliance on musical terms and references, not only provides their analysis with a suitably deterritorialized set of vocabulary, but it also corresponds to a major trend in the writing and criticism of short fiction in general, and particularly within the postwar period: the explanation of the short story as a form through analogies with other art forms. Such explanations accentuate any discussion of the short story as minor in two regards. Firstly, they focus on qualities imbued to short stories by their formal limitations and structural compression, emphasizing the minor scale on which they operate. This is particularly the case when, as in *Towards a Minor Literature*, the analogy is to music or photography. But the use of such language also positions the short story as a form whose identity is dependent upon a similar, but more complex, art form in whose shadow it operates—namely, the novel. Figuring the short story as an essentially corollary form could be seen as an act of diminution, reducing it to a secondary tier of artistic production, precisely as midcentury critics had. From the perspective of the countercultural politics of the short story, however, such a conceptualization in fact galvanizes the short story as a form uniquely placed to disrupt the major narratives enforced by the novel.

Such a reading applies equally well to stories as apparently disparate as Bowles's, Williams's, McCarthy's, and Welty's—or even to those of writers normally understood as conventional midcentury practitioners of the genre, such as Salinger or Cheever. Indeed, Cheever's 1954 story "The Country Husband" provides an excellent example of the ways in which a writer traditionally understood as conventional, perhaps even formulaic, could use the short story as a minor form to articulate precisely such a combination of disruption and entrapment.[118] This story, first published in the pages of the *New Yorker*, has recently been republished as part of that magazine's retrospective anthology *The 50s: The Story of a Decade*, in which Jonathan Franzen identifies it as an exemplar of "the main template for the *New Yorker* story" that Cheever crafted over the course of the 1950s.[119] While Franzen notes the archetypal imagery that Cheever employs, suggesting that it is "to Cheever, even more than to *The Man in the Gray Flannel Suit*, that we owe a core-cultural suite of images of the fifties: the fathers working in Manhattan, the commuter trains, the autumn leaves on suburban lawns, the overwhelmed young mothers, the willfully forgotten war, the drinking," he also recognizes that in spite of his apparent conformity, Cheever was simultaneously "chafing against the confines of the stereotype, exploiting the fact of these confines by letting his main character chafe against them."[120] Not only does Cheever self-consciously draw attention to the constraints of the short story, emphasizing its physical limitations, he also thematizes enclosure, so that the characters are trapped by their own awareness of their limitations.

From the first sentence, Cheever's prose strains against the temporal confines of the story, announcing the narrator's ironic self-awareness of the conventions of storytelling and the generic expectations of the short story by beginning with the phrase "To begin at the beginning" (420). This playful sense of limitation, however, develops into a more sustained tension between the desire for action and an inertia that borders on stasis. The protagonist, family-man Francis Weed, observes that all but one of his suburb's "other marriages were intact and productive" (437), suggesting a pervading belief in the possibility of growth—that his world is predicated on a capitalist sense of productivity. But his neighbor, the lonely and unconventional Clayton, punctures this delusion by arguing that in their community, forward momentum is not possible; what is "really wrong" about Shady Hill, he claims "is that it doesn't have any future. So much energy is spent in perpetuating the place" (437). This paradoxical combination of effort and stasis is reflected syntactically in the constant impasse in Francis's arguments with his wife. Even when she tries to leave him, their stichomythic conversation, in paired oppositional statements, affirms both the strength of their feelings and their inability to make any progress: "'You can't go, Julia.' 'I can't stay. I know that'" (440). Throughout the story, Cheever places reminders of this domestic containment and dependence through the use of the photograph on Francis's office desk, which ties together his economic, domestic, and social roles through the terrible stasis of the image in which "his children in their photograph laughed and laughed, glazed with all the bright colors of summer" (443). Here, rather than cheerful, the framed photograph is a shuddering reminder of the obligations Francis hopes, but is unable, to escape.

Indeed, the story is not only structured around compression, with the narrative pushing against the boundaries of the story, but it also draws attention to the characters' own awareness of their limitations. Julia is introduced as constrained by her own internal feelings of emptiness, so that although she "was well liked and gregarious," her "love of parties sprang from a most natural dread of chaos and loneliness" (426). This feeling is described as "insatiable"—suggesting again a sense of both constant exertion and limitation. We later learn that, for Francis, a veteran of the Second World War, "it was not his limitation at all to be unable to escape the past; it was perhaps his limitation that he had escaped it so successfully."

While this helps to develop the sense of frustration and insipient violence underlying his actions, it also helps make sense of the desperate, fruitless activity of the party-going suburb, where everyone "seemed united in their tacit claim that there had been no past, no war" (428). The irony of their behavior is that they have chosen to be confined; their trap is of their own making, and over the course of the story, Francis grows more aware of this, thinking of "the strenuousness of containing his physicalness within the patterns he had chosen" (433). This pattern of containment is even reiterated through the imagery of office stationery, so that "on the letterhead of his firm there was a drawing of the Laocoön, and the figure of the priest and his sons in the coils of the snake appeared to him to have the deepest meaning" (433). Like the story itself, his life is bound and confined, where the act of struggling only reinforces the enclosure, so that the system of entrapment works on both a micro- and macrostructural level.

Cheever underscores this tension with the imminent threat of collapse, with the narrator reminding the reader at crucial points that the apparently orderly and controlled world of the story could implode at any moment, that with one wrong step the "card house would come down on them all" (433). This is echoed later when Francis is getting changed to sit for a family portrait photograph, in a scene that reiterates his containment within the domestic sphere: "he thought of Anne Murchison, and the physical need to express himself, instead of being restrained by the pink lamps of Julia's dressing table, engulfed him" (436). Again, not only is Francis trapped, but that very awareness of his entrapment compounds his containment. And this pervasive claustrophobia is drawn together with the threat of collapse in the final images of the story, which initially reminds the reader of how arbitrary the narrative selection has been, with the last scene taking place "a week or ten days later" (445). We are reminded that "the village hangs, morally and economically, from a thread," before the narrator draws us to an image that echoes an earlier comment, where a party host likened his feelings of love to Hannibal crossing the Alps. The final words of the story—"then it is dark; it is a night where kings in golden suits ride elephants over the mountains" (446)—suggest the potential splendor of the squalid, suburban love, while proleptically gesturing to its collapse; as with Hannibal, all their effort will only lead to destruction.

Not only does Cheever's story reflect the disruptive aesthetics of minor literature, but its insistent use of the photograph as a metaphor for containment suggests another particularly influential account of the short story as a literary genre, which adopts both the language of minor literature and an alternative artistic analogy. Developed by the Argentinian author Julio Cortázar, a contemporary of McCarthy, Bowles, Williams, and Welty, it was first published in English in 1983 and noted that the genre of the short story was still "exotic" outside of Latin America, echoing the terms used by U.S. critics. Rather than working solely within a literary register, Cortázar set out a paradigm for understanding the short story that figured it in direct contrast to the novel and drew on visual media to explicate their formal distinctions. Using the analogy of cinema and photography, "in that the film is in principle 'open ended' like the novel, while a good photograph presupposes a strict delimitation beforehand," Cortázar placed equal responsibility on the author and the form itself for the sense of compression in the short story, just as the limitation of the photograph is "imposed in part by the narrow field of the camera cover" and in part by "the aesthetic use the photographer makes of this limitation."[121] Cortázar's analogy, therefore, provides a productive framework for thinking about the relationship between the short story and the novel, focused around presence and absence; while a film generates its plot, its aesthetics, and formal distinctions from the accumulation of details—even on a basic level, the technology of film relies on the compound effect of many images—a photograph instead generates its meaning from what it omits and excludes. In the same way, while a novel generates its meaning from the accumulation of material, whose individual sections—like a film still—have meaning only in relation to the rest of the text, the short story generates meaning through its omissions.

From this particular perspective, the short story is defined by its gaps. This focus seems apt, given that, as Cortázar rightly emphasized, even in terms of its designation as a "short" story, this form is distinguished by its brevity. Once a piece exceeds a certain number of words, it strays into the territory of either the novella or the short novel, whose nebulous dimensions can be nonetheless safely distinguished from what would be accepted as a short story. Much more than any other literary form, therefore, short stories are defined by their limitation. In this sense, any

writer who chooses to compose a short story is foregrounding the process
of selection, determining what material is chosen to be included. Given
that, in a novel, the author could have conceivably included any, and as
much, material as they wanted, the selection of plot and description for
a short story, and its location within the narrative, becomes much more
noticeable; because it is defined by its limitation, the act of selection
and placement is much more prominent. Equally, the author's omissions
are registered with greater intensity, precisely because there is so little
material. If there is a disjuncture in the narrative, information about characters or events that the reader feels is missing, or if the larger context
of the events is unclear, because of the scale of the short story, such gaps
feel proportionately more significant than they would in even a short
novel. One of the factors that made the containment culture of Cold War
America such a successful ideological narrative was its totality. Within the
specific field of literary studies, for instance, by emphasizing qualities of
growth and development, any isolated or individual action could be rendered part of a sequence that followed a politically acceptable trajectory.
The short story undermined grand or totalizing narratives by isolating
incidents and emphasizing the absences around them and within them.
If we return to Deleuze and Guattari's ideal of the short story as sonic—a
syntactical scream—it is clear that their conceptualization of minor
literature is predicated upon the same understanding of the effect that
discrete, isolated, and internalized literature has in undermining the
totality and expansiveness of major literature.

Cortázar's use of photography to account for the peculiar structural
effects of the short story has a secondary effect, beyond the way that it
helps develop a model for understanding the form as a minor literature.
it gestures to the frequent intersection between short fiction and other
artistic forms. Alongside his large body of short fiction, his several novels,
including the uniquely experimental *Rayuela* (*Hopscotch*), and several
works that defy classification, Cortázar was an enthusiastic photographer;
his theoretical recourse to the form is certainly not accidental. One of
his more curious works is his long poem *From the Observatory*, which was
inspired by, and accompanied by photographs of, an eighteenth-century
Indian observatory. Such an investment in another art form, while not
unique in literature, is striking given that several major postwar short

story writers were themselves highly regarded in other modes of artistic expression; of the countercultural authors on which this book focuses, it is noteworthy that Bowles was, for more than a decade, better known as a classical composer than author and was an avid amateur photographer, while Welty's fiction was written in tandem with an extensive and intricate photographic practice. The specific implications of these alternative praxes naturally differ; together, however, they suggest a pattern of writers turning to the miniaturist aesthetics of other forms as a means of developing the introversion and minimalism that characterizes short fiction as minor literature.

As the following chapters elaborate, the specific textual strategies adopted by these different authors each enacted their own form of resistance to the cultural and critical pressures of postwar American society. What I am suggesting, however, is that their works, and those of others similarly resistant to containment culture, should be considered part of a coherent response to the cultural pressures that demanded a literary enunciation of nationalistic values. The obvious irony of America's containment culture—restricting authors to a limited number of ways of expressing a very specific model of freedom—was not lost on contemporary authors. With his usual keenly critical eye, Williams noted the extent to which this consensus had rendered American culture rigid, arguing that "contemporary American society seems no longer inclined to hold itself open to very explicit criticism from within."[122] Even novelists who actively positioned themselves and their work as countercultural—such as Jack Kerouac, with pieces like *On the Road*—still organized their texts along the same formal and thematic lines that were advocated for by cultural critics like Trilling. As Williams argued, instead of "moving forward" and replicating the critical model of progress and growth, short story writers instead articulated their criticism of American culture through form, and a formal "retreat" into compression and isolation.[123] It is this idea of a retreat that aligns these authors' strategies with the idea of minor literature advanced by Deleuze and Guattari, whose recurring image of Kafka's writing as a burrow articulates the compelling way such writing serves to undermine the totalizing structures of major literature.

chapter two

Mary McCarthy and the Containing Mask

In an interview for *Paris Review* in 1962, Mary McCarthy described her novel *The Group*, then in the final stages of being written, as "the history of the loss of faith in progress, the idea of progress."[1] In its published form, the novel—"a kind of mock-chronicle"—traced the lives of a group of eight young women following their graduation from Vassar College in 1933 until their reunion at a funeral in 1940. Although McCarthy compressed this chronology over the course of composition—shifting its original conclusion in the early 1960s first to "the inauguration of Eisenhower" in 1953, then to a date shortly before America's entry into the Second World War—the contrast between the novel's ostensible forward movement and its thematic interrogation of progress creates an ironic double register that is characteristic both of her writing and her position in American culture. Despite her profile as an outspoken and often acerbic critic of contemporary culture and criticism, McCarthy nonetheless maintained a prominent position inside the cliques of several major intellectual magazines, most notably the *Partisan Review*. And given how fluently she moved between the genres of autobiography, criticism, and fiction throughout her career, it should not be surprising that it has become a trope, when assessing her work, to note the difficulty of distinguishing invention from experience. This bivalent tension between inside and outside, progress and decline, underpins her use of form and offers a strategy for reading her work that bypasses questions of static identity and rewards fresh attention to her first two volumes of short stories, *The Company She Keeps* and *Cast a Cold Eye*.

After her own graduation from Vassar College in 1933, McCarthy began a career that straddled literary, political, and cultural criticism, academic teaching, autobiography, travel writing, and literary fiction. The wealth of biographies McCarthy has inspired attests to the enduring fascination her personal life has held, particularly her Trotskyite beliefs, marriage to the critic Edmund Wilson, detailed correspondences with the Jewish intellectual Hannah Arendt, and long-standing (and public) feud with the dramatist Lillian Hellman. Of her fiction, *The Group* was undoubtedly the most commercially successful work; however, the official classification of this and other of her books as novels has drawn attention from the way she deliberately challenged conventional generic structures. This has been compounded by her association with the dominant figures of postwar cultural criticism, particularly Lionel Trilling and Phillip Rahv, whose writings yoked a need for a particular strain of liberal imagination in American prose to a cultural narrative oriented squarely around progress—a critical confluence her own writing determinedly undermines.

But this is not to say that her books were received straightforwardly as fiction; McCarthy was frequently accused of masking her own biography with a veil of fiction, while her memoirs were themselves critiqued for their distortion of fact. Indeed, when her 1949 satiric novella *Oasis* was reviewed in the *New York Times*, Donald Barr argued its failure was that it drew too much on real life, and "readers outside [McCarthy's] circle can get little from [it] except a vague sense of defamatory brilliance and a few fine scene," while her entry in the *Columbia Companion to the Twentieth-Century American Short Story* continues to emphasize the "share[d] characteristics and themes" between her *Memoirs of a Catholic Girlhood* and her first published fiction, *The Company She Keeps*.[2] What this emphasis on distilling truth from stories (or applying the facts of biography to unlock her fiction) has occluded, however, is the extent to which within her fiction she self-consciously plays with the literary genres of novel and story, and the way this manipulation of scale plays out across her writing, regardless of classification. By focusing on McCarthy's use of isolation, stasis, and repetition, this chapter shifts the discussion of McCarthy away from biography to show the way her writing insistently engaged in a formal critique of the power structures of midcentury America.

Alongside her 1942 debut, *The Company She Keeps*, 1949's *The Oasis*, and 1963's *The Group*, McCarthy published sixteen other books in her lifetime, including the 1950 anthology of stories *Cast a Cold Eye*, the 1952 novel *The Groves of Academe*, and a range of nonfiction works, most prominently her initial biography, *Memories*, and its intellectual successor of 1987, *How I Grew*. These were preceded by almost a decade of work as a literary and theater critic, however, through which McCarthy established both a personal reputation as a sharp, witty personality and the intellectual credentials of a highbrow critic. Her career as reviewer began almost immediately after she left college, with regular book reviews for the *New Republic* and the *Nation*. These roles—coups in themselves for a female graduate with few social connections—developed into McCarthy's first major foray into the critical arena, coauthoring a series of reviews for the *Nation* on the state of contemporary criticism. She later explained that she had been chosen for this "large-scale attack on critics and book-reviewers" because her own reviews stood out as "rather harsh" and that the tone of her pieces "was a great sensation at the time," making several important figures "very mad."[3] The implications of her biting evaluations of her (much senior) peers were twofold; the reviews established her credentials with other intellectuals as a piercing mind, but they also helped her to recognize her own ability to play the insurgent, critiquing the culture of contemporary criticism from within. In 1937, her ability to perform this role was amplified by the refounding of the *Partisan Review*. Formerly a Stalinist mouthpiece, the magazine was revived chiefly through the efforts of Phillip Rahv and William Phillips, becoming one of the most prominent voices in midcentury criticism. The change in the magazine's ideological leaning acted as a kind of weathervane for pre- and postwar criticism more generally, with its shift from a Trotskyite leftism to a conservative nationalism mirroring the position of liberal critics like Trilling.

McCarthy later remarked that her own position in the magazine was often tenuous; never a committed Marxist, she felt even more alienated by the magazine's postwar conservative reversal. For her, the role of partisan instead entailed challenging established voices and developing her own nuanced and transgressive critical approach. With hindsight, her criticism from the 1930s and 1940s is particularly exceptional for its sophisticated synthesis of literary and critical approaches—and in her reviews themselves, she frequently called on other writers to appropriate fictional techniques and perspectives in their reviews, while suggesting writers needed to avail themselves of a more critical perspective. This tendency to break down genre boundaries, in terms of both style and structure, culminated most controversially in *Memories of a Catholic Girlhood*, which McCarthy structured around a dialogic pattern of asserting the truth of her narrative before undercutting it in appended critical notes. Beginning the volume with the assertion that, although "some readers, finding [parts of the book] in a magazine, have taken them for stories," she could "not understand the reason for these doubts," as her "record lays a claim to being historical."[4] This claim to authenticity, invoking the historical conventions of autobiography, is undercut after the first chapter, when McCarthy explains, in an italicized critical commentary that "there are several dubious points in this memoir," before admitting that she "believe[d]" one episode to be "pure fiction" (47, 48). This ironic movement from an invitation to read the work as biographically and historically accurate to revealing her narrative as fiction reflects in more overt terms the pattern she established more subtly in her earlier short fiction. In *The Company She Keeps*, especially, McCarthy's prose rejects the confines of either fictional or critical conventions, instead playing with multiple perspectives and shifting structures of interiorization and exteriorization, in order to implicitly critique the same authority and stability of cultural norms that *Memories* more explicitly confronts.

Given her prominent status as a public intellectual and the complexity of her formal experimentation, it is surprising that McCarthy's fiction has not received more sustained critical attention. I would suggest that one factor that has occluded the sophistication of her style is its sense of aesthetic completion—even when it makes readers uncomfortable, the ease of her style—often registered by others in terms of her eloquence in putting down her rivals—smooths over the transgressions of her generic hybridity. In her *Memories*, McCarthy quickly defines herself through a predominating quality: "a passionate love of beauty" (17). From an early age, moreover, she associated the aesthetic with a spiritual (rather than physical or political) regime, which was tied intrinsically to a sense of unfairness. Explaining that her "ugly church and parochial school provided me with my only aesthetic outlet," McCarthy emphasized that her sense of beauty was governed by—even defined by—the power structures through which she accessed it. Although it was through the church that she accessed the aesthetic, this was always contingent upon an external hierarchy; "equality was a species of unfairness which the good sisters of St Joseph would not have tolerated" (16). Rather than suppressing her desire for the aesthetic, these conditions instead instilled a simultaneous revulsion and attraction toward structures of power, so that when she "threw" herself "into it with ardor, this sensuous life," to the point where although "a desire to excel governed all my thoughts," she was still "much attracted by an order for fallen women called the Magdalens" (16), craving at once the position of prodigy and outcast.

Later, McCarthy developed a more nuanced appreciation for the possibilities offered by containment, which developed through reading Latin. Studying Caesar's famously clipped style, she recalls "recogniz[ing] the beauty of an ablative absolute and of a rigorous code of conduct" (166). As her *Memories* relate, she went on to reject the Catholic Church and its demands, but her writing continued to be governed by a paradoxical desire for closure and compression, and a resistance to the hierarchies that perpetuate control and containment. In her critical and literary career, these hierarchies manifested in the form of the political narratives of a nationalistic United States, and even in *Memories,* the way that she figures religious containment is commensurate with political control. But in keeping with her "passionate love of beauty," McCarthy figured her resistance to political containment in terms of a personal resistance, directed by aesthetic judgment. At the end of her commentary on her religious growth, culminating in her rejection of Catholicism, McCarthy reveals that her resistance is based on an uncompromising sense of personal judgment: "I do not mind if I lose my soul for all eternity. If the kind of God exists who could doom me for not working out a deal with him, then that is unfortunate. I should not care to spend eternity in the company of such a person" (27). The resistance to political conformity enacted through her fiction invokes, implicitly, the same logic of resistance. But as with Catholicism, or Caesar, she cannot resist the allure of aesthetic enclosure.

McCarthy and the Critics

To develop a model of writing that coordinates form and style in a way that opposes cultural expectations of literary production and undermines national political narratives demands a sophisticated conceptualization of both the role of literature and the broader relationship between critic, text, and society. Bowles, Welty, and Williams stand out not only for their idiosyncratic use of form but also for their clear articulation of their works' opposition to the constrictive demands of critical and social values. Where they couched their works' oppositional impetus in terms of their other artistic media, however, the countercultural approach that McCarthy adopted in her writing grew directly out of her role as a literary critic. Her career as a writer began not simply by reviewing books or theater but by explicitly critiquing other critics, through a series of articles published in the *Nation*. Not only did these pieces garner her a large audience, but they allowed her the chance to openly cultivate a metacritical voice, through writing articles that explicitly questioned what literary criticism ought to achieve and how it ought to do so. More specifically, these pieces allowed her to grapple with problems that would prove central to her own fictional output: what relationship content should bear to form; how a work's aesthetic concerns should match up to social issues; and to what extent literature should conform to expected structures and affirm popular tastes. The style of writing and playful tone that she emphasizes in her criticism heavily inflected her later literary style, and although her own reviews do not always live up to the kind of criticism that her early reviews implicitly demand, McCarthy's ironic awareness of this gap informs her stories' obsession with the double register of failure.

Beginning in October 1935, the *Nation*, the New York bastion of left-wing cultural criticism, began publishing a series of articles entitled "Our Critics, Right and Wrong." The byline of the pieces identified the authors as "Margaret Marshall and Mary McCarthy," although McCarthy would later maintain that the inclusion of Marshall, who was then assistant literary editor for the magazine, was simply to act as a "restraining influence" on the younger McCarthy, whose attitude was noticeably more confrontational.[5] The articles were originally conceived of as a four-part series surveying the landscape of American criticism, but they proved to be so successful that the editors extended the series to a fifth piece. For later readers—especially those inured to theory-laden, partisan justifications of specific strands of literary analysis—these three-page overviews can seem quaint or naïve. At first glance, they seem to simply lampoon other critics for inconsistency and poor judgment, or what they title an "anarchy of standards" that levels literary analysis to personal taste ("Our Critics I"

472). This impression was exacerbated by their sly humor, which is characteristic of McCarthy's criticism elsewhere, as in her analysis of one critic, for whom "literature stirs in him simply a number of vague, often undocumented associative thought processes" ("Our Critics III" 595). In the series' first instalment, the touchstone for their critique is the Pulitzer Prize–winner Thornton Wilder, for whom they seem to hold utter contempt. After satirizing the excessive praise that his (clearly unworthy) work had received, they wonder "how many" critics actually possess "sober judgment" or "the sense of proportion, the discriminating taste which once would have assigned Mr. Wilder to the humble niche he now occupies?" ("Our Critics I" 468). However, beneath the veneer of outrage and dismissal, these articles began to develop a metacritical argument that was more sophisticated than quibbling over the value of particular writer and that prefigures the sustained social critique of her fiction, particularly the concentric stories of *The Company She Keeps*. Indeed, it not only attacks the critical establishment but asks readers to consider why books should be reviewed at all and how they themselves evaluate what they have read. The first review concludes that "criticism in America during the last ten years has on the whole worked for the misunderstanding of works and the debasement of taste," implicitly asking the reader to consider the value of works beyond their adherence to contemporary trends ("Our Critics I" 472).

One way that these reviews invite such a reading is by challenging the idea of the totality of literary value. Arguing that critics treated literature as something that was either priceless or worthless, the articles point out that the language critics use falls at the extreme end of the spectrum, harpooning the archetypal reviewer, "his well of superlatives not yet dry" before detailing a myriad of specific examples (often framed in terms that caustically emphasize their hazy relationship to the original prose) ("Our Critics I" 494). Asking the reader to think beyond this idea of absolute literary value and question the "oracular certainty" of reviews, these articles also critique judgments that are based on emotional reactions. Through what I read as a conscious use of irony, these essays appeal to the readers' emotions as they pass judgment on precisely such appeals, attacking writers who "reduce the critical world to a quivering jelly of uncritical emotion" ("Our Critics I" 469). Rather than undermining the metacritical position of the articles, however, such appeals invite the reader to go beyond their own initial reactions, to think about why texts might be manipulating their feelings. As such, they heap contempt on one particular reviewer, for whom "ignorance is her fetish," and who is "easily swayed by her emotions," encouraging the reader to instead take a more removed look at how works are encouraging certain reactions, and to consider why they might do so ("Our Critics II" 544). These articles also suggest the potential implications of taking an emotionally guided and totalizing position: it leads to an eventually hypocritical position, which is ultimately driven by personal egoism; McCarthy and Marshall maintain that "the history of American criticism during the last ten years has been a history of inflations and deflations: the first, raucous, hyperbolic; the second, apologetic, face-saving, whispered" ("Our Critics I" 471). But they also identify a less private, more social context that influences critics: the financial exigencies of newspaper and book production. They note that newspapers are "busily engaged in turning literature into merchandising," and in spite of their critical tone, they go so far as to acknowledge that although "literature is art," it is "at the same time, merchandise" ("Our Critics V" 717). This recognition is not made in order to excuse reviewers, however, but rather to emphasize the need for a criticism that separates a work's commercial and artistic merits.

This final, contentious domain is where the articles articulate their clearest vision for the future of criticism, and where McCarthy's later concerns are most explicitly foreshadowed. While they never contend that a book's appeal to a larger reading public should be considered, McCarthy and Marshall nonetheless argue that criticism needs to come from an intellectual perspective and needs to evaluate works in terms commensurate with their sophistication. They take explicit issue with "a group whose most notable characteristic is its militant anti-intellectualism," which they suggest manifests in obsession with a work's superficial plot, and ease of access. "For this group," they contend, "literature must be 'exciting,' history and biography must read like fiction, and fiction must above all be entertaining and easy" ("Our Critics II" 452). The problem that they identify with such an approach is that it reduces literature to mere entertainment, overriding any other possible function. Equally problematic, however, is the alternative position, where a critic "treats books primarily as news" ("Our Critics III" 596). They argue that such a slavish insistence on the relationship between a novel and the real world leads to reviews that "are in the nature of reports" and that such a reading "seems to be more interested in books dealing with general questions than in purely literary productions" ("Our Critics III" 596). What both these critical positions lack is an analysis of the connection between form, style, and content, instead reducing literature to pure narrative movement, or social commentary.

Ultimately, these articles conclude that the problem with contemporary criticism lies in broader social conditions: an absence of a nuanced understanding of the role of literature and a refusal to question why works might subvert their readers' expectations. Arguing that the existing culture is predicated on absolute values, and consequently absolute judgments, McCarthy and Marshall explain that critics are "unequipped to deal with complicated artistic or intellectual problems" and that they "instinctively resist them" ("Our Critics II" 452–53). They suggest that this pattern is contingent on the moral demands that their culture places on literary production—an observation that McCarthy would continue to make thirty years later. Concluding that, at their heart, most critical judgments "are old-fashioned-American, moral and personal, not aesthetic," where a reviewer might react negatively to a work, "not because it was a bad novel, but because its heavy dose of sex offended his moral sensibility," these articles insistently call for a model of criticism that is aware of stylistic complexities and that does not dismiss writing because it is unconventional (or praise work simply for conforming to taste). They explicitly link this need to developments in literature itself, arguing that "important novels demand from genuine critics new turns of thought, new patterns of prose" ("Our Critics II" 544). Most crucially, in light of McCarthy's subversive approach to literary form, this argument implies that critics need to be complicit in changing readers' minds, and asking them to view ideas from new perspectives—much as these articles consistently attempt to do.

What stands out most obviously about McCarthy's ideal mode of criticism, then, is the way that it flows out from literary expression, with a sophistication of language and structure that is commensurate with the most innovative prose. Implicit within this model, however, is also a kind of feedback; the kind of evaluative, searching perspective she asks of critics, she suggests, also should inflect fiction. Certainly, her own fiction is conspicuous for the incisive and analytical perspective that it adopts. And while it is fiercely concerned with aesthetic patterning on the one hand, and social criticism on the other, these concerns are not developed in a way that is governed by ideology (a stance her criticism insistently resists). Instead, her prose cultivates the register of the critique—provoking in its reader an appraisal or interrogation. In this respect, the title of her anthology *Cast a Cold Eye* is particularly suggestive, reflecting her stylistic approach to the subject of her stories. It was her career as a reviewer—and particularly the metacritical impulse of her work for the *Nation*—that supplied her with the toolbox to construct such penetrating inward looks at characters and ideas. As her own urgings would suggest, moreover, this gaze was tied to complex strategies of representation and thought. Her insistent themes of stasis and enclosure attest to the fact that one of her key fictional concerns was that of containment—whether through the power imbalances of gender relations, social dynamics, or political systems—and in structural terms, she interrogates these ideas through the techniques of mirroring and layering. These controlled perspectives are reflected throughout her criticism, where they form the foundation for her idiosyncratic mode of analysis.

From her earliest reviews, dating back to the years after she graduated from Vassar, McCarthy's critical prose suggests several stylistic preoccupations. One central concern is the positioning of perspective. Not only do her reviews reflect a sophisticated conceptualization of the contingency associated with specific perspectives, but they frame this concern with spatial language, figuring it in terms of proximity, distance, and angle. This recurs in even the most unlikely reviews; in a 1940 account of a series of books about the start of the Second World War, she makes the observation that "it is paradoxical that the closer we are brought by technological means to events, the less we know about them."[6] And her own prose in this review telescopes in and out of the books, playing with the broadest lens of the survey before subjecting individual phrases to intense scrutiny. But even as she employs multiple perspectives within her own critiques, she also suggests the limitations of such an approach, explaining that "the reason for the fragmentariness" of a particular book on saints is "the feebleness of the conviction behind it."[7] This "feebleness" translates, in stylistic terms, to the sense of movement in a text, and her reviews are constantly attuned to the interplay between stasis and energy, or the moment when, although a work "first appears to be no more than a static account," it eventually "turns into a story."[8] This syncopated style would have a more prominent place in *The Company She Keeps*, but even her early reviews suggest a keen concern for the way that expectations of progression could be subverted and redirected.

These concerns were most clearly articulated, however, in retrospect, when McCarthy returned to the *New Republic* in 1962 to review Vladimir Nabokov's *Pale Fire*. Not only did the distance from her earlier criticism give her a clearer perspective on her literary values, but her ability to recognize the qualities of prose that she saw as important was honed by her own (now extensive) literary career. Nonetheless, there is a clear continuity between the critical practice she outlined in 1935 and the way she read Nabokov's genre-crossing work—indeed, the latter review acts as kind of coda to "Our Critics," endorsing *Pale Fire* as the ideal "important new novel" to which she argued critics needed to respond. Describing the work as "pretending to be a curio," she concluded that "it cannot disguise the fact that it is one of the very great works of art of this century, the modern novel that everyone thought dead."[9] McCarthy attributed much of the work's stature to its generic hybridity, through a chimerical description of it as the "centaur work of Nabokov's, half poem, half prose, this merman of the deep," which she evaluated as "a creation of perfect beauty, symmetry, strangeness, originality, and moral truth." As this language suggests, she was interested in the work in large part for its careful patterning and balance, which it deploys both structurally and thematically, so that "repetitions, reflections, misprints, and quirks of nature are taken as signs of the presence of a pattern" (24). This patterning is coupled with a structure designed to facilitate multiple perspectives, where the recursive patterning is matched with tessellated points of view that interact in uncomfortable ways. Suggesting that the overall effect was "like those houses of memory in medieval mnemonic science," she noted that although *Pale Fire* was structured as "a novel on several levels," these levels did not interact through a linear arrangement, or "the customary 'levels of meaning' of modernist criticism" (21).

Instead, they reflected distorted or false versions of the novel's central images back at one another, so that "each plane or level in its shadow box proves to be a false bottom; there is an infinite perspective regression, for the book is a book of mirrors" (22). Given her earlier emphasis on enclosure and containment, what is most salient about McCarthy's description is its ironic awareness of the infinite possibilities offered by an inherently limited space—the productive potential of compression. Her optical imagery, moreover, focused around mirrors and perspective, suggests a peculiar kind of craft on Nabokov's part: funneling the reader's vision, so as to dislocate or disorient them. The final conclusion that she reaches—that the novel forces the reader to evaluate their assumptions about rational logic—is also her highest form of praise. Asserting that "the real, real story, the plane of ordinary sanity and common sense, the reader's presumed plane, cannot be accepted as final," she suggests that Nabokov's success in *Pale Fire* is a recalibration of perspective, achieved through a technocratic attention to structure and reflection.

Insurrectionary Aesthetics: McCarthy as Double Agent

In his scathing review of *The Group* in 1963, Norman Mailer astutely emphasized this discrepancy between McCarthy's outsider persona and her success in navigating the closed world of critics and reviewers. Casting her as America's "First Lady of Letters," an iconoclastic "Joan of Arc" who had assumed the role of "our saint, our umpire, our lit arbiter, our broadsword," Mailer suggests in mock disgust that the success of her novel may reveal that McCarthy had "conspir[ed] with the epigones," or that she was, herself, merely a hack.[10] Mailer's incredulity was no doubt exaggerated by the phenomenal success of *The Group*, which had inspired a slew of glowing reviews and would go on to top the *New York Times* best-seller list for nearly two years. But the core of his review constituted an attack on the work's apparent acquiescence to the conventional expectations of literary form and content. Until *The Group*, McCarthy's work had been characterized by either formal obtuseness (the unstable point of view in *The Company She Keeps*), overtly intellectual subject matter (the academic setting of *The Groves of Academe*), or a combination of the two, as in the long story or short novel *The Oasis*, which satirized a utopian academic community. By contrast, *The Group* seemed to follow a traditional novel-istic arc, following the growth of a group of eight young women through a roving third-person narrator. Pleasingly, for critics, this growth was linked to external social change, and its focus on the domestic details of life in the 1930s suggested both a broad appeal and potential social ben-efit for its readers. Today, this unnuanced reading of her work continues to exert a hold on the text, with contemporary writers like A. S. Byatt maintaining that "its intention was literary, storytelling, shocking rather than forwarding a cause."[11] The terms in which McCarthy's work has been misread suggest her success not only in infiltrating the midcentury critical establishment but also, paradoxically, in critiquing it from within.

While the commercial success of *The Group* was generally reflected in its critical reception, its endorsement was not quite as universal as Mailer's critique suggested. But even in those reviews that attacked McCarthy's work, critics nonetheless drew specific attention to the qual-ity of her prose. The values that influenced this assessment were twofold. On the one hand, as Charles Poore suggested in a review for the *New York Times*, McCarthy's prose wed subject matter to style, where the astute reader was "rewarded by the miraculous precision [McCarthy] displays in making her prose fit her characters." Her novel thus replicated the voices of her characters clearly and uncritically. This sense of stylistic integrity was combined, in critics' eyes, with witty humor, to the extent that Poore could claim the novel was written "with amazingly unflagging jubilance."[12] And on a larger scale, despite routinely classifying the novel as a satire, critics maintained that McCarthy's style was ultimately posi-tive, endorsing the changes undergone by the characters. While a satire would normally be understood as critical, reviewers suggested that the chief value of McCarthy's style lay in its clear and unbiased reproduction of reality. So in an otherwise harsh review in the *Chicago Tribune*, Richard Sullivan could still note that "it has been remarked many times that the prose that Mary McCarthy writes is fine and sharp" and acknowledge that she "writes unquestionably with knowledge and authority as well as sharpness."[13] For its initial readers, then, the novel's success came from McCarthy's ability to convey a detached authority on the narrative, using humor to subtly endorse its action—a reading that clearly ran against McCarthy's professed aim to critique the idea of progress.

In fact, this strategy of misreading is closely linked to the perspective that critics understood the novel to have on American culture, both in its recent past, and present. Writing for the *Wall Street Journal*, Edmund Fuller noted that "McCarthy has drawn a bead on American society and its education of women" through a fundamentally analytical gaze, whereby "everything it touches is called into question"—suggesting that the novel's chief aim was that of interrogation.[14] But as Arthur Mizener argued, in another review for the *New York Times*, this interrogation was carried out in a detached tone—McCarthy's "voice is cool and reasonable, and her eye is fixed, not on her own emotions, but on the revealing particulars of people's lives."[15] Using similar terms, Tom Fitzpatrick noted in a review of *Venice Observed* (an account of Venice republished in 1963 to capitalize on the success of *The Group*) that "Miss McCarthy is an excellent reporter," emphasizing this same sense of detached, accurate attention to detail.[16] This suggests that *The Group*'s reception was guided by a sense of its documentary function: McCarthy's writing was simply a record of what she and her peers had experienced. Insistent references to her nonfiction reinforce this interpretation—Mizener, for instance, suggests that the "precise, commonsense voice" that McCarthy adopts in *The Group* "is perhaps most appealing in her autobiography." From this perspective, the novel could clearly be construed as offering strong social benefit to its readers, offering an unbiased viewpoint on the way American society had developed in the previous decades.

With hindsight, this concerted reimagining of *The Group* as a progressive text that optimistically—even joyfully—charted social progress in America through an inquisitive but detached lens may seem willfully perverse. Even without McCarthy's own guidance regarding the novel's critique of progress, the strength of her satire indicates an intensely critical attitude toward social conventions and patriarchal authority. That such a reading was possible, however, can be attributed in large part to McCarthy's use of form. In critics' eyes, McCarthy linked a socially progressive movement to a formal use of narrative progression, through a style that Fuller described as a "shifting, episodic narrative pattern." In spite of the setbacks faced by many of the characters, such a style could be seen as suggesting forward movement and positive change because McCarthy's own voice was seen as absent; her lack of authorial interpolation lent her narrative structure greater authority in interpreting the text. Explicitly linking style and form, Fuller stressed that "the book does not 'say' anything. It shows us behavior"—the lack of explicit judgment lent the narrative structure greater power in suggesting development and growth.[17]

Mailer's sometimes vindictive reviews drew attention to these same formal elements of her collection, but unlike other reviewers, he suggested that there was a tension between *The Group*'s apparent form and its narrative movement, declaring it to be "a book which could be said to squat on the Grand Avenue of the Novel like a shabby little boutique, a place which offers treasure in the trash" (1). Mailer's condemning tone should not obscure what is an astute observation: *The Group*'s overarching narrative, and individual chapters, resist the forward moment that was closely associated with the novel and that gave it such prominence in midcentury criticism. Indeed, Mailer argues that the work repeatedly sets up an expectation of novelistic conventions before rejecting them: "Let's refine Comrade Mary's problem a little further. A collective novel in which the most interesting character is missing, a collective novel in which none of the characters have sufficient passion to be interesting in themselves, yet none have the power or dedication to wish to force events. Nor does any one of the characters move critically out of her class by marrying drastically up, or savagely down" (2). In Mailer's eyes, the novel's failure lay in this repeated structural bathos, promising a certain narrative arc, then failing to deliver. Cannily, he suggests that McCarthy was herself aware of this process, noting that she "is too much of an old pro not to see the odds"; he even suggests that she may be deliberately undermining audiences' expectations, where "her characters will come from one class and make no heroic journeys to other classes, they will not look to participate in the center of the history which is being made, and they will be the victim of no outsize passion" (2). While he does not endorse this strategy in any way, he does inadvertently provide an explanation for why McCarthy may have adopted it. Noting that the characters seem trapped "because they have neither the interest to break out of the cage of their character, nor even the necessity" (3), Mailer provides a reading of the novel that links the lack of forward movement to a commentary on the restrictions of individuals. He suggests, moreover, in another critique of the work, that this commentary could reflect on the recent, rather than

distant past, when he notes the "atrocious anachronism" that the characters, "while engaged in the activities of the thirties," nonetheless have "a
consciousness whose style derives directly from the fifties" (3).

In spite of his clear intentions otherwise, then, Mailer presents an alternative reading of the novel, in which McCarthy has deliberately undermined the novelistic structure of her work, to reflect on the restrictions
on identity in postwar (rather than prewar) America. It is telling that, in
order for the book to be read positively by critics, it needed to be understood as recording with an unbiased eye the changes in American society,
within a structure that endorsed that growth. If it were read critically,
however, then the attention to detail became not a technique to show
development, but stultifying or static—suffering from "the taint of the
monotonous and overindulgent," in Mailer's words—and the work as a
whole was judged "a fail[ure] as a novel" (2) because it questioned the idea
of personal growth. On the one hand, this reflects critics' investment in a
narrative of growth and social progress, where a novel's formal structure
needed to correlate to a narrative of growth. On the other hand, it suggests
a possible act of insurgency on McCarthy's part: deliberately undermining
the relationship between formal progression and social progress.

While the formal demands of critics certainly played a part in *The Group*'s
misreading, by 1963 the pressure on authors to conform to a formal and
thematic narrative had abated from the intense "critical McCarthyism"
of the late 1940s and early 1950s. Instead, what compounded the tendency to reimagine *The Group* as a neutral account of social progress was
McCarthy's already well-established reputation as a critic and nonfiction
writer. Her reputation for frank self-exposure was marshaled in support
of the accuracy of *The Group*'s details of its characters' lives, and this colored the novel's wider reception as an honest work tied closely to reality.
Mizener, in a generally positive evaluation of the work, still noted that
"the book will be widely read as a titillating insider's report of the life actual Vassar girls lived," and suggested that "to some extent . . . McCarthy
has asked for this." Indeed, he suggested that this was part of a larger
problem with her work, where readers over-identified, or mis-identified,
characters and narrators with McCarthy and her peers. Not only had she
"written a good deal of the kind of autobiography that encourages readers
to take her literally," but her style more generally had "a personal intensity

that makes the reader very aware of the author." In the case of *The Group*, Mizener argued, this kind of reading was further encouraged given that "her previous fiction . . . seems to invite the reader to identify the originals of the characters."[18] In Mizener's eyes, this stylistic obfuscation of accuracy, inviting readers to treat fiction as fact, was not a deliberate stylistic choice. Although Mailer, by contrast, was able to see this as deliberately contributing to McCarthy's intended tone in the novel, he dismissed this strategy through another personal attack, arguing that it is a symptom of "vanity"—"the accumulated vanity of being over-praised"—and concluding that McCarthy was "simply not a good enough woman to write a major novel . . . she has failed" (2). For both of these critics, McCarthy's writing outside of fiction influenced the way that her fiction was read. But rather than considering the possible thematic implications of such generic destabilization, they instead dismissed it as, at best, a distraction, or at worst, a symptom of vanity and authorial overreaching.

This pattern of reading was prefigured in the reception of McCarthy's first work of fiction, *The Company She Keeps*, which was also insistently framed in terms of McCarthy's public persona and intellectual credentials. In a review for the *New York Times*, John Chamberlain introduced her as "the sharp-eyed wife of Edmund Wilson," positioning her in relation to her well-established husband.[19] In another review for the *New York Times*, Edith Walton similarly noted that although "personalities are usually irrelevant to a book review," in "the case of Mary McCarthy," it seemed "the reader should know something of her background and of her familiarity with the world which this first novel depicts." Although for Walton—as for readers of *The Group*—this familiarity simply lent the narrative a greater degree of authenticity, in that "much of [McCarthy's] own experience, unquestionably, is reflected in that of her heroine," for most readers McCarthy's proximity to the intellectual circles that the work depicts helped them to recognize the criticism in which it was engaged.[20] Writing in the *New Republic*, the novelist and critic Malcolm Cowley summarized the book as "a comedy of life among the New York intellectuals," suggesting that the work's primary aim was to critique the tenor of contemporary criticism.[21] Chamberlain's verdict echoed Cowley's; he described the work as a "collective portrait of bohemian and radical New York," particularly its "partisan reviewers," and suggested that its "satire is administered as gently and as murderously as a cat administers death to a mouse."[22] Where, for *The Group*, McCarthy's reputation influenced readers to view the work as accurate and progressive, in the case of *The Company She Keeps*, aligning McCarthy's public persona with her work helped in emphasizing its overtly critical, even partisan tenor.

But as these readers noted, McCarthy's persona did not simply sit outside the text; it added credibility to her satire. As in *The Group*, McCarthy's prose deliberately destabilized the boundaries between the genres of fiction and nonfiction—a fact to which critics were keenly alive. For Walton, this transgression was to the detriment of the work. Noting that it was "as strange and provocative in form as it is in content," she emphasized "how obliquely, how deviously the story takes shape." This deviousness was derived from McCarthy's blurring of the lines between author, narrator, and protagonist, and Walton agonized that "it seems to me a pity that her viewpoint is so personal, and that some of her characters are modelled so viciously and unfairly on actual literary figures."[23] This perspective was not limited to Walton, either. Initial readers of *The Company She Keeps* repeatedly criticized McCarthy for her fiction's precarious relationship to reality, as in Chamberlain's conclusion that "either viewpoint [factual or fictional] would, I think, be acceptable, but a mixture of the two is disturbing. One cannot escape the impression that Mary McCarthy is too close to her heroine."[24] The most generous assessment came from Cowley, who praised the quality and earnestness of the prose, suggesting that McCarthy "has learned the difficult art of setting down everything as it might have happened, without telling a single self-protective lie." But again, the disruptive quality he can identify and praise ultimately undermines the work as a whole—although it has "the still unusual quality of having been lived," *The Company She Keeps* is ultimately neither "a likeable book, nor is it very well put together."[25] Curiously, beneath the superficial spitefulness of their critiques, none of these readers seemed disturbed by the destabilizing lived quality of McCarthy's prose, in and of itself. Instead, it was the ends to which she deployed this strategy that perturbed them. Chamberlain concluded that although *The Company She Keeps* "has very definite merits . . . its values, I feel, are suspect."[26] In other words, critics could recognize the adroitness of McCarthy's writing but rejected the social critique that it enacted.

This tendency for readers to register the stylistic incongruities of McCarthy's earlier work is further reflected in their keen interest in the text's formal ambiguities. While Cowley and Walton identify it as a novel, a reviewer for the *Chicago Daily Tribune* described it as a "book of short stories," explaining that it is "called a novel in six parts, but is only a novel in the sense that the reader knows Margaret Sargent infinitely better at its end than at its beginning."[27] McCarthy had initially developed the book as a series of stories, and the shifting perspectives and formal discreteness of each episode seem to contradict the work's marketing as a novel. Even when discussing the work through the terminology of the novel, critics acknowledged the work's interplay between compression and movement, falling back on the terminology of photography to account for its fragmented and containing aesthetics. Chamberlain described McCarthy as having "photographically and psychologically 'shot' her heroine from six angles," and while his review acknowledges the skill with which McCarthy executes this approach, he concludes that the effect was unsettling: "The book is almost too penetrating," giving "the uneasy feeling of [the reader themselves] being under an X-ray."[28] Echoing this language, Walton summarizes the novel as "a series of six episodes which are virtually short stories," in which the reader "is given varying facets and aspects of the girl's personality as seen from a variety of angles." For Walton, this shifting perspective "seems distorted,"[29] and more broadly the language that critics summoned to account for the effect of this multiple exposure was localized around compression and restriction. This certainly applied to Cowley's observation that McCarthy's characters have "a peculiar air of coming from nowhere, having no relatives and believing in nothing, as if their well cut opinions were delivered in a box with their clothes."

Kept by Her Company: McCarthy, Form, and Social Critique

How can this interpretation of *The Company She Keeps* be reconciled with the reception of McCarthy's later work? Within the context of *The Group*, these same techniques of shifting perspective, compressed focus, and contrapuntal movement were understood in opposite terms, as part of a progressive and socially optimistic narrative. While subjected to a much harsher critique, *The Company She Keeps* also elicited a much more nuanced reading, with critics attentive to the work's play with genre and form—regardless of whether they endorsed the ends to which these strategies were deployed. In recent years, *The Group* has replayed its earlier commercial success, most prominently through Candace Bushnell's contemporary reimagining of the work as the *Sex and the City* essays (alongside their filmic translations). But in terms of literary style, *The Company She Keeps* left a clearer impression on readers and authors. A year after its publication, Orville Prescott noted in a review of Helen Howe's *The Whole Heart* that "in its oblique method of presenting a character through his impact on others it recalls Mary McCarthy's bravura *The Company She Keeps*," and other reviews in prominent periodicals such as the *New York Times* and *Chicago Daily Tribune* drew on McCarthy's debut work to similar ends.[30]

This legacy does not necessarily reflect a more stable interpretation of the book. Indeed, the play of scale and perspective that these first readers noted continue to trouble readers—a situation which McCarthy's own conflicting accounts of the book serve to exacerbate. As is clear from the initial reviews, it was marketed as a novel and, on publication, generally understood as such. The *Columbia Companion to the Twentieth-Century American Short Story*, however, treats it as a "series of interlocking stories," and a *Guardian* review of its 2011 reprint classifies it as "really six short stories tenuously held together by dint of McCarthy's intensely autobiographical style."[31] The insistence with which later readers identify the book as a short story collection seems to suggest that, in retrospect, the anthology is more fragmented than initial reviewers could observe. And in interviews about her work, McCarthy's accounts of her conceptualization of her writing indicate a deliberate blurring of lines between different forms, supporting this interpretation. When her interviewer for the *Paris Review* referred to *The Company She Keeps* as a novel, McCarthy explained that although "about halfway through" the writing process she began to think of the work as a novel, this was only in the sense of the chapters telling "a kind of unified story" where "the same character kept reappearing." So despite deciding "finally to call it a novel," McCarthy's conceptualization of the finished work was "a story, one story" which was composed of chapters explicitly written "as short stories."[32] This explanation reflects her sensitive awareness of the nuances of literary

structure—evident in her praise of generic hybridity in her criticism—
and her deliberate transgression of those structures. It also suggests that
she wrote with an eye to the aesthetics of scale and containment—a
suggestion borne out by the work itself.

From the contents page it is clear that the volume is arranged as a
series of discrete stories rather than a continuous novel. And although
the acknowledgments page attributes the original publication venues for
"certain of these episodes," the stories themselves offer no suggestion that
they are part of a connected narrative or that their female protagonists
are necessarily the same person; in several of the stories she remains
unnamed, so that it seems inaccurate to refer to her as Miss Sargent, as
the second story names her, or Meg, as she becomes in the fourth. This
narrative isolation or fragmentation is reiterated in the stories' structures, which McCarthy has crafted to accentuate their sense of being
contained—even in a story like "Rogue's Gallery," which covers a large
expanse of time, the story is crafted in a way that resists momentum, so
that the opening line, "Mr. Sheer fired his stenographer in order to give
me the job" (23), already implies an end point and a specific bracket of
time. This renders the collection, as a whole, more a sequence of static
moments than a larger, organic and novelistic trajectory. Such an observation might seem merely a generic quibble, but McCarthy's use of
stasis and containment is essential to the social critique that her stories
articulate and can be seen particularly in the case of "The Man in the
Brooks Brothers Shirt," a story that had earlier been published in the *Partisan Review* and that develops a sustained critique of the contemporary
discourse around identity.[33]

McCarthy's choice of setting immediately suggests a predominating
theme of enclosure: almost all of the story takes place over a single train
ride, beginning with the protagonist's observation that "The man who
came into the club car was coatless" (63). Although she immediately
rules him "Out of the Question," the way that she conceptualizes the
"trip West" as a discrete space, outside of the normal flow of time, implies
an understanding of identity as contingent upon context and suggests
a desire to make the most of the opportunity to act outside of normal
societal restrictions—she feels "a curious, shamefaced disappointment, as
if she had given a party and no guests had come." McCarthy consistently

emphasizes the claustrophobia of the train's confined spaces, playing on the resonances of the word "compartment"—as when the epony-mous man invites her back to his—and the suspension of normal social codes—as when, "in the cultural atmosphere of the Pullman train," the author Vincent Sheean became "a titan" (64), rather than someone to be disdained. This sense of physical segregation is exacerbated by the affair into which the married man, a sales rep from a Cleveland steel company in monogrammed Ivy League attire, inexorably draws her. As their flirting and intimacy grow, the protagonist begins to feel trapped in a "whole strange factory," with the sense that "she did not know how to turn it off" (92)—transforming her into the raw material that her interlocutor processes and transforms. In spite of her earlier disappointment, she recognizes that "a compartment was something she had not counted on" (67); McCarthy's wording suggesting that the man's sexual aggression is placing her into a state of unwanted confinement.

Such a reading is reinforced by the protagonist's own frustration at being coerced into a constricting role, which emphasizes the intersection between physical and social constraint. Forced to decide on whether to accompany him to her room, "she felt bitterly angry with the man for having exposed her—so early—to this supreme test of femininity," she reveals her own sense of being forced into one of two compromising po-sitions: "she would either go into the compartment, not wanting to (and he would know this and feel contempt for her malleability), or she would stay out of the compartment, wanting to have gone in (and he would know this, too, and feel contempt for her timidity)" (68). Once they have slept together, rather than subsiding, this containing pressure increases; McCarthy repeats the motif of enclosure within the sheets of the bed, the attended bath on the train, and within the developing relationship. The man shows a fetishist obsession, viewing her as a "rabbit's foot," and wants to "keep her in an apartment in New York" (91). However, McCarthy does not limit this containment to her female character; when, in the brief epilogue outside the train journey, the man comes to visit the woman in New York, he feels "claustrophobia" (101) in her Greenwich Village apartment, trapped in an environment of which he is not in control.

The initial freedom that McCarthy's protagonist feels outside of the normal social conditions afforded by the train is replaced with a recognition of the limitations that the developing relationship places on her identity. In what could be considered a neurotic register, she obsesses about roles, types, and classifications; at one point she admits that she is interested in the man because he might be "the one who could tell her what she was really like" (78). And the story is charged with an almost schizoid dynamic, as she longs for the man to confirm her identity but resists the characterizations he tries to impose on her. As her biography is revealed—a biography that echoes McCarthy's own—it is revealed that this drive dates back to a rejection of the Catholic faith: "when she rejected the Church's filing system . . . she had given away her sense of herself" (78). Although, in their first conversation, she attempts to convey a certain appearance, "sustaining her end of a well-bred, well-informed, liberal conversation" (63–64), his remarks force her into an extreme posture, in which she feels confined—"he had trapped her features in an expression of utter snobbery" (67). She appears most comfortable when her persona remains fluid, as when they are talking in his compartment, but with the door open "exactly as if they were drinking in a show window" (68). Here she can maintain an open, unrestricted identity, where, "if for the people outside she was playing the great lady, for the man across the table she was the Bohemian Girl." It is during this brief moment of equilibrium that McCarthy's prose reaches its highest lyricism, through free indirect discourse that suggests a moment of almost beatific personal revelation: "As these multiple personalities bloomed on the single stalk of her ego, a great glow of charity, like the flush of life, suffused her" (69). The "idyll" of this revelation is shattered, along with any hope for the future of the affair, when near the end of the journey she finally realizes that he has been continuing to understand her as a type. When he declares that he does not love her because she is "a Bohemian," but because she is "underneath all that . . . just a sweet little girl" (98), this assertion clarifies their relationship for her, affirming that it was based simply on a "misunderstanding." Her ultimate refusal to be bound to a type is signaled when, in the final sentences of the story, she tears up a letter from him, as "it would have been dreadful if anyone had seen it" (101), thus tying her to another's closed perception of her identity.

Despite her own resistance to classification, McCarthy's protagonist is nonetheless fully aware of her own tendency to class others by type, particularly the man whose perspective she rejects. The title of the story itself suggests a type of man—one who would wear a brand of clothing associated with a certain Ivy League education and lifestyle—and in interviews, McCarthy has reinforced this view, describing the story as "the one about the Yale man."[34] Conscious of her own attempts to understand the man in terms of a restricted identity—to "whitewash him" (72)—the protagonist acknowledges that she is attracted to him "on the basis of one of two assumptions, both of them literary: (a) that the man was a frustrated socialist, (b) that he was a frustrated man of sensibility, a kind of Sherwood Anderson character" (72). Using a phrase that reinforces the artificiality of such constraints, however, McCarthy suggests the hypocrisy of such a position, as the man's actual "personality kept popping up, perversely, like a jack-in-the-box, to confound these theories" (73). Shifting tack, she offers him alternative roles that he could play—unconscious here of the extent to which her actions mirror his and instead believing that "she was offering to release him from the chains of habit, and he was standing up and clanking those chains comfortably, and impudently in her face." The irony of her recognition that "she knew . . . that somewhere in his character there was the need of release" is that her plan for this release is her own constraining image of how he should be. So although on a surface level, McCarthy's narrative could be read as a straight protest against the limitations that social conventions place on identity, the satirical edge of her portrait of the protagonist suggests that, in fact, such confinements are inevitable and identity is necessarily limited, the possibility of fluidity cut off by the exigencies of human interaction.

In the particular "Bohemian" identity she tries to cultivate, her role as a reviewer and contributor to the *Liberal* periodical and her allusions to a deceased mother and family in Portland, the protagonist of "The Man in the Brooks Brothers Shirt" bears an uncanny resemblance to McCarthy herself. Acknowledging this similarity in biography, however, as in many of the stories in this anthology (the Miss Sargent of "Rogue's Gallery," for example, is writing a memoir), is to overlook the sharp dissonances between the protagonists of the different stories. It is hard to reconcile the heroine of "Cruel and Barbarous Treatment" with that of "The Man in the Brooks Brothers Shirt," even though the impending divorce in the former reflects the protagonist's status in the latter. Yet as John Crowley noted in an article in the *Explicator*, the original jacket notes for the first edition of *The Company She Keeps* explicitly identified the main character of all six stories as the same Meg Sargent.[35] Whether we want to attribute these notes to McCarthy or not, I would suggest that the dissonances between the characters and their shared identity are part of a deliberately destabilizing strategy on McCarthy's part. The references to "types" that pervade the collection reinforce this interpretation, as do the frequent shifts in temperament and attitude of the protagonist(s). If we return to McCarthy's dual conceptualization, of the chapters as stories in and of themselves but the entire book telling a metastory, then it follows that the individual characters could be considered individual iterations of a larger pattern. By juxtaposing radically different views or versions of the same character against one another, both within the individual stories and across the collection as a whole, McCarthy suggests the impossibility of reconciling freedom of identity with the limitations of an individual existence.

This critique reflects McCarthy's own fascination, as a critic, with works that could present a narrative through a patterned, compressed structure—a perspective that contrasted so clearly with her contemporaries, as their reviews of *The Company She Keeps* attests. Such a pessimistic alignment of claustrophobic structure and regressive narrative movement ran directly against the critical priorities that emerged in midcentury American critical culture. While the Great Depression had led to government initiatives designed to reinvest Americans' faith in their nation on an abstract level, it was the threat of the ideological conflict that culminated in the Second World War that impelled cultural critics to increasingly argue for a model of fiction oriented around the articulation of individual freedom—a tendency that was exacerbated by the cultural politics of the Cold War. But it was during the prewar years that an American tradition of liberal democracy had begun to be linked to a particular, nationalistic model of literature, with Dewey, writing on the cusp of war in 1939, declaring that "the attainment of freedom is the goal of [America's] political history."[36] This kind of position was similarly adopted by critics like Trilling and Rahv, as well as more broadly by venues like *Partisan Review*. As a prominent intellectual, involved with many of the critics who argued for an increasingly nationalistic model of writing, McCarthy's critique of the naïve possibility for individual freedom of identity, uninflected by social conditions, jarred with her cultural context. Using a form of the short story that was emphasized by its closure and containment, moreover, her writing could be read as a resistance to the imposition of political agenda onto literary expression. The priorities of McCarthy's contemporary critics extended beyond assessing the quality of a text, or concern with the details of what it communicated, to the kind of generic structures around which it was organized. For a text to communicate something that could contribute toward the political agenda of an America engaged in a global ideological struggle, it needed to enunciate in its form the same qualities of freedom that its characters and actions expressed. This meant, in general terms, a novelistic mode of expression. McCarthy's approach in *The Company She Keeps*—ostensibly acquiescing to these demands, then undermining them from within—exemplifies her insurgent spirit. It also emphasizes why, its commercial success notwithstanding, *The Group* failed to be read as a social critique. Structurally, McCarthy played the game too well, producing a work that could be read unironically as a novel, and consequently as a narrative of growth.

Indeed, the valorization of *The Group* by the majority of its readers enacts, on a small scale, the critical metanarratives that were guiding American fiction in the mid-twentieth century. If critics were opposed to writing that undermined a narrative of growth, then their expectations were certainly antithetical toward the short story, not simply on a structural level but based on their dedication to cultural production that enunciated a democratic model of individual freedom. While Mailer's resistance to *The Group* suggests a sense of discontinuity between form and narrative movement, he mostly resists the work's autobiographical aura. Even if it was not praised for doing so, *The Company She Keeps* was still recognized by critics as a transgressive work that resisted attempts to situate it within a novelistic tradition, defined by its ability to articulate a universal model of individual autonomy. This is because it is precisely such a model of individuality that McCarthy's stories destabilize and undermine. Rather than a coherent series of events through which her heroine grows and develops a clearer understanding of her world and her own place in it, her stories instead present a fractured protagonist, whose individual "episodes" are disjointed and fragmented. Well aware of the political implications of form in contemporary literature, McCarthy used the inherent limitation of the short story form as a way to offer a counternarrative to the model of democratic freedom that critics encouraged through their advocacy of works that drew on a romantic tradition of personal growth. Rather than attending to development, McCarthy instead almost obsessively focuses on her characters' conformity to various types and classifications, to suggest the extent to which behavior is patterned and conditioned by different social settings.

Structurally, this is manifested in the relationship between individual stories and the larger form of *The Company She Keeps*. While individually fragmented, the pattern of each story is reiterated on a macroscale, so that the individual stories can be read as miniatures of a larger pattern. But rather than nihilistic, there is a certain joy in McCarthy's writing, and even as she satirizes both the power structures that confine her heroines and their attempts to break free from them, she also celebrates them for having achieved at least a level of recognition that they are bound to these patterns of behavior. In *The Company She Keeps*, this paradoxical awareness is effected through the work's attention to aesthetic completion—reflecting the implicit desire for beauty expressed insistently in both her *Memories* and her criticism. Rather than simply patterning the text through repeated motifs, she uses a technique of shifting perspective that refracts identity through a series of lenses, creating a sense of expanding and contracting perspective. It is this playing with scale that invites more overt comparison between McCarthy's stories, memoir, and *The Group*. All three texts unsettle the reader's expectations of continuity and movement through changes in voice, magnitude, and generic conventions; however, it is in *The Company She Keeps* that these stylistic conventions most successfully enact a form of countercultural critique.

Within her *Memories*, McCarthy plays most obviously with scale, sequence, and perspective. The narrative is presented in two distinct voices: the narrative history, conveyed in a series of discrete episodes, and the commentary to each episode, presented in italics. The very use of the word *Memories* in the title signals a sequence of potentially distinct and untrustworthy moments rather than a strictly factual and sober narrative. Publishing the stories independently, without any indication of their ontological status, confounded this issue—as the bibliographical details to the book note, "the following chapters originally appeared in the *New Yorker*, some of them in somewhat different form." Not only are the reader's expectations of generic stability thus unsettled, the polyphonic dialogue draws attention to McCarthy's other stylistic experiments. She explains, early on, that she "wished that [she] were writing fiction," as "the temptation to invent has been very strong;" however, she quickly admits that "there are cases where I am not sure myself whether I am making something up" (3, 4). As the narrative progresses, other commentators are marshaled, including uncles, siblings, and friends, and McCarthy's critical voice is blended with those of her relatives. She confesses that "most of my memories of him [her father] are colored, I fear, by an untruthfulness that I must have caught from him as a child," and that "many of my most cherished ideas about my father turned out to be false" (11). The commentary also highlights McCarthy's own disingenuity in structuring the work, explaining the ways in which events have been reordered or amplified to shape a certain effect. She describes one "example of 'storytelling,'" in which she "arranged actual events to make a good story out of them," while freely admitting to having invented other episodes, as she could "have no idea if this story is true or not" (164, 14). The effect is to destabilize the reader's perspective, and transform what was marketed as an autobiographical portrait into a meditation on the instability of identity. By scrutinizing her memories through a series of lenses, each perspective accompanied by a self-analysis, McCarthy encourages the reader to acknowledge how contingent identity is upon the structures through which it is viewed.

Where this earlier work almost frenetically asked readers to question its presentation of events, however, *The Group* achieved its popular success in large part because it obscured its own formal experimentation. The work presents a series of detached views on the eponymous group of Vassar graduates, with each chapter focusing on a separate young woman, shifting in tone, emphasis, and chronology. As critics' easy classifications of the work as a novel attest, these shifts were not of great enough magnitude to confuse the question of the work's genre. McCarthy's well-established reputation as a public intellectual, cemented by her "candid" reflections in *Memories*, encouraged readers to identify the work as a biographically inflected fiction, so that ideas of a crossover between the conventions of fiction and nonfiction were registered in terms of subject matter, not style. Indeed, where her earlier novel pointed so clearly to its corruption of truth with fiction, the lack of commentary in *The Group* led readers to engage with it as a simple roman à clef, so that the irony of such an equation was lost. Perhaps what most distinguishes *The Group* from *The Company She Keeps,* however, is the kind of idea that they each critique. Where McCarthy's stories are focused around the specific power imbalances that contain the single protagonist's identity, *The Group* is expansive in its viewpoint, leveling out the individual experiences of each character in order to focus on a singular containing force: the concept of progress. As a novel about an idea, the differences between each character —although engaging in and of themselves—are thematically redundant. As Paul Giles appositely notes, this is not, in itself a problem but rather, "from another ideological angle," constitutes "one of the novel's great successes, for McCarthy is concerned not with the independence of the 'spirit' but with the interdependence of destinies."[37] Through her shifting perspective on her own past in *Memories*, McCarthy suggests the extent to which individual identity is determined by others; in *The Group*, her structure suggests that the identities of whole groups or classes is similarly determined. But rather than a political or cultural critique, this is an existential one—and in this sense, readers who saw *The Group* as a personal narrative were correct, insofar as it questions the parameters through which individual identities are constructed.

The success of *The Company She Keeps* lies in the way that it effects these shifts in perspective and scale through an ongoing interplay between novelistic and short story conventions. As the reviews of her work attest, the different expectations around the structure and content of each of these forms were predicated on their respective sizes—as were the cultural assumptions about their social relevance. Upsetting this neat schema, McCarthy draws the reader into questioning the genre of the collection almost immediately, as the first short story, "Cruel and Barbarous Treatment" (which is narrated through a compressed third-person voice), moves into the second, "Rogue's Gallery," which is narrated in the first person. Where the earlier story located the reader in a broad, departicularized scene, moreover, with characters identified

not by names but by social function, the second invokes an immediacy
and closeness that seems jarring by comparison. Opening with the declaration that "Mr. Sheer fired his stenographer in order to give me the
job" (25), "Rogue's Gallery" invites a reading as a separate, even discrete
narrative. This destabilization of any traditional novelistic trajectory is
coupled with ironic reflections that seem to prefigure McCarthy's technique in *Memories*; while the narrator reflects that being hired "puzzled
me at the time," she also creates a distance from events by commenting
on them as if from a place of superior knowledge—"I see now that he
must have owed her money." This contrasts with the continuity in focus
that McCarthy cultivated in the first story. Here, McCarthy juxtaposes the
proximity of her narrator's initial observations with a detached reflection,
creating the effect of a visual zoom in and out.

McCarthy also suggests a slightly mocking self-awareness, when the
narrator reveals her earlier naivety, admitting that "later on, after I had
quit, I, too, would make regular calls to collect my back pay," encouraging
the reader to notice the difference between her earlier actions and words
and later reflections. But even though this style seems to provide a closer
understanding of Meg's personality and perspective than in the first story,
by conveying her recollections through an inflected first-person voice,
this nonetheless sits uncomfortably in contrast to the portrait that the
first story had prepared. It is hard to reconcile the sincere image that
begins "Cruel and Barbarous Treatment"—"She could not bear to hurt
her husband. She impressed this on the Young Man, on her confidantes,
and finally on her husband himself" (2)—with the witty, playful tone of
the second story, especially as the former seems to convey the sense of
free indirect discourse. In juxtaposing these distinctive voices and inviting
the reader to understand them as the same character, McCarthy creates
two separate effects. On the one hand, she emphasizes the narrative
disjunction between the two episodes, unsettling the work's status as
novel. On the other, she invites the reader to consider the possibility
that individual identity can appear radically different, depending on
perspective and context—a conclusion that the narrator herself reaches.
Considering the way that Mr. Sheer was metonymically "listed as The
Saville Galleries," she notes that although "the plural conveyed a sense
of endless vistas of rooms gleaming with collector's items," in reality

"The Saville Galleries consisted of two small, dark, stuffy rooms whose natural gloom was enhanced by heavy velvet drapes" (26), and of course, ultimately consisted of a diminutive con-artist. In contrast to *The Group,* which creates narrative and thematic flow by levelling the difference between multiple distinctive voices, *The Company She Keeps* disrupts narrative flow by introducing schisms in a singular voice and asking the reader to think about the multiplicity of identity—and the structures that contain it.

Part of the way that she facilitates this kind of structural critique of identity is through the work's adroit blending of genres. Rather than directly contrasting two kinds of prose, as in *Memories,* McCarthy uses subtler prompts to coax the reader into making the kind of judgments about a fictional work that are nominally the domain of nonfiction. "Rogue's Gallery" is somewhat unconvincingly annotated as "an extract from memoirs begun by the heroine" (26), suggesting immediately that the work is meant to be read with an awareness of different literary conventions to those at play in the first. Rather than following the cues of an omniscient third-person narrator, the reader is now at the mercy of a willful and potentially untrustworthy first-person account of personal experiences. Now in the territory of the metafictional, the reader is invited to consider the implication of Meg being in control of her own representation and how this contrasts with a detached observation of her actions. Beyond this particular episode, moreover, this shift in voice inflects the way that subsequent chapters are read. Even on the smallest scale, the use of the word "heroine" to describe the narrator sounds suspicious. A much grander title than any used in the first chapter, it suggests that the annotation may in fact be attributed to Meg, beyond the story itself—in which case, it can be read as a subtle indication that the anthology as a whole may be a product of Meg's literary efforts. But even if the reader doesn't go so far as to read the entire book as a metafictional act of self-representation, this phrase, "an extract from memoirs," nonetheless asks us to question the narrator's truthfulness, and by extension the reliability of the narrative at large.

In this way, McCarthy foregrounds the slim distinction between a deliberate fiction and a subjective memory, providing conflicting cues about which side of this line the story should fall. But more crucially, she forces the reader to reconsider the kind of judgments that are contingent on the classification of a text. From this perspective, *The Company She Keeps* prefigures the dialogic commentary of *Memories*, by working into the fabric of the narrative less coercive and overt prompts to reflect on the process of interpreting a text. In "Rogue's Gallery," for instance, Meg exposes the mental processes behind her recollection and narration, through phrases like "I know this because" or "for I remember," which invite us to question the extent of her knowledge and the reliability of her memory on these issues. Inconsistencies within the narrative suggest that she may not, in fact, have had access to certain pieces of knowledge that she claims to possess, and McCarthy emphasizes the limitation of Meg's knowledge through direct reflection on her part—she muses, for example, that certain "explanations, taken separately or together, do not satisfy me. They may be one or all true, but there must have been something more" (38–39). These prompts do more than force the reader to evaluate Meg's reliability, however, and in fact suggest that her identity is contingent upon her access to knowledge, in much the same way that McCarthy's identity in her *Memories* is tied up in the narratives she can access about her own past. Although, to an extent, this is an external form of limitation—for Meg, it is tied to her status as a woman, not privy to knowledge that society withholds for men alone—McCarthy also stresses that this is an internally driven process. In one of the anthology's more comic moments, Meg notes how Sheer "had succumbed to the spell of his own salesmanship," so that the painter of miniatures, Monsieur Ravasse, "had become interchangeable with the Kaiser in his mind" (29). This is where *The Company She Keeps* is most distinct from *The Group*: it openly explores the way that individuals are culpable in their own containment.

The final story of the book, "Ghostly Father, I Confess," does not close the book in a traditional sense, bringing the narrative arc to a conclusion, but instead acts as a final framework, structurally containing the preceding stories. On its own, it seems deceptively simple; of the book's six stories, it has the most contained narrative, following a single, uninterrupted sequence of events, and focuses on a clear interaction, between a woman and her psychiatrist. The reader becomes quickly aware that the two are discussing some of the events of the previous stories, offering a dialogic interrogation that emphasizes Meg's containment. The description of the session itself is couched in terms that draw attention to the way Meg performs a particular role for the psychiatrist. Explaining one of her dreams, Meg notes, "I must have dreamed that just to please you. It's custommade. The womb fantasy"—and in spite of the psychiatrist's plea not to "worry about what *I* think" (250), McCarthy makes it clear that Meg's responses are guided by his expected responses. This is confirmed by small moments throughout the story, such as when Meg "knew without looking that she had coaxed a smile out of him," that highlight how her company, to take the words of the title, keeps her identity fixed. It is in this final context that Meg becomes most aware of her own containment, which she frames it in terms of movement: "It was a phrase that came to her lips a dozen times a day." "She would find herself hammering her fist on her knees and crying out to herself in a sort of whispered shriek, 'I can't go on, I CANNOT GO ON'" (258). The story thus draws the reader's attention back to the lack of narrative movement and asks them to link this to a personal sense of claustrophobia or limitation. With the same metafictional flourish that always characterizes McCarthy's style, however, the discussion within the therapy session turns this theme into a kind of puzzle, as Meg and her psychiatrist try to determine *why* she feels trapped and limited. Framing her act of self-representation in the terms of a detective story, Meg imagines that her "fugitive, criminal self lay hiding in a thicket" (257), detached from but within her mind or memory. In trying to account for her own identity, she cannot avoid imposing external narrative forms onto it, and although she stubbornly claims to "reject this middle-class tragedy, this degenerated Victorian novel where I am Jane Eyre or someone in Dickens" (263), McCarthy makes it clear that the only way Meg can try to understand her identity is by turning it into a story and confining it within a narrative. She recognizes, moreover, the double-bind of this process, where the only way she can understand her identity is through limiting it. This is where McCarthy articulates her clearest resistance to critics yoking personal growth to narrative movement, for as this sequence of stories makes clear, the act of narrating one's own experiences is inherently to limit them. It is for this reason that "the subject" of childhood "frightened" both Meg and her doctor: "it suggested to them that the universe is mechanical, utterly predictable, frozen" (262).

On the one hand, McCarthy seems to emphasize Meg's own culpability in this act, regardless of any external system. Her psychiatrist observes that she tends to crave being contained in other aspects of her life, noting that it is "unfortunate that you should have chosen to marry exactly the kind of man who would make you feel most enslaved and helpless" (281). But Meg links this idea of containment to an external regime, specifically a political one; she recognizes that her situation is like that of "the small state, racked by internal dissension," that "invites the foreign conqueror," because external regulation and confinement "is sweeter than responsibility" (282). Whatever personal judgment this implies, it also suggests that the narratives through which she defines herself are externally enforced. Reflecting on her own process of self-definition, she notes the way that she seems to be playing a part that has been set up for her—"always there was this sense of recognition, this feeling that she was only repeating combinations of words she had memorized long ago" (293) so that she is not able to distinguish between an authentic identity and an imposed one, and she ultimately wonders "whether the false self was not the true one" (294).

From this perspective, the tension that McCarthy establishes between novelistic and short story conventions in *The Company She Keeps* worked to emphasize the divisions in Meg's identity—which although apparently singular, is fractured and compressed. The patterned stasis of the stories, culminating in "Ghostly Father I Confess," highlights the extent to which Meg's identity is externally enforced and dependent on containing narrative structures. At the same time, McCarthy uses a style and structure that invites the reader to engage in biographical terms with the text, interrogating the episodes as a kind of detective story, where the culprit is Meg's true identity. But the book concludes with the assertion that there is *no* true identity—that Meg is at once "the Nazi prisoner, the pseudo-Byron, the equivocal personality who was not truly protean but only appeared so" (303). While this epiphany struck many contemporary readers as pessimistic—and McCarthy certainly uses this moment to emphasize that identity is ultimately limited, contained by a process in which the individual is culpable—it also has a more positive aspect. Observing that she has the ability to distinguish between the different narratives she imposes on her life—"she could still distinguish the Nazi prisoner from the English milord"—Meg seems to reflexively suggest that she can exert some control over it through the act of critical awareness, as long as "the inner eye has remained alert" (304). Invoking the same kind of critical consciousness that her reviews urged readers to adopt, *The Company She Keeps* asks its readers to at least recognize the way their identity is being corralled by external narrative structures, even if they are unable to avoid this process of containment.

chapter three

Tennessee Williams and the New School of Decadence

In both critical terms and the public imagination, Tennessee Williams's work exists as an iceberg. Although he is universally recognized as one of two canonical American playwrights, along with his contemporary Arthur Miller, his reputation rests on a handful of plays (and their film adaptations), masking an enormous body of writing across a range of forms and genres, most of which is critically and commercially unseen. The same can be said of his personal life. A seemingly inexhaustible subject for biographers, Williams's public image nonetheless rests on a few choice performances of identity, which, as John Lahr notes in the preface to his 2014 biography *Mad Pilgrimage of the Flesh*, remain largely uninterrogated; in Lahr's words, "almost none" of the more than forty volumes written on Williams "risks interpretation."[1] Until recently, this narrow focus has also tended to mask Williams's complex political engagement; however, recent critics, beginning with David Savran's *Communists, Cowboys, and Queers*, have started to acknowledge his sophisticated resistance to coercive political narratives. As Savran emphasizes, Williams "was a figure who called himself a revolutionary and meant it, a playwright who produced a new and radical theatre that challenged the Cold War order."[2] But even a discussion such as Savran's limits itself to Williams's better-known works. By moving his short fiction to the center, rather than periphery, of this line of criticism, I want to emphasize the way that Williams deliberately adopted different literary forms in order to articulate a personal resistance that was unavailable to the public genre of his plays. I also want to draw attention to Williams's nuanced conceptualization of the relationship between form, identity, and politics, which suggests broader strategies for how short fiction can be read in midcentury America.

Given Williams's almost unassailable position at the summit of American theater, it can be hard to consider his earlier writing retrospectively without falling into the trap of seeing it as naturally leading toward his major dramatic works. This tendency is reflected in the kind of criticism that his short stories have largely received; by far the prevailing critical treatment of his short fiction has been based around comparing it to the theatrical work that it often prefigured. Most famously, his early success *The Glass Menagerie* had been drawn from an earlier story, "Portrait of a Girl in Glass," and the way that such stories have acted as prototypes for their extended theatrical counterparts has occupied most of the critical energies expended outside the realm of Williams's plays. Indeed, as Dennis Vannatta notes, in the only extended critical consideration of Williams's stories to date, Williams has been a "victim of the understandable but regrettable tendency among readers and critics to become so blinded by the writer's brilliance in one genre that they overlook perhaps lesser but certainly worthy accomplishments in another." Vannatta suggests that "this tendency is exacerbated in regard to the short story," but he does not consider why Williams was drawn to what has often been understood, by both critics and authors, as a minor form—especially given his deep attraction to the theater.[3] But from his letters and notes it is clear that, especially until his abortive Boston production of *Battle of Angels* in 1939, but indeed for most of his first decades of writing, Williams dedicated a considerable portion of his literary energies to short fiction. Buoyed by the publication of his kitschy tale of sororial revenge in Ancient Egypt, *The Vengeance of Nitocris*, alongside the work of Robert E. Howard in the pulp magazine *Weird Tales* in 1928, he devoted himself to entering short story competitions and submitting works for publication in journals. Although the rate at which he produced new short stories flagged over his career, Williams nonetheless ultimately published seven anthologies of stories, an oeuvre rivaling that of authors for whom the form is their main literary mode. Yet despite his notorious hunger for success, instead of employing a conventional publication model for his first volume of stories, *One Arm*, Williams convinced his friend James Laughlin (the founding editor of New Directions) to print a very limited run—1,500 copies—that was to be available by subscription only. Laughlin was careful to avoid any advertising for the book and issued no review copies; in effect, *One Arm* was privately distributed, and as such, received no critical attention and generated little public interest. The question of why Williams would *privately* publish work on which he had sometimes spent years strikes at the heart of his self-image and sense of place in a larger literary lineage.

"Critical McCarthyism": Williams and the Culture of Criticism

By 1948, Tennessee Williams had not only enjoyed the breakout success of *The Glass Menagerie* but had produced the work that would place him at the forefront of the American dramatic canon—the Pulitzer Prize–winning *Streetcar Named Desire*. So it is worth asking why a figure so famous for his skills at self-promotion made the decision to publish his first anthology of short stories privately, in a small run, with no advertisements, available only by subscription. Although republished six years later in a public form, the covert release of *One Arm* constituted a strategic retreat from the public sphere that, I believe, signals Williams's resistance to mainstream U.S. culture and suggests a divergence between his work in dramatic and prose forms. His turn to an alternative mode of publication reflects his cultivation of an alternative literary voice, working in different ways to his public, theatrical writing and aligned with an alternative, European literary tradition. My general contention is that Williams drew on such a model of writing with deliberately oppositional motivations, as a way to undermine the cultural norms of the wartime and early Cold War United States, and that he conceptualized himself as part of a broader movement engaged in such a countercultural retreat. From this perspective, the lack of critical engagement with this aspect of Williams's work is a result of his own attempts to articulate a private form of political and cultural dissidence.

Along with recognizing the political implications of Williams's work, Savran introduced an interesting term to the discourse around his plays: the diptych. The term suggests a bifurcation in Williams's writing, with shared themes present within the context of different frames or scenes. As a strategy for elevating the status of Williams's short fiction to that of his plays, it is particularly useful, as it acknowledges that "Williams's diptychs are often written in different media."[4] It also draws attention to one of the major problems that Williams faced as a playwright, which certainly contributed to this bifurcation—overtly homosexual content. As Savran astutely notes, many of Williams's "texts almost certainly remained stories, in part, because their subject matter would have prohibited their production as plays during the 1950s."[5] This restriction was even more pronounced in Williams's screenplays, where even plays without any overtly "aberrant" sexuality provoked intense public debate around their censorship. The idea of a diptych, then, suggests that Williams turned to short fiction as it offered a more permissive form to explore otherwise taboo ideas, and thus suggests reading them as a more personal form of expression than his plays. At the same time, this approach still demands that his stories be read *in tandem* with his plays, leading to an ultimately secondary role as a thematic corollary to the more serious theatrical work. In doing so, it ignores the way that Williams deliberately staged these works in isolation from his plays, in a form of aesthetic retreat exemplified by *One Arm*.

Indeed, the publication of Williams's first volume of stories suggests that he conceptualized the work as belonging to a separate sphere from his plays, characterized by a private sense of joy. When he received his first copy of the book, he wrote jubilantly to Laughlin, announcing that it was "the most beautiful book you have yet made, and I am crazy about it."[6] His enthusiasm for the book never seems to have waned, either; he continued to reminisce about it even in a 1977 interview with William S. Burroughs. A slim volume, with eleven often miniaturist stories, *One Arm*'s size belies the efforts Williams put into its creation. Indeed, Williams's satisfaction with the volume could be understood as the natural corollary to the "torment" he suffered in writing it. When Laughlin praised the finished draft of the title story, focusing on the eponymous one-armed boxer, Williams clarified his difficulties in composition: "The work on One Arm was so long-drawn-out and tormented by my inability to fuse matter with style and the sensational with the valid, that I was unable to read it myself without a clear perception, but if what you say about it—if you are not just being kind—indicates that I have done the second thing at least acceptably this gives me a wonderful feeling!"[7] The volume as a whole can be understood in the same terms, as a labor of love, and Williams's intimate revelation of a "wonderful feeling" suggests a close personal connection to the book's reception. His notes testify to the protracted composition of this story, and he had equally entertained the idea of publishing a book-length collection for some years. By 1946 the project had taken a clear shape, with Williams revealing to a friend that "Laughlin is talking about bringing out a book of them [his stories], perhaps privately, at $5 a copy."[8] And when, two years later, it was printed, *One Arm* contained a note, slipped inside the cover, asking booksellers to sell the volume "by personal subscription rather than general display" as the publishers were "particularly anxious that the book should not be displayed in windows or on open tables."[9] Such a closeted publication might provoke knowing winks at the author's then-private sexuality. Savran, for one, explicitly identifies this as a reason for Williams choosing the short story form, arguing that "*One Arm* and *Hard Candy* are so filled with stories that are explicitly and even graphically homoerotic that it is difficult not to read Williams's petition parodistically."[10] But it is worth acknowledging that these instructions reveal a care and protectiveness toward the collections; Williams confided to Laughlin that he was "nervous over the advertising on *One Arm*" and did not "think the book should be publicized and sold through the usual channels" as "only a few of us will understand and like it, and it is bound to be violently attacked by the rest."[11]

The very intimate terms that Williams uses with Laughlin suggest a personal rationale behind publishing *One Arm* privately. But in other letters, Williams also implies that a political awareness informed his decision. Given the analysis that he raises, in these letters and elsewhere, of the political motivation underpinning contemporary cultural criticism, it is worth considering what a withdrawal from the world of criticism might represent to him. Williams linked his inability to develop particular themes for the theater not simply to the prevailing cultural views but specifically to the politics of the Cold War and critics' acquiescence to the nationalistic narratives used to contain individuals within restricted social identities. This connection, foreshadowed in his fears of a "violent attack," was made explicitly after Williams and Laughlin decided to rerelease *One Arm*, this time in a public edition, in December 1954. Among the several predicted attacks that the volume drew, Williams singled out a review in *Time* to which he responded in a letter that—perhaps understandably—the magazine chose not to print. Suggesting that their review revealed a "type of intolerance, bordering on persecution, in [their] attitudes towards arts, theatre and literary,"

Williams declared the review (and by extension others like it) to be "a piece of critical McCarthyism."[12] While invoking national politics in defense of literary style might suggest a shade of paranoia, I would argue that it instead evinces Williams's sophisticated political and artistic awareness and helps more clearly define the social implications of his approach to short fiction

At a most basic level, Williams was opposed to a model of individual identity that was static and fixed; his continued experimentation in dramatic form—leading to intense critical scrutiny during the latter half of his career—attests to his resistance to being restricted to a limited style. His use of the figure of Senator Joseph McCarthy to characterize attempts by critics to limit artistic expression suggests that this personal independence was linked to a broader opposition to imposing a fixed identity from outside. His claim links such an imposition of conformity to geopolitics, in that it suggests that domestic culture was being curtailed on the basis of Cold War ideology—and in doing so, Williams aligns cultural dissonance and political dissidence. At the same time, however, short story writing remained a secondary mode of expression for Williams, with theatrical work later completely displacing any other form of literary expression. For a long time, he resisted distributing his short fiction widely, and indeed he cultivated it as a private form, through which he could stage a retreat from the world of publication and production—with all its attendant acquiescence to public and critical demands. Where a writer like Mary McCarthy used the conventions of the short story in a confrontational way, challenging her readers' expectations of literary form, Williams instead used the short story for its internalizing, inward-facing aspect. For all their lurid use of rape, cannibalism, and violence, Williams's stories operate in a private register that contrasts markedly with the exhibitionism of his plays.

Even as they were first being produced, it was clear that Williams's theatrical career had been made by his first two major plays: *The Glass Menagerie* (1944) and *A Streetcar Named Desire* (1947). Those he had failed to seduce with the fragile nostalgia of the former, he won over with the bristling energy of the latter, and it was in terms of *Streetcar* that his future work would continue to be judged. Williams later expressed frustration at the way these earlier works fixed critics' conceptualization of his other, more overtly experimental plays, but it is easy to understand why they dominated expectations surrounding future work: they were received immediately as classics. Joseph Wood Krutch's review in the *Nation* of *Streetcar*'s original production suggests the extent of this canonization. Initially emphasizing his skepticism toward Williams, Krutch opens his review by noting that when Williams "was being hailed as the best new playwright to appear in a decade" for *The Glass Menagerie*, Krutch himself "was among those who were inclined to wait and see." This reservation quickly dissipates, however, with Krutch proclaiming that "the new work is sure and sustained where the former was uncertain and intermittent," before concluding that "everything is perfectly in key and completely effective." His observations about Williams's focus on his "mastery" of his craft; he argues that "the difference in merit" between his first two plays "seems to be almost entirely the result of the author's vastly increased mastery of a method which is neither that of simple realism nor frank fantasy."[13] The play's success, then, lay in its cultivation of a peculiar register that drew on the two major modes of contemporary theater and its attendant appearance of formal perfection.

In spite of the overwhelming endorsement that *Streetcar* received, however, not all of its reviews were positive. One of the most glaring attacks on the work came from another author who was herself opposed to the kind of critical McCarthyism Williams decried: Mary McCarthy. Writing in *Partisan Review* in 1948, McCarthy's response to Williams's play oddly echoes the kind of politically motivated restriction of cultural expression that characterized her namesake. What complicates this equation is the superficially Marxist criterion that McCarthy uses to attack Williams: his crass commercialism. Describing Williams as possessing "a talent which is as rooted in the American pay-dirt as a stout and tenacious carrot," it is hard to miss the sneer in her assertion that "whatever happens to his characters, Mr. Williams will come out rich and famous."[14] But these latter comments—typical of McCarthy's often scathing tone—are simply her assessment of Williams's character. Her critique of the play itself, conversely, relies on a socially conservative and restrictive mode of analysis: for McCarthy, Williams's play is a sham because it is morally bankrupt. In part, this is a product of the play's queer subtexts, and in several instances she seems to attack Williams as a closeted homosexual, describing her impression that, "like the Southern women he writes about," Williams has "been mortified by the literary poverty" of his core material and "the pettiness of the arena which is in fact its grandeur."[15] Because—she implies—of this homosexual "pettiness," Williams is unable to limit himself to the domestic, socially realistic material that forms the foundation of the play and that would have made the finished product worthwhile—even "a wonderful little comic epic." Instead, however, he subverts the social realism of his work and, "addicted to the embroidered lie," structures the play around the deceit of the audience. In other words, McCarthy expected his play to be restricted to the conventions of "the literature of domestic realism," and his resistance to its tropes and structures condemns the work to censure.

Given her own insistent focus on quotidian details in *The Company She Keeps*, perhaps it is not surprising that McCarthy's harshest critiques are reserved for the work's relationship to everyday life. She even suggests that its antirealist register heralds the decline of culture at large, asserting that "if art, as Mr. Williams appears to believe, is a lie, then anything goes."[16] Along with its overt manipulation of the audience, the work's resistance to the conventions of reality is construed as a kind of pornography-by-stealth. Indeed, McCarthy implies that Williams is attempting to corrupt his audiences, listing his use of "clarinet music, suicide, homosexuality, rape, and insanity," as if they represent a logical sequence or progression inherent to the work.[17] Although this critique stands out as anomalous, among the otherwise glowing responses to *Streetcar*, McCarthy's violently (and surprisingly) normative demands are typical of the reception of many of Williams's later plays. More importantly, they prefigure the terms used to critique *One Arm* when it was reissued in a public reprint, which inspired Williams's claims of critical persecution.

The reviews that greeted this public edition of *One Arm*—in such prominent venues as *Time*, the *New York Times*, and the *Chicago Review* —bore out Williams's invocation of Cold War politics, insofar as the reviewers explicitly linked their aesthetic judgments about the volume to an imagined set of social implications. Robert Roth, in the *Chicago Review*, suggested that the republication of the book was an act of "knocking for admission into the house of American fiction and into the canon of

Williams's mature artistic production," an ambition he categorized as "an unfortunate one," given that "the difference in power between the plays and the stories . . . is chasmal."[18] He ostensibly attributed this gap to Williams's awkward style of writing, dismissing him as "remarkably unsure of himself in handling narrative"—but for Roth, this difficulty was also explicitly tied to the kind of subject matter Williams was dealing with. Arguing that "with its diverse elements of the pathetic, the disgusting, the terrible, the comical, and the purely psychiatric, this material would present any writer whose ambition was more than journalistic with difficult aesthetic problems," he relies on an interpretive maneuver that suggests that material is poorly written because the subject matter is unconventional or that the work has unappetizing social implications; Williams's stories cover ground that is "too new both to public and private morality for him to be able to depend upon any ready-made, 'generally accepted' responses to it."[19] In other words, his short stories were read from the same perspective that McCarthy had adopted regarding *Streetcar*. Williams was attacked for not handling material that was socially acceptable and for presenting it in a way that did not guide the reader safely through uncomfortable waters (given the lack of social context for reading such material).

Refiguring this same critique in the *New York Times*, James Kelly also questioned whether the stories were "the recorded fantasies of a cynical young man with an overpowering need to shock," before defining them as "lurid studies of perversion, madness and human decay."[20] This charge, which levels an olfactory accusation of homosexuality, echoes McCarthy's snide observation that Williams's "work reeks of literary ambition as the apartment reeks of cheap perfume."[21] It emphasizes, moreover, the extent to which his short stories were judged on the basis of social utility and positive representation; clearly, critics felt it to be incumbent upon a writer like Williams to offer a hopeful, progressive vision of society rather than a critical one. In identifying this trend in attacks on his own work, Williams registered a fact that McCarthy and Bowles also observed: contemporary reviewers and critics placed an insistent pressure on authors to construct texts that would reinforce socially and politically normative behavior. Just as, within canon-forming texts like F. O. Matthiessen's *American Renaissance*, the ideal American text—necessarily a novel—was characterized by its ability to articulate a model of individual autonomy, reviews like those of Kelly or Roth emphasized the need for writers to present socially adjusted, progressively developing individuals. In their schema, the ideal author was a figure who could offer a vision that led to a better (in the context of America's hegemonic agenda, a freer, more democratic) society. In other words, across authoritative and popular iterations of contemporary U.S. criticism, literature was being directed toward a vision that realized the Cold War ideal of freedom both thematically and structurally.

In order to contextualize this critical trend—and Williams's resistance to it—it is worth considering what else was published in the same issue of the *Partisan Review* in which McCarthy savaged Williams's erstwhile masterpiece. On the one hand, the vestiges of the magazine's communist origins can be seen in articles such as "The Soviet Literary Purge" and "The Morale of the Red Army in Germany." But, at the same time, the magazine's swing toward a conservative, nationalistic position can be seen not only in McCarthy's theater column but in the book and art reviews that follow it. McCarthy's peer and sometime-friend Elizabeth Hardwick, reviewing Truman Capote's *Other Voices, Other Rooms*, appropriates the same set of aesthetic judgments in critiquing the work as a "parody" of "our recent Southern fiction," characterized by the moral decay of "withering homosexuals, and dainty sadistic women."[22] The work's failure is again linked to narrative decline and subversion of reality, with Hardwick concluding that although elsewhere "the charm and capriciousness of Southern fiction, the extravagance of character, the comedy of provincial life, the love of gentility and pretense, had the appealing quality of having been observed firsthand" in Capote's work, these values became vices, because they had been made "literary and clever" and "divorced from character."[23] Nor is this line of critique unique to prose; in his column on poetry, Leslie Fiedler attacks Robert Frost's latest volume on the grounds of the same disingenuity, asserting that the poet "shocks us by suggesting that ultimately his poetry cannot mean as much to him as it may to us."[24] Such an ironic distance from an author's work, maintained by a fixation on technique, was understood as undermining the sincerity of a work, suggesting a movement of decline rather than progress, where the decay of an individual was mapped outward onto a model of social collapse.

This same metonymic figure is present in Clement Greenberg's art column, which, in this issue, focused on the decline of cubism and the European avant-garde. Today, Greenberg is remembered as the first major champion of Jackson Pollock and a specifically American model of abstract expressionism that—like Trilling or Matthiessen with literature—he linked explicitly to a narrative of democratic freedom. In this piece, he makes the obverse distinction: that European modernism was in a state of collapse that was linked to specifically political narratives and motivations. Declaring that, on surveying European art of the last decade, "any remaining doubt vanishes as to the continuing fact of the decline of art that set in in Paris in the early thirties," Greenberg attributes this trend to "exhaustion on the part of those who in the first three decades of the century created what is known as modern art."[25] He dismisses the later work of artists like Pablo Picasso, Jean Arp, Joan Miró, or Kurt Schwitters as "repetitious and retrograde," and in doing so, invokes the same dichotomy of progress and decline that saw writing like Williams's condemned as socially reprehensible. Crucially, he argues that the decline of European visual artists is "coincident with Marxism," and the hope that he expressed for future artistic development is instead placed on an emerging, democratically American tradition. Noting "on the other hand, how much the level of American art has risen in the last five years," Greenberg stresses that "the conclusion forces itself, much to our own surprise, that the main premises of Western art have at last migrated to the United States, along with the center of gravity of industrial production and political power."[26] My contention is that such a paradoxically constrictive model of democrat art, whether visual, theatrical, or literary, is precisely what Williams's stories react against.

The New School of Decadence

Alongside the culturally coercive reviews by McCarthy, Greenberg, and Fiedler, the editors of *Partisan Review* also published two quite different pieces that troubled their increasingly nationalistic and democratic regime. Both of these pieces, moreover, overtly influenced Williams in his decision to publish *One Arm* privately, along with his stylistic choices within those stories. The first was a short story by Paul Bowles, "Under the Sky," which described (in antirealist and uncomfortably visceral terms) both drug use and the rape of a blond tourist. The second was an essay by Jean-Paul Sartre titled "For Whom Does One Write." The third in a series of meditations on writing, Sartre's piece unpacks the relationship between author and society through historical reflection, drawing attention to the way the spread of literacy increased the writer's burden of accountability to a reading public. Emphasizing that, as the expectations of society grew, writing became an increasingly "ceremonious affirmation that author and reader are of the same world and have the same opinions about everything," his observations reflect obliquely back on the normalizing demands that critics placed on contemporary prose.[27] The alternative that this essay offers is the anachronistic model of the feudal scholar-monk, for whom "the writer's mission was to prove his autonomy" through an act of social and linguistic retreat into a form of writing that was defined by its limited audience and inaccessible style.[28] Regardless of historical context, Sartre's piece seems to conclude that these two responses, retreat and internalization, or conformity and externalization, are the only options available to the writer. Explaining the ultimate literary bind, he maintains that "it is inconceivable that one can practice freedom of thought, write for a public which extends beyond the restricted collectivity of specialists, and restrict oneself to describing the content of eternal values or a priori ideas."[29] From this perspective, it is clear that Williams's decisions to turn to short fiction as an internalizing form and to use a private mode of publication were motivated by more than an awareness of the need to maintain his reputation: they were, in the context of contemporary discourse, logical ways to resist the dominant political and cultural narratives and expectations.

The connection to Sartre is more than one of coincidence in publishing, for during the 1940s, Williams read almost obsessively in French literature. Not only did he reference Sartre privately in letters and later publicly in a review of Bowles's *The Delicate Prey*, but his prose in *One Arm* bears obvious traces of his wider conversance with French writing— particularly his passion for the quintessential enfant terrible, Arthur Rimbaud. At the same time as reporting to Laughlin on the progress of his stories, he wrote asking for "all you have of Rimbaud," and his turn toward French aesthetics, particularly at a time when (as Greenberg emphasized) transatlantic aesthetic and political power was shifting in the opposite direction, is significant in two respects.[30] On the one hand, it informed his literary practice, helping him develop a style of short fiction that opposed, in form and in content, the expectations of contemporary critics. On the other, it aligned his writing with an alternative intellectual tradition, characterized by its historically regressive, rather than progressive, direction of vision. In both senses, this influence contrasts with the tendency in Williams's plays toward experimental growth and avant-gardism. Perhaps the clearest enunciation of this oppositional stance came in 1950, in the pages of the popular weekly paper the *Saturday Review*, with Williams's review of Bowles's short story collection *The Delicate Prey*. The review in question marked William's second public intervention on behalf of his friend, with whom he enjoyed a long friendship (one of the few to last throughout Williams's life), along with a productive working relationship. For the public, the two were strongly conceptually connected, as Bowles had composed the scores for several of Williams's plays—most notably *The Glass Menagerie*, whose score proved almost as successful as the play itself—and had set a series of Williams's poems to music. Like his earlier review of Bowles's debut novel, *The Sheltering Sky*, Williams's piece for the *Saturday Review* both cannily acknowledges the subtleties of Bowles's prose and endorses his style and critical position, this time in the context of Bowles's second book, the short story collection *The Delicate Prey*. Where *The Sheltering Sky* had received almost unanimous critical acclaim, however, Williams was swimming against the tide in his praise of Bowles's short stories. Indeed, he directly addressed the critical disquiet that these stories had induced, suggesting in a striking phrase that Bowles was being marginalized for belonging to what Williams described as a "New School of Decadence."[31] Williams's coinage of this term is, like so many of his critical comments, more a reflection of his own insecurities about his writing than it is an assessment of Bowles's work—however accurately it may be applied to *The Delicate Prey*. As such, it is of particular interest for the way that it marries social commentary to formal aesthetics, within an overtly transatlantic framework.

Indeed, Williams's conceptualization of a New School of Decadence is particularly enticing in part because it is so gesturally defined. His use of the phrase is not developed elsewhere, and within the article he does not explicitly explain either how he expected the idea of decadence to be understood or who the other members of this school might be. As a term that refers back to late nineteenth-century French poetry and the so-called School of Decadence, which included, among others, Williams's pet poet, Rimbaud, along with Charles Baudelaire and Paul Verlaine, Williams's designation of Bowles as the emblem of a new iteration of the movement suggests a particular, transnational aesthetic position. It also helps contextualize Bowles's well-known preoccupation with patterning and structure by situating this tendency alongside the intricate use of poetic form by such writers. This particular interpretation is supported by Williams's argument, developed in his review of Bowles's stories, that the constitutive authors of this new movement could be defined by their "personal lyricism" and their withdrawal into the "caverns" of their "own isolated being[s]." In the case of Bowles, Williams extends this idea of an idiosyncratic poetics to define his entire approach to writing: Bowles's "dominant theme," according to Williams, was "the fearful isolation of the individual being." In this sense, he evokes a more histor-ically inflected concept. In their recent anthology revisiting the original Decadent movement, Jane Desmarais and Chris Baldick suggest that "when we speak of being decadent in our own times, we will refer usu-ally to some form of private self-indulgence," while for the fin-de-siècle writers and artists aesthetically associated with the term, "Decadence was an idea with a far greater provocative power and cultural resonance than it [has] in our current looser usage" and could thus be considered, broadly, as a movement that "embodied a peculiar post-Romantic form of protest against modern civilization and against inherited literary and cultural assumptions."[32] By associating Bowles's aesthetic position with a retreat from society, therefore, Williams suggests that, beyond any sty-listic tendencies, his putative literary movement is characterized by its critical relationship to contemporary U.S. society. Indeed, in the essay's most incisive moment, Williams argues that "contemporary American society seems no longer inclined to hold itself open to very explicit crit-icism from within."[33] As his later reaction to critics shows, Williams held an inherent interest in developing a form of insurgent writing that could critique contemporary society, and as such, he positioned Bowles's writing at the forefront of decadent literature precisely because he was

"apparently the only American author whose work reflects the spiritual dislocation (and a philosophical adjustment to it) of our immediate times."[34]
In spite of his somewhat nebulous definition of the term, therefore,
Williams's use of "decadence" had two clear qualities: a deliberate, or
staged, aesthetic isolation and a critical stance toward the values of midcentury America.

What was it about Bowles's stories that prompted Williams to inter-
cede so self-consciously—indeed, defensively—on their behalf? Despite
Williams's oft-referenced hero-worship of Bowles, he must have also
felt at least a small sense of responsibility for Bowles's anthology (and,
given Williams's tendencies elsewhere, this was likely to have been felt
rather strongly). Before the 1940s, Bowles was best known as a classical
composer, and despite finding venues for individual stories in traditional,
high-culture publications such as *Harper's Bazaar* and *Partisan Review*, he
was unable to secure a publishing deal for either his novel, *The Sheltering
Sky*, or a collection of short stories. As Evan Brier rightly notes, it was
only on the strength of Williams's recommendation that New Directions
agreed to take on Bowles as an author; Williams acted as "Bowles's agent
in deed, if not in name, and if it had not been for his intervention, it is
likely that New Directions would never have published Bowles."[35] Bowles
himself readily noted the importance of his friend's support, explaining in
one interview that "he couldn't have been a better friend. No one I know
has so consistently stood behind my writing as Tennessee."[36] With the specific case of this anthology, moreover, Williams had given Bowles counsel
regarding certain stories, suggesting they ought to be reworked. He noted,
in an anecdote that Bowles also enjoyed repeating, that "Bowles asked
me to read a short story of his"; in an uncharacteristically squeamish
response, Williams explained that this story, the eponymous "Delicate
Prey," "shocked" him, so much so that he "advised against its publication
in the states."[37] Given the content of some of Williams's own short stories,
it is unsurprising that Bowles found this advice "incomprehensible" and
promptly ignored it. Nonetheless, Williams's personal and professional
intercessions regarding this work would justify, by any standard, his
further steps to support his friend's fiction.

Such an explanation, however, does not account for the personal
implications that Bowles later identified in Williams's review, which are

equally evident in the defensive tone and self-reflexive account of decadence that Williams provides. Instead, I would contend that it was the
peculiarly aggressive and constraining tenor of the reviews of Bowles's
work that stirred a sense of personal grievance in Williams. John Bak
notes that in all of his writing on behalf of other authors, Williams "talks
as much about himself and his own developing troubles with audiences
and critics as he does the writer whose work he is apparently praising,"
to the extent that "non-fiction prose" became "his best line of defense
against the mounting criticism against him and his work."[38] Following this
pattern, in his earlier review of *The Sheltering Sky*, Williams summarized
the general critical response to the text by suggesting that, in focusing
on the "external aspect" of the novel, critics had only perceived it as "an
account of startling adventure"; he "suspect[ed] that a good many people,"
including critics, would ignore those internal aspects of the text, which
he characterized as "a mirror of what is most terrifying and cryptic within
the Sahara of moral nihilism, into which the race of man now seems to be
wandering blindly."[39] Not only did Williams presciently identify Bowles's
own sense of his texts' relationship to society, but he also emphasized the
very qualities that critics would castigate Bowles for in his short fiction.
In this respect, the two reviews can be read as complementary, articulating Williams's disquiet at the critical misreading of Bowles's work, and
the latent implications for readings of his own.

Although Williams did not elaborate on his proposed literary movement in writing elsewhere, Bowles himself took up the subject in a letter
he wrote to Laughlin, at this time their mutual editor at New Directions.
In his response to Williams's review, Bowles set out his own feelings
about this possible movement and at the same time divulged details
about Williams's motivations that had been communicated privately.
Helpfully, Bowles explained which authors Williams had in mind when
coining the term: the members of this "school" were to have been Bowles,
Williams, Gore Vidal, and Truman Capote. Over the decade preceding
the publication of this article, all four of these authors had developed
personal relationships with one another and had written a reasonable
body of short stories—including Capote's volume savaged by Hardwick
in *Partisan Review*—in addition to their other fictional output. Bowles
also noted that Williams had hoped that the negative terminology used by

critics to dismiss not only Bowles's work but that of the other members of this schools "could be combatted by means of a manifesto." Conceding that the term "decadent" could be applied to his work, Bowles invoked the same framework that Williams deployed, admitting that he had "no great objection to being called decadent, if the word is used in such a way that it is clear the user considers my work to be a reflection of the period in which it was written, a period which by every cultural standard is assuredly a decadent one."[40] Bowles's understanding of the word "decadent," then, was predicated upon a similar stance toward contemporary culture to Williams's—not exactly oppositional, it instead reflected the flaws of a society that both authors envisage as failing, or in the terms of decadence, falling down.

Where Williams suggests that adopting this attitude toward contemporary society constitutes a form of retreat, however, Bowles frames it instead as a form of intellectual and aesthetic honesty. Elsewhere, Bowles articulated a more general understanding of the world as stemming from exactly this kind of de-*cadence*, suggesting to one interviewer that he "never expect[s] anything to be put right" because "nothing ever is"; instead, "the future will be infinitely 'worse' than the present, and in *that* future, the future will be immeasurably 'worse' than the future we can see. Naturally."[41] The conversation between both authors' concepts of decadence, therefore, offers two related but distinct definitions. From Williams's perspective, the aesthetics of decadence involve a performative retreat from a compromised society and, in doing so, offer a criticism of its values. Bowles, on the other hand, despite viewing contemporary American society as equally (if not significantly more) compromised, registers the aesthetics of decadence as a reflection—or rather a deliberately constructed representation—of the flaws from which Williams argues that his own work retreats. This disjunction reflects the extent to which, although ostensibly advocating on behalf of Bowles, Williams here had his own work firmly in mind. Not only does Bowles explicitly state that Williams intended to include himself in the New School of Decadence, but his assertion to Laughlin that "lumping together such disparate writers" was "manifestly ridiculous" suggests the extent to which he understood Williams's concept as largely self-reflexive.[42]

Bowles's reading of this is appropriate, however, given that decadence is, in and of itself, an inherently self-reflexive concept, movement, and style. In the introduction to his influential 2002 study *Decadent Subjects*, Charles Bernheimer notes that, today, this understanding is perhaps more prevalent than ever. Explaining the context of writing his work, Bernheimer notes that in his friends' "endorsement of decadence" he "felt that envy was mixed with disapproval," conceptualizing this as "envy for the potential unraveling of my stable identity through the subversive force of perverse desire," and imaginings that his "self's bourgeois coherence—and its expression in writing—would explode and disintegrate."[43] As Baldick and Desmarais note, however, this idea of retreating inward was originally intimately associated with a reaction to a society external to oneself. To be decadent was to choose an internalized, private identity, in opposition to joining the collective of society. It implied a resistance to dominant tastes and demands, as well as rejection of the democratic ethos and the enlightenment ideal of progress. It is telling that, in their attempts to exercise cultural control, midcentury critics used terms like "decay" and "retrograde" to describe works that did not conform to the expected democratic values: in doing so, whether consciously or not, they drew upon the discourse of decadence. The fear behind such inward regression was not simply a metonymically linked opposition to Soviet totalitarianism but was instead motivated by a conceptualization of individual identity that was organized round the principle of growth. Decadent aesthetics, as Bernheimer suggests, followed the alternative trajectory, where human life culminated not in an uplifting moral and intellectual apotheosis but a violent and rupturing self-destruction. It is no wonder, given his yoking of political and literary resistance, that Williams turned to Rimbaud as his exemplar of decadence. For in life and art, Rimbaud exemplified this trajectory.

Born in 1854, Rimbaud famously flourished, creatively speaking, over a brief period—roughly the three years from seventeen to twenty. During this time, he established a reputation for personal rebellions of the kind that might be termed delinquencies: alcoholism, petty theft, and poor grooming. These minor instances of resistance to social conformity, however, paled in comparison to his literary disregard for convention. His years of creative activity were bookended by *A Season in Hell* (1871) and *Illuminations* (written circa 1874) and marked by a deliberate deconstruction of the self. Accounting for his physical decay, Rimbaud wrote to his friend George Izambard that, in order to achieve a profound poetic vision, "the idea is to reach the unknown by the derangement of the senses." In the case of *Illuminations*, this physical decay also manifested, textually, as an incomplete work, which was published without Rimbaud's involvement by his friend and erstwhile lover, Verlaine. What earned this work its seminal status as countercultural text was Rimbaud's withdrawal from the conventional model of publication, and its association with a conformity of taste and ideology. Regardless of Rimbaud's hopes for his future reputation, the convoluted history of its publication, detached from any authorial control (or, as it appeared, desire) accentuated the poet's image as the extreme iteration of literary outcast. It also directly contributed to Williams's conceptualization of *One Arm*, reflected in his letters to Laughlin regarding its limited circulation and withdrawal from the capitalist exigencies of conventional publication.

Interestingly, given popular tendencies to associate the two as renegade homosexual playwrights, Williams figured his admiration for Rimbaud in direct opposition to his disdain for Oscar Wilde. Describing the latter as "soft-headed," Williams argued that Wilde was "the biggest fool of his time" for trying to overtly challenge the status quo, going on to explain: "You just can't win against those establishment people. Wilde should have known that. He didn't have a chance!"[44] Instead, his idea of decadence as a retreat mirrors Rimbaud's turning away from cultural establishments and embracing of the unsavory, visceral underside of society. Nor was he the only writer to consider Rimbaud a crucial model for future literary development in America. Around the same time as Williams was writing *One Arm*, an American novelist with an even closer connection to French aesthetics—Henry Miller—began an abortive series of articles on Rimbaud, of which two were published in the New Directions' annual publication, *New Directions in Poetry and Prose*, and later republished as *The Time of Assassins* in 1956. In his preface to this collected edition of the essays, Miller explained that it was his "sincere belief that America needs to become acquainted with this legendary figure now more than ever," linking this urgency, like Williams, to a coercive political regime that enforced a violently normative model of identity. Arguing that the demands of conformity were limiting creative expression, he proclaimed that "never was there a time when the existence of the poet was more menaced than today. The American species, indeed, is in danger of being extinguished altogether."[45] For Miller, the only way to challenge the prevailing culture of containment was to look outside of America, to an alternative tradition. Whatever their personal difference, in their use of Rimbaud as a model for aesthetic renewal and political resistance, Williams and Miller were on the same page. Like Williams, moreover, Miller connected the experimentation of Rimbaud to an aesthetic retreat, which was metaphorically realized by his physical collapse and early death; Miller concluded that "perhaps in fleeing from the world, Rimbaud preserved his soul."[46] Interest in this kind of decadence was not limited to these two authors, either. Laughlin solicited Miller's articles in part because New Directions had just published a new translation of *Season in Hell*, which proved a commercial success for the small press. From this perspective, Williams's ideal of retreat from society clearly tapped into a broader, decadent discourse that saw retrogression and internalization as the only viable resistance to American politics and criticism.

On the one hand, then, the concept of a New School of Decadence is particularly useful in reading Williams's work, as it helps contextualize his defiantly vulgar, visceral content, and private model of publication. It also emphasizes the political motivations behind these choices and helps to clarify the kind of critique they offer on his contemporary society. From the point of view of literary form, moreover, it offers a framework for reading Williams's use of the short story that, while complementary, is not contingent upon his plays. But his place as a decadent author is not as straightforward as his use of the term might suggest. At the same time as reveling in what Rimbaud might have termed the "scum" of society, many of Williams's stories in *One Arm* tend, at least on the surface, to replicate the subject matter expected of conventional fiction: reflections on "American adolescence," refracted through ostensibly heteronormative relationships. This is why Williams's particularly idiosyncratic reading of Rimbaud is so important. The quality he emphasizes in Bowles's fiction— the "fearful isolation of the individual"—is also the quality he drew most from his reading of Rimbaud. With their persistent and overwhelming focus on unease, or perhaps dis-ease, coupled with physical and spiritual isolation, these stories enact a far more unsettling destabilization of the "socially beneficial" narratives contemporary critics espoused than their stock settings might connote. In these stories, it is the ostensibly conventional, even trite, subject matter that Williams uses to stage a protest against prescriptive social norms. Indeed, rather than the more lurid stories, I argue that it was this sharp contrast between subject matter and treatment that so unsettled critics when the volume was republished. While explicit accounts of homosexuality may have made reviewers of the volume squeamish, by presenting "straight" relationships in ways that destabilized the kind of traditional relationships and narratives that critics and politicians prescribed, Williams actively undermined the model of generative growth that was being demanded not only of the writers he termed "new decadents" but of any American writer in the postwar period. He was particularly sensitive to such moralistic prescriptions, and his references to "critical McCarthyism" in his unpublished letter to *Time* reflect his awareness that the negative reviews he himself received were motivated by the collection's destabilizing potential. His espousal of a new school of literature, therefore, reflects his own stories' broad investment in critiquing contemporary culture.

Fractured Form: *One Arm,* Style, and Identity

Decadence could readily be used as a productive framework for reading the wider body of Williams's work; however, it is in the context of *One Arm* that it yields the most complex analysis. As a concept tied closely to Williams's insecurities regarding both his own short stories and those of a friend whose work he had endorsed and coaxed into publication, it signals a break in his thinking about form that was tied specifically to an internalized and private mode of writing. The language that he used to express his fears for his short stories, should they be widely published—the fear of "a violent attack"—reflects his growing awareness of the violent normativity governing contemporary criticism. It also suggests that, in distinction to his plays, he saw his short stories as politically motivated, advancing a countercultural perspective that would antagonize mainstream readers and reviewers. The personal anxiety that was tied to this particular anthology, moreover, evinces Williams's understanding of writing decadently as a process closely tied to the deconstruction of personal identity. Drawing explicitly on the model of Rimbaud, he wrote these stories with an insistent focus on corporeal collapse that is emblematized by the title character's fractured body. Indeed, this thematic focus guides Williams's use of the short story form, which is governed by a sense of fragmentation and imminent decay.

Despite the unconventional publication of the volume as a whole, a handful of the stories in *One Arm* were more widely disseminated through magazines. It is perhaps unsurprising, however, that these stories tended to conform, at least on the surface, to the expected domestic narrative model of individual growth. The most obvious example is Williams's early piece "The Field of Blue Children." Here, Williams carefully constructs an uncomfortable tension between the apparent completion and unity of the story as a whole, and the restlessness and suspended collapse of the prose and imagery. The protagonist, a college student named Myra, suffers from a "restlessness" that "she could not understand," which manifests as a yearning desire to find "something still further to give the night its perfect fullness" and prevent it from "slipp[ing] from her fingers."[47] Williams suggests that the only way Myra is able to find solace is through poetry, which allows her to attain a sense of completion; as Myra begins to write poetry, she adopts the maxim *"Words are a net to catch beauty!,"* which allows her, for a while, to feel that she "understood what she wanted" (80). This urge to enclose a poetic form of beauty leads her to a night of passion with the socially isolated aspiring poet Homer Stallcup, who leads her to a field of dancing blue flowers. Rather than constraining the poet—and thus, the poetic impulse—Myra instead succumbs to a greater, roiling openness, which Williams registers through the textual restlessness of initially clipped, staccato phrases, which collapse into a rolling awareness of existential possibility that spirals into defeat:

> She thought of the view from her window at night, those nights when she cried bitterly without knowing why, the dome of the administration building like a white peak and the restless waves of moonlit branches and the stillness and the singing voices, mournfully remote, blocks away, and the smell of the white spirea at night, and the stars as clear as lamps in the cloud-fretted sky, and she remembered the choking emotion that she didn't understand and the dread of all this coming to its sudden, final conclusion in a few months or weeks or more. (85)

Instead of accepting the chance to articulate something greater, and more emotionally authentic, Myra rejects Homer, falling into a conventional marriage that brings to an end, both personally and stylistically, Myra's earlier restlessness. But years later, overtaken by a moment of unarticulated longing, she returns to the field, where she falls "to her knees . . . sobbing" (87). Confronted with the rush of the aesthetic induced by her memories, Myra's response is to quash her feelings, asserting a violent normativity. She leaves, believing that she has "now left her troublesome youth behind her" (87), but ironically highlighting the extent to which conventional expectations have suppressed her creativity. For what she has left behind is the yearning for more, which Williams so clearly associates with the poetic and the unconventional.

This enduring, unarticulated potential for an idiosyncratic model of poetic expression contrasts with the more caustic tone that Williams adopts in "Night of the Iguana," which satirizes the staid, conventional understanding of creativity and imagination. Like "Blue Children," however, "Iguana" is intimately concerned with the confining and restrictive implications of conventional social structures, using the compressed form of the short story to articulate a narrative that resists these constraints. The close third-person narration is refracted through the perspective of Miss Edith Jelkes, a former instructor of art who has "suffered a sort of nervous breakdown and given up her teaching position for a life of refined vagrancy" (257). Alone with two other guests at an off-season hotel in Acapulco, Miss Jelkes observes these two men reveal an apparently homosexual relationship, whose freedom in the empty Mexican resort is manifested in the younger man's open nudity, which provokes in "the spinsterish side of her nature" a sense of "squeamish distaste" (262). This ostensible openness, however, is contrasted with the architectural claustrophobia that frames their relationship: Williams accompanies the rising sense of constraint with the capture of an iguana, which is fastened beneath the hotel's verandah, where it "makes the most pitiful attempt to scramble into the bushes just beyond the taut length of rope" (264). Miss Jelkes's attempts to articulate her horror at the treatment of the iguana to the men further elides any difference between their respective situations, reading homosexuality as a form of physical restriction. The older of the men, however, rejects her insinuations, suggesting that the animal is not "capable of feeling half as badly over its misfortune as you seem to be feeling for it" (265), before noting that she has "a real gift . . . for vicarious experience" (266). Later, though, as the men's relationship begins to implode, his response is revealed to be part of a self-defense mechanism; he explains to her, "I have to depend on myself" (273). The story closes with Jelkes discovering that the iguana has been freed, and gaining a sense of independence herself, feeling that "in some equally mysterious way the strangling rope of her own loneliness had also been severed" (275). Her need to exist through a virtual experience of other peoples' lives, Williams suggests, has been replaced by a newfound awareness of authenticity and integrity.

In both of these stories, Williams depicts sexual relationships on the brink of collapse; "Angel in the Alcove" marks a departure from this critical register, instead suggesting a broader possibility for the acceptance of difference. The narrator of "Angel" opens by explaining how the perennial "suspicion" of landladies has "left [him] with an obscure sense of guilt" (136). Despite the narrator's explicit homosexuality, however, Williams flattens out this guilt to encompass society at large, irrespective of sexual inclination. Indeed, the persecution to which the narrator is subjected is detached from any specific accusation, and the landlady regularly reads him any item "concerning an act of crime in the Quarter" (136). The story's climax comes with the ejection of another more notoriously homosexual character from the boardinghouse, and Williams suggests that this particular act of persecution is part of a wider trend of suspicion and approbation in contemporary society. This model of persecution is juxtaposed against the eponymous angel, who offers comfort and the possibility for acceptance. After a nocturnal encounter with another man, the narrator expresses concern about the spectral angel's "attitude . . . toward perversions of longing" (138). And assessing the apparition, he divines that "she had permitted the act to occur and had neither blamed nor approved" (138). This disarmingly earnest story contrasts with the cynical attitude that characterizes much of the volume, suggesting a genuine hope for a less hostile society.

While such stories are underlined by a more aspirational tone than that which characterizes McCarthy's or Bowles's relatively nihilistic work, they nonetheless confront the dominant model of fiction, oriented around encouraging the heteronormative "growth" and "social cohesion" that was advanced by contemporary critics. Williams's oppositional use of the short story form is important because it offers a structure that is compressed and fragmented, in contrast to the extended growth suggested by the social novel in its various guises. Indeed, the recurring criticism that Williams's stories were "unshapely" suggests not so much an artistic failure as the high level of craft with which he structured his short fiction. In a story like "Blue Children," Williams deliberately juxtaposes the possibilities of Myra's expansive, uncontrollable poetic urges against the constraining pressures of marriage on a social level with the short story on a formal level. Equally, the freedom that Miss Jelkes feels she has attained is ironically hemmed in by the claustrophobic pressure of the storm clouds around her and the sleep that cuts over her bemused observations. Structurally, then, Williams uses the short story as a way to restrict his narratives and accentuate the tension between stifling social and geographic pressures and an internal aspiration toward openness and freedom.

In spite of the self-consciously oppositional stance toward mainstream midcentury America that Williams adopts across these stories, which is accentuated by the intensely crafted aesthetic principles that dictate their structure and style, reading these stories is problematized by the fact that Williams never intended for the volume to be widely distributed. Indeed, despite having published several of the stories in literary magazines, Williams clearly intended the criticism of contemporary society that his anthology enacted to be limited in its impact, with the finished book instead staging his stories as a private performance of resistance rather than a more overt call for social change. When advising Bowles against including the story "The Delicate Prey" in his collection on the grounds that it was too violent and lurid for an American audience, Williams justified his apparently hypocritical stance on the basis of this very model of private distribution. In his *Memoirs,* Williams recalls:

> Bowles asked me to read a short story of his later. This story was "The Delicate Prey" and it shocked me. This seems odd, I know. And I think it was quite incomprehensible to Paul that I, who published such stories as "Desire and the Black Masseur" should be shocked by "The Delicate Prey." I recognized

it as a beautiful piece of prose, but I advised against its publication in the states. You see, my shocking stories had been published in expensive private editions by New Directions and never exhibited on a bookstore counter.[48]

Here, Williams justifies both his aesthetic approach and his choice to only circulate his book privately. Not only did he consider the material too confronting for a general audience, but—following the logic of his explanation—he had only adopted that particular style because he was confident that its eventual readers would not find it difficult to swallow.

Such a perspective immediately contrasts with, say, McCarthy's ambitions for *The Company She Keeps*, which she designed as a broader social satire, intended to be widely read. Similarly, Bowles's articulated a very public ambition for his collection, which helps to explain the two authors' differing perspectives on decadence as a social response. Arguing that his work was merely a reflection of the current degradation of society, Bowles published his stories with a view to dramatically changing his readers' perspectives (although not, it should be stressed, with the idea of thereby effecting specific changes in social structures). Although he acknowledged that "human behavior is contingent upon the particular culture that informs it," he strongly believed that writers should "reject, at this moment in history, the mass society."[49] For Bowles, the success of any given text could be measured by the extent to which it provoked its reader to reconsider social constructs, since it is only if "a writer can incite anyone to question and ultimately to reject the present structure of any facet of society" that "he's performed a function."[50] Instead of "proposing changes" in a specific way, however, Bowles saw his short fiction as simply "trying to call people's attention to something they don't seem to be sufficiently aware of," subsequently engendering shifts in perspective and, more broadly, engaging them in social critique. Williams's characterization of Bowles as an author "retreating from contemporary society," then, not only misrepresents his intentions with *The Delicate Prey* but also helps delineate Williams's own aesthetic agenda.

The particular story that Williams isolated to justify his reluctance to circulate the stories widely is one that has achieved a certain level of notoriety for its central figure: sadomasochism descending into cannibalism. Given the salacious subject matter of "Desire and the Black Masseur"—a story in which a timid corporate drone becomes addicted to visiting his increasingly violent black masseur, until he is finally beaten to death and eaten—critics have generally tended to align it in with the traditional reading of his plays, as a story about sublimated homosexual desire and the guilt associated (principally by Williams himself) with such socially marginalized forms of desire. Several variations on this interpretation have been advanced: most recently, Nathan Tipton has argued that the "violence" of the story should be read "as an allegorically-rendered lynching narrative."[51] While a useful critique, fundamentally such critical approaches are predicated upon the same perspective as the story's first reviewers and, crucially, ignore Williams's imagined audience. In his *New York Times* review, Kelly suggests that these stories demonstrate that "to Mr. Williams, imagination, violence and surrender of self to others are simply the means for overcoming the guilt of incompletion."[52] Read as a story intended for wider circulation, "Desire" would therefore fulfill a kind of ritual expiation and/or communal contamination, implicating the reader in the processes of sublimation. Indeed, from Bowles's point of view, this would be the point: engendering a shift in perspective regarding social and cultural norms. Williams, however, was at least initially opposed to such a sweeping (and, for someone who was as established as Williams was, risky) attempt at challenging the American public. As he explained to Laughlin, the volume needed to be privately distributed "because only a few of us will understand it and like it, and it is bound to be violently attacked by the rest."[53] Such a selective readership helps explain why Williams's idea of decadence, as conceptualized in his review, was characterized by a retreat from society; seeing contemporary American society as unwilling to accept criticism, he wanted to stage a tactical withdrawal. Unlike his plays, which—at least initially—presented their ideas through socially acceptable narratives, Williams intended his stories to be received by those sympathetic to alternative perspectives, structuring them with a different kind of audience in mind. This strategy also helps explain why his proposed manifesto never eventuated; as he perceived it, his own "decadent" work was actually characterized by a voluntary withdrawal from society and, as such, was scarcely in need of a public articulation of its principles.

    This aesthetic of withdrawal is embodied, quite literally, in the title story, "One Arm," which opens the collection and establishes Williams's key themes of fragmentation, introversion, desire, and self-destruction. In this case, they are manifested in the young one-armed boxer-cum-hustler of the title, Oliver Winemiller, who is eventually imprisoned and executed for the murder of a stockbroker client. Given the success of other stories in periodicals, or as adapted for the stage (as with "A Portrait of a Girl in Glass"), it is worth considering why Williams chose this particular story as the entry point for his collection. Apart from the rich symbolism of the story, in retrospect it also stands out as one of the most *crafted* works in the collection, in that it seems ideally suited for the short story form. Indeed, it is telling that although Williams later adapted the work for the screen, he was unable to generate any interest in the work. In 2011, however, an adaptation by Moisés Kaufman debuted in New York, which met with decidedly ambiguous reviews. Although critics praised the acting and appreciated Williams's source material, they tended to emphasize its awkward fit with the longer play form. Writing in the *New York Times*, Ben Brantley noted that "despite the grittiness of its subject, 'One Arm,' as a story, is essentially a lyrical allegory in which the third-person narrative is as dominant as that in a Grimm's fairy tale." As Brantley rightly suggests, the story itself is written in an elevated, allegorical register, which works through metaphors and symbolism that are not readily mapped outward onto the stage, or expanded into a longer narrative. Because of its insistent emphasis on fragmentation, moreover, it defies the more coherent narrative demands of a play, so that, "while Ollie finds redemption before the final curtain," on the stage, "his tale never achieves the same apotheosis."[54] The failure of "One Arm" to be translated to the stage signals the key distinction between Williams's plays and stories: working through different registers, they rely on contrasting narrative movements, toward cohesion on the one hand, and collapse on the other.

Although a streak of nihilism permeates the collection, it is in "One Arm" that Williams's emphasis on the drive toward destruction most clearly invokes the spirit of decadence. Indeed, Williams opens the story with a description that yokes the physical with the spiritual through the imagery of time's decay. After losing his arm in a car accident, Winemiller "looked like a broken statue of Apollo, and he had also the coolness and impassivity of a stone figure" (7). The external rupture of his physique, moreover, is linked explicitly to an internal breakdown where, once "the arm has been lost," the young boxer "was abruptly cut off from his development as an athlete and a young man wholly adequate to the physical world he grew into" (10). In terms that recall Rimbaud, Williams imagines Winemiller's foreclosed feelings as an inarticulable force, that manifest as "a realization that whirled darkly up from its hidden laboratory and changed him altogether in less time that it took new skin to cover the stump of the arm he had lost" (10). Rather than responding to his physical and emotional mutilation with pure pity, however, Williams imbues this figure of decay with an erotic charge that destabilizes all those with whom he comes into contact. This urge is figured in hemispheric terms, with the pseudo-Apollo standing "as a planet among the moons of their longing, fixed in his orbit while they circled about him," so that when he is arrested and his impending execution publicized, his former lovers send hundreds of letters to his jail cell. The fragmented form of the protagonist elicits a violent passion in others, and Williams suggests that Winemiller's hopeless self-destruction is fundamentally attractive—more attractive, certainly, than wholeness or completion.

On the one hand, Williams's erotics of fragmentation suggest an innate desire for broken or damaged aesthetic objects. The one-armed hustler had "the charm of the defeated . . . a quality which acts as a poultice upon the inflamed nerves of those who are still in active contention" (16), so that his attractiveness was predicated on an inability to grow. On a deeper level, however, the erotic pull of his broken form implies that completion is itself unattractive, where the ideal of wholeness is merely a façade. Congruent with the logic of the other stories in the collection, the insatiable hunger elicited by the one-armed body suggests a desire that goes beyond social conventions—even that those conventions are forcing people into limited roles. Initially, Winemiller's accident gives him freedom from those restrictions, allowing him to pursue his own destruction without inhibition. Once he is imprisoned, he is afforded a second revelation and becomes aware of the social conventions that restrict others. It is only once he is confined that "autoerotic sensations began to flower in him," which grow precisely as he becomes aware of his own captivity, so that "every morning he seemed to wake up in a space that had mysteriously diminished while he slept" (22). In terms that reflect a much greater awareness than his earlier, impulsive actions would suggest, he describes the letters he receives from former lovers as "bills from people I owe. Not money, but feelings" (30), acknowledging the extent to which conventional relationships burden the individual. This is reinforced when he is visited, the day before his execution, by a Lutheran minister, to whom he explains, "I am lonely and bottled up the same as you are. I know your type."

Like Winemiller, the priest acts as an allegorical figure who manifests precisely the desire for destruction that the disfigured hustler tends to elicit in others. Williams conveys this through a fable-like memory associated with the priest: visiting a golden panther at the zoo. His earlier desire to be raped by this caged animal is projected outward onto Winemiller, to the extent that "from the moment that he had seen this photograph the Lutheran minister had been following out a series of compulsions so strong that he appeared to himself to be surrendering to an outside power" (24). Much like the sadomasochistic urge in "Desire and the Black Masseur," this compulsion leads to an erotically charged massage; however, here the priest ultimately denies his desire and leaves the prison hysterically. Like the unpaid debts of emotion that he has left his letter writers, Winemiller's role as embodied fragmentation means that he cannot satisfy the priest—can only leave him aware of his confinement and inarticulable desire. Appropriately, Williams closes the story with a sentence that reminds the audience of their own fragmentation, noting that "death has never been much in the way of completion" (32).

As I have argued, however, rather than crediting Williams's emotional honesty with the bravery that its subversive aesthetics demonstrated and that Williams acknowledged in his defense of Bowles, critics instead equated writing that undermined mainstream narratives with that most pernicious of social vices: pornography. In the same way that Bowles was castigated as a "pornographer of terror" because his stories did not enforce conventional behavior, once *One Arm* was widely reprinted, its first edition was retrospectively classified as a form of smut. Revealingly, when Roth explained that the volume "first appeared in 1948 in an expensive limited edition," it was to suggest that it enjoyed in that form a "semicovert reputation and comparative immunity from implacable critical scrutiny not unlike what are often accorded the privately circulated erotica of an otherwise justly famous writer."[55] Although Roth was quick to suggest that "no one would complain about this," his review, alongside others of this volume, decried the translation of what he considered a private form of literature into the public realm. In this sense, Williams's cries of critical McCarthyism ring true: in the immediate postwar decade, the American critical establishment was unwilling to accommodate fiction that did not have a social benefit or that broke from a strictly controlled image of "democratic" behavior. As a text that not only challenged aesthetic values but presented lurid material in a way that was divorced from any moral instruction—and indeed encouraged "antisocial" behavior—*One Arm* necessarily ran against the grain of contemporary critical and national values. The context of the volume's publication, moreover—circulated privately among those whom Williams believed would be sympathetic to his overtly critical perspective—suggests that Williams's short story writing was important to him as an alternative form of expression through which he could articulate a social critique unavailable to his plays. This has broader applications, beyond the case of Williams, for thinking about the way that writers used the short story as an ancillary form to their "main" register—and also for considering the way that American authors turned toward European modernism as a form of personal retreat, under the increasing political pressure of the Cold War to produce a certain nationalistic and socially beneficial model of fiction. It directly contrasts, moreover, with McCarthy's model of countercultural writing. Where Williams saw contemporary society as in a state of irrevocable decay, McCarthy merely saw a world compromised by hypocrisy. Her public mode of resistance, therefore, relied upon a veneer of conventionality, whereas Williams's internalizing model of withdrawal resisted any possibility of critical rehabilitation.

chapter four

Paul Bowles's Verbal Violence and Patterns of Words

During the 1930s and 1940s, Paul Bowles enjoyed an almost singularly diverse artistic career. A prominent classical composer, responsible for the "Tennessee Sound" that accompanied Williams's first major theatrical successes, Bowles was also a highly regarded translator, whose profile was such that Jean-Paul Sartre commissioned him to translate his play *Huis clos,* which Bowles rendered in tellingly claustrophobic terms as *No Exit.*[1] His poetry was published in major avant-garde magazines, such as *transition,* and he was an important contributor to the American surrealist magazine *View.* The short stories he wrote over this period, which he would continue to consider as his most important works throughout his life, found publication in such venues as *Harper's Bazaar* and *Mademoiselle,* alongside the intellectual redoubt of the *Partisan Review.* With clearly articulated antidemocratic beliefs and a perspective on concepts of progress and civilization that has often been read as nihilistic, Bowles provides the ideal test case for the concept of minor literature. Writing with the explicit aim to undermine his readers' belief in freedom and individual growth, Bowles also sought to establish an alternative literary tradition that ran counter to the dominant narrative of the American novel.

The relatively limited focus with which critics have hitherto considered Bowles's writing can be attributed in large part to his long-term residence in Tangiers. Indeed, his popular image and later career were both shaped by this self-imposed exile in Morocco, where he lived for more than half a century. Along with the question of geography, however, the relatively narrow focus of criticism can also be attributed to the forms in which different examples of Bowles's works were produced. Certainly, the works that have received the most critical attention have been those set in Morocco or North Africa; although at the start of his career Bowles used Latin America and even the United States as the setting for his writing, over the long term his writing increasingly reflected his involvement in the culture of North Africa, particularly Tangiers. Equally, however, these North African works were published in a form that critics have been predisposed to prefer: the novel. Not only were all of Bowles's first three novels set in North Africa, but the work that occupied the latter stage of his authorial career was also decidedly novelistic. Beginning in 1964 with the text *A Life Full of Holes*, Bowles enjoyed a secondary literary career recording, transcribing, and translating Moroccan oral storytellers, whose work Bowles generally produced into the form of novels; over the next thirty years, Bowles translated and published more than twenty works by Moroccan authors.[2] Given the intersection of North African setting and novelistic form, it is not surprising that Bowles's work within the genre of the short story has been critically occluded.

Bowles's first volume of short fiction, *The Delicate Prey*, was dedicated obliquely to the American master of the short story form, Edgar Allan Poe: "To my mother, who first read me the stories of Poe."[3] This subtle nod belies the extent to which Bowles actively styled both his personal life and his style of writing on his earliest literary influence; he explained the dedication of *The Delicate Prey* in a letter to David McDowell, at Random House, as follows: "The introduction should be 'For my mother, through whom I first became acquainted with Poe.' As a small child, I used to be read to by her, and the first short stories with which I came in contact that way were Poe's *Tales of Mystery and Imagination*. They also made the greatest impression; and she told me the story of his life, so that I resolved then to go to the University of Virginia, which I did, solely because he had attended it."[4] Although sometimes reticent to discuss his own writing from a theoretical perspective, maintaining the position that he had "never been a thinking person," Bowles not only openly drew inspiration from Poe but, more broadly, was invested in the short story as a literary genre.[5] While his novels may have proven financially successful, his model of short story, I will argue, had much greater long-term repercussions for the development of the form. Recognized today as one of its most important twentieth-century practitioners, Bowles was invested in the form of the short story to the point that he constructed his first novel, *The Sheltering Sky*, as an extended short story—a formal development of short fiction rather than a text constructed with the stylistic principles of a novel.[6]

Alongside its descent from Poe, the same volume of stories, *The Delicate Prey*, reflects another neglected aspect of Bowles's earlier literary career: his involvement in interwar European artistic culture, particularly the movement of surrealism. Despite the wider connotations that the adjective "surreal" has since accumulated, the surrealists themselves were originally an exclusive, self-regulating group of largely French, German, and Spanish artists. Although never a member of this group, Bowles was closely affiliated with them—indeed, along with the poet and editor Charles Henri Ford, he was the American writer most involved in the surrealist movement. This involvement was not limited to writing, however, and included musical compositions, magazine editing, and acting in surrealist film; during the 1930s in Paris, and the 1940s in New York, Bowles's artistic production continually intersected with the movement. In terms of his writing, moreover, Bowles was not only involved in the production of explicitly surrealist works—which ranged from poetry, to editorials, to collections of "surreal" documents—but was also consciously reworking aspects of surrealism into an idiosyncratic artistic practice. Perhaps more interesting than narrowly surrealist work, Bowles's short fiction offers an access point into the way that aspects of surrealist art became part of a more general American idiom. The stories collected in *The Delicate Prey* were written at a period where Bowles was transitioning from closely surrealist work into a style that followed a narrower, more precise, and closely structured aesthetic regime, and, while attentive to many of the same concerns as surrealism, they reflect a distinctive, technocratic approach.

Aside from the theoretical considerations that influenced his use of the form, Bowles also considered himself to be best suited to writing shorter texts. Indeed, this tendency was a natural carry-over from his earlier work as a composer, where his musical compositions increasingly tended toward minimalism and were characterized by short song forms rather than extended pieces. The relationship between Bowles's two ostensibly distinct modes of cultural production, however, has also remained unexplored territory. From the early 1930s until the late 1940s, Bowles's primary career had been as a classical composer, and he offers a unique example of an artist who found equal success in both music and writing. Although many modernist writers had attempted to bring a musical aesthetic to their fiction, Bowles stands out as an author whose compositional practices drew on years of experience within a musical, rather than written, medium. Composed at the juncture of his musical and authorial praxes, *The Delicate Prey* represents a synthesis of artistic practices, aesthetic priorities, and political motivations.

Fundamentally, reading Bowles's short fiction within the framework of minor literature is to position his writing within a context that emphasizes closure and containment. Taking their cue from *The Sheltering Sky* and its endless Saharan landscapes, critics have figured Bowles in terms of expansiveness and freedom, often invoking the spirit of existentialism in the process; even Bowles's first critics considered his works to be populated by "the existential school of characters, who find no reason to live."[7] From such a perspective, Bowles can be easily recuperated within the same countercultural tradition as the Beat generation, with studies as recent as those of Raj Chandarlapaty and Rob Wilson continuing to deploy Bowles as a parallel to Jack Kerouac, Allen Ginsberg, and William Burroughs.[8] Despite Bowles's distinctly countercultural ambitions, however, his position toward society and stylistic approach to writing diverge considerably from those of the Beats. Invested in establishing an alternative literary tradition, Bowles was fundamentally opposed to the ethos of individual freedom that motivated the form and underpinned the social implications for authors such as Kerouac and Ginsberg. Characterized by compression and claustrophobia, Bowles's writing instead evinced his intrinsically antidemocratic political beliefs and opposition to the narratives of social and political progress espoused by the American government and reinforced by cultural criticism in the postwar period. This critical stance was heightened by Bowles's awareness of the rapidly increasing influence that American culture was having on a global scale, where the "trend of this century is being set by America for the entire world."[9] In short, considering Bowles as a writer of minor literature is to present a figure quite distinct from the benign Moroccan guru of popular imagination. This Bowles is Jorge Luis Borges's first English translator, who adapted Frederico García Lorca's work for the stage and traveled extensively through Latin America. He is a collaborator with Alexander Calder and Max Ernst who worked with Salvador Dali to produce a ballet based on the poetry of Paul Verlaine. This Bowles studied under musical luminaries Aaron Copland and Virgil Thomson and was awarded a Guggenheim Fellowship to facilitate his work as a composer. Above all, this is a writer who saw his writing as "an exhortation to destroy" and who considered writing to be nothing more than "patterns of words."[10]

A Pornographer of Terror: Bowles and the Critics

Despite the extensive body of work he produced across his career, Bowles has been permanently defined by his first two volumes of prose, which were published little over a year apart. While Bowles placed higher value on his short stories, it was his first novel, *The Sheltering Sky,* which "seemed to locate his fictional vision for good in the minds of his readers."[11] In particular, his juxtaposition of rootless, disengaged Americans with alien North African landscapes and people established a pattern of conflicted representations of modern society that derived directly from Bowles's own often deeply antagonistic feelings toward Western "civilization."[12] *The Delicate Prey* followed in 1950, an anthology of short fiction collecting works he had published in a range of literary journals over the previous five years that cemented his reputation for shocking violence and fine, almost delicate form, which James Lasdun has described as "the combination of refinement and delinquency."[13] Like *The Sheltering Sky,* these stories take place in a detached, alien landscape and are written with what Joyce Carol Oates described as a "superlunary authority."[14] Both texts were able to generate a large amount of critical attention, from the *New York Times* to the *Kenyon Review,* while also taking a firm hold on the general public and "entered the travel guidebooks as something like required reading."[15] The critical reception of these works, however, swung sharply from the almost universal praise that greeted *The Sheltering Sky* to the general censure contemporary critics applied to *The Delicate Prey.* American critics reacted almost as violently against *The Delicate Prey* as they had thrown their support positively behind his debut novel. This dramatic shift illustrates both the critical pressure on authors to produce works that aligned with nationalistic narratives and the short story's suitability to offer a counternarrative to precisely these expectations.

The impact of *The Sheltering Sky* was instantaneous. David Dempsey's "Cross Section" in the *New York Times* in January 1950 summed up "a

score of nineteen critics rapturously in favor, eight slightly less enthusiastic, and only one . . . wholly against"—with a swathe of high-literary
comparisons in tow, including Hemingway, Eliot, and Faulkner.[16] The
tide of positive reception culminated in the inclusion of the novel by the
arbiter of American value William Carlos Williams, at the top of his list
of "Best Books I Read This Year."[17] And, despite the extent to which the
novel suggested serious problems with being American, this should not
be that surprising. While critics consistently took issue with aspects of
Bowles's characterization, they were drawn to a quality of "adventure" in
the journey of the protagonists, Kit and Port Moresby, which took them
into the emptiness of the Sahara and offered a contemporary parallel to
the American frontiersman heading into the West, as a "chronicle of startling adventure."[18] Moreover, the journey that the Moresbys undertook
appeared to be personal quests for freedom from society, or from themselves, and seemed to voice an idea of individual freedom—of a desire to
break free from external constraints—that resonated with readers. Cyril
Connolly evaluated "the courage and intelligence of their despair" as
being the "adolescence" of Hemingway's The Sun Also Rises "fully grown
up"; they captured an essential quality of the modern individual.[19] The
characters' desire to escape the "sheltering sky" of the title even seemed
to inflect the formal qualities of the text as a novel; chafing at the constraints of a traditional novelistic structure, it was initially rejected by
his publishers because, from their perspective, it failed to conform to the
expectations of the form. So The Sheltering Sky was a success on both a
popular and literary level. It offered a tale that conformed to popular expectations of the generic framework of the adventure story, to the extent
that it could be recuperated within it and easily consumed (Tennessee
Williams slyly suggested that "a good many people will read this book
and be enthralled by it without once suspecting it contains a mirror . . .
of moral nihilism").[20] But it also offered a vision of a search for freedom
that, at a critical level, could be integrated within a literary model attuned
to the political exigencies of Cold War America.

    Despite this critical success—or indeed, because of it—Bowles himself
rejected his debut novel. In one of his final interviews, with Gilles Herzog
in 1996, Paul Bowles lamented the critical and popular obsession with The
Sheltering Sky; suggesting that critics reproached him "for not having per-

petually re-written" the same novel, Bowles declared that he had only "one thing to say: 'I'd really like to forget [*The Sheltering Sky*].'"[21] Bowles himself clearly prioritized his short fiction and considered himself preeminently suited for the short story form. He explained to Phillip Ramey that "short, simple pieces were the most satisfying" and that he was "least ashamed of some of the short stories, more so than the novels."[22] These priorities are evinced in *The Sheltering Sky* itself; Bowles wrote the novel only in order to secure publication for his short fiction and composed it with the same set of concerns as his short fiction. In his article on the publication history of *The Sheltering Sky*, "Constructing the Postwar Art Novel," Evan Brier aptly draws to the fact that Bowles began work on the text only after he was unable to get an anthology of short stories published. While he had found a venue for individual pieces in both avantgarde journals, such as *transition* and *View*, and popular publications, most notably *Harper's Bazaar*, Bowles wanted to reach a broader audience through a published collection. The volume that eventually came out— *The Delicate Prey*—would remain the book Bowles considered the most successful, and closest to his heart.[23] In 1947, however, when Bowles initially attempted to publish this collection, he was informed by publishing house Dial Press that he would require a published novel first. The writing of *The Sheltering Sky* was motivated, therefore, by Bowles's desire to gain a wider audience for his short fiction; as Brier stresses, Bowles explicitly "set out to write a novel as a way to get his short stories published."[24]

From this perspective, the critical backlash against *The Delicate Prey* can be attributed, in large part, to the cultural pressures to produce novelistic fiction that promoted individual growth and reinforced the democratic narratives of American cultural identity. This structural bias is particularly evident in critics' frequent disquiet at elements that had been praised in *The Sheltering Sky*. Overall, the strongest sense across the reviews was that the work was irrelevant—simply "a bit of exotic reporting."[25] As such, critics were clear that they were not criticizing Bowles's skill as a writer: Charles Jackson praised the technical aspects of his writing as "crystal clear, economical, unrhetorical, sophisticated,"[26] while Leslie Fiedler thought that he "escaped completely the sort of enmity to language" that other contemporary short story writers seemed to bear ("Style" 170). If anything, reviewers were supportive of Bowles's technical abilities—instead, they foregrounded his need to change the macrostructures of his writing so that he could reach the level that they considered him capable of reaching. Jackson revealed that he "look[ed] forward to the day when such a forthright and honest writer as Paul Bowles returns to his native scene [of America]"; if the stories of *The Delicate Prey* had been "truly stories . . . rich with life and meaning," then he "would have been absorbed and moved, and he would have learned and felt and believed."[27] So it was not that critics had lost faith in Bowles's skill but that they felt his writing was dealing with subject matter that, in a crucial sense, did not matter; literature required a subject that possessed "meaning," that could "absorb and move" the reader.

In *The Sheltering Sky*, Bowles had seemed justified in sending the Moresbys to North Africa: critics like Prescott could equate its status as "a novel about the Sahara" with being "also about the spiritual wasteland in which its characters wander."[28] But in the stories of *The Delicate Prey*, the qualities of the landscape that were able to be extrapolated out to a metaphorical framework for the novel become major flaws, disconnecting his work from reality. Barbour was content to reduce them to "a bit of exotic reporting,"[29] while Fiedler suggested that "his work denies the world of our every-day" ("Style" 170). Clearly the use of deliberately foreign settings was jarring for contemporary critics, and Jackson's critique offers a clearer picture of why this was the case. Such landscapes have, he argues, the "connotation of romantic and far places" appropriate to "escape literature"; Bowles had used his settings for entirely the opposite purpose, to practice "brutality and horror" upon his reader.[30] Jackson juxtaposes Bowles's use "the remote, the strange, the untypical" against where he ought to have set his work: his "native scene" where he could give "personal, intimate, and, shall we say, down-to-earth stories or glimpses of the small town in which he was brought up."[31] In other words, Bowles's stories were disconnected from "reality" because they failed to deal with relevant issues within an *American* setting. If he had merely intended to provide escapism, then these settings would have been more critically acceptable. But because his stories are challenging and confront their reader, aspiring to some *meaning*, they ought to have been located somewhere *real*. Bowles's critics were very concerned with what the stories would mean to their reader: Jackson, for example, is desperate to find the stories "rich with life and meaning" and to "have learned" from them. Detached from American life and the issues relevant to the reader, his stories were pointless as fiction; they were not "truly . . . stories." For contemporary critics, therefore, the use of a specifically *American* setting was not only a question of geography but closely tied to particular kinds of narrative structures and thematic concerns. Jackson hoped that, in a future *novel,* Bowles would give his reader "personal, intimate, and, shall we say, down-to-earth glimpses of the small town in which he was brought up. For it is the native and the personal, reflections or refractions of everyday living—particularly American adolescence, never a tired theme when well done—that are universal that will prove to be the stuff of our literature, and that Paul Bowles could do so well."[32] From this perspective, the idea of meaningful literature necessarily entailed particular patterns of the growth and development of an individual—note the emphasis on American *adolescence*—which in turn suggested specific models for understanding progress on a national scale. This configuration reflects the increased critical pressure toward representation, where critics expected fiction to present narratives where the protagonist's development reflected, on an allegorical level, the democratic freedom that distinguished America from the Soviet Union.

Naturally such bias was not always conscious, although it manifests almost universally in the expectations critics expressed regarding the characters of *The Delicate Prey.* The overwhelming response to the anthology was that its works were "less story and characterization than scenes and places described with great originality." As Jackson explained, there was nobody with whom the reader could relate in the anthology, a situation that Fiedler put down to Bowles's "total inability to make intellectual notions as real as feelings, to specify men thinking as convincingly as he can specify men undergoing castration" ("Style" 170). While critics wanted to "take part in" the stories themselves and become invested in their characters, they found themselves cut off from them, unable to relate to these "undeveloped" figures.[33] Thomas Barbour summarized the reaction, declaring that *The Delicate Prey* was "lacking any . . . penetration of character."[34]

The distance that Bowles set up between the characters and his readers formed only part of the problem. In *The Sheltering Sky,* despite feeling

a similar distance between themselves and the characters at times—
Prescott, for example, was "suspicious" that Port and Kit were ultimately
just "decadent parasites"—critics still valorized many elements of the
Moresbys' representation.[35] But even with Port's existential quest in mind,
critics still questioned his suitability as a literary role model: simply put,
the Moresbys were too lifeless for readers to emulate. Fanny Butcher put
it most succinctly when she claimed that "the reader has no feeling whatever for the people to whom the horrors or the ecstasies happen."[36] While
this was embedded within most of the criticism of The Sheltering Sky to
some extent or another, it emerged as an overt critique of The Delicate
Prey, where the question of his characters' freedom and ability to offer
a model for the reader became much more insistent. The obvious lack
of responsibility shown by the characters—to society, their families, or
themselves—was an important concern, with Charles Jackson particularly
concerned by the way "a young sailor is finally accepted by his hostile
shipmates only after deliberately perpetrating a cruelty that surpasses
their own.[37] The question of the characters' morality, and of the morality
of Bowles's storyworlds as a whole, placed The Delicate Prey under much
greater scrutiny—what was the point in reading about such morally
ambiguous, if not completely amoral, characters? Jackson described his
"active anger at having to put up with ["A Distant Episode"] at all," and the
sense pervaded that the amorality of the characters in the anthology was
too great for "proper" literature; indeed, Thomas Barbour condemned the
collection as "not fiction."[38] But underlying this was an essential question
about the characters' agency. Did the inhabitants of these stories actually
demonstrate any ability to direct their actions or display any desire to
do so? Or were their actions subsumed by the impulse of the narrative,
driven by something outside of them? Fiedler suggested this second
possibility, arguing that Bowles's fiction operated by "devising ingenious
literal levels for allegories of the unconscious"; rather than true characters, the figures in Bowles's fiction were actually components directed
by the allegorical machinery of the stories ("Style" 160). The consensus
of critics that the characters were uninteresting, not merely by virtue of
being distant but because they failed to model ethical behavior for the
reader, was fundamental to the negative judgments of the anthology.

    If critics were concerned with the morality of Bowles's fiction, then perhaps the most decisive factor in their rejection of the anthology could have been the violence that is symptomatic of *The Delicate Prey*. Certainly, his overwhelming use of violence—shocking, graphic, and visceral—was one of the more contentious issues for critics. Advertisements for the book deployed it as a major hook for potential readers, and even in 2011, the Modern Classics edition published by Penguin, collecting three of Bowles's most famous stories, proclaimed them to be "unbearably tense tales from sun-drenched and brutal climes," telling titillatingly of "vengeance, abandonment, violence and cruelty enjoyed and suffered, in a surreal realm of horror."[39] On original publication, Bowles was condemned as "a pornographer of terror,"[40] as a writer who produced "such unspeakable horror and brutality that there is no sense in trying to describe it" (Fiedler, "Style" 170). The language used here is an important indicator of why the violence of these stories was viewed as so repugnant. It was not simply that Bowles was depicting horrifying events; Fiedler accepts that "we must, somewhere between the limits of squeamishness and abandon, learn to come to terms with horror" ("Style" 171). But Bowles presented his violence in a titillating way, in an approach that ran counter to any social use that its deployment could perform—he seemed "a secret lover of the horror he evokes" ("Style" 170). Rather than offering an image of violence that could help society grow, his use of violence seemed to actively frustrate growth. On a more particular level, the violence cut off the potential for the individual characters to grow within the stories. Some of the highest praise for *The Sheltering Sky* came for its ability to show the development of the individual in the modern world, "an allegory of the spiritual adventure of the fully conscious person into modern experience."[41] In *The Delicate Prey*, however, the insistent violence cuts off any possibility for such growth, and, as such, the text remains "characterless." Bowles's violence, then, was characterized as something that served no function and reduced his stories to "a vehicle for the vicarious enjoyment of sadistic perversion."[42] Moreover, it made his texts socially irresponsible, as it actively frustrated both the reader's and the characters' growth—implicitly aligning it with the model of oppression and stagnation imaginatively mapped onto the Soviet East.

Perhaps the best illustration of this is in the reception of the most controversial aspect of Bowles's prose, the graphic violence. Fiedler argued

that *The Delicate Prey* "compels from us the shocked, protesting acceptance of terror as an irreducible element of being. The whole impact of
his work is the insistence on the horrible" ("Style" 170); while it may
engage the reader with the story to some extent (by shocking them), it
also alienated them through its depiction of action to which they could
not relate. Moreover, it offered no productive message, served no social
purpose. Instead, it confronted the reader with the reality of the opposite:
violence, severance, and decay. The most suggestive critique of Bowles's
fiction—Jackson's unflattering portrait of the author as a "pornographer
of terror"—is particularly interesting in that it supposes a level of in-
tentionality behind his aesthetic strategies. This is certainly reflected
in Bowles's own conceptualization of his writing, which focuses almost
obsessively on compression and introversion. In a phrase that curiously
echoes William Carlos William's aesthetic of "no ideas but in things,"
Bowles described a literary manifesto that matches his own praxis surprisingly well: "there's nothing in writing except words, patterns of words"
(*Conversations* 213). In this formalistic interpretation of the writer's role,
which contrasts starkly with the liberal ideal of "unpatterned fiction," he
emphasized the craft that is so apparent in his work, but he also directly
confronted the idea that fiction should be (or even could be) meaningful;
as he argued explicitly, "what's in a novel is not important . . . it's how it's
told" (*Conversations* 213).

One way in which he set about achieving this level of patterned fiction
was through the relationship between characters and setting. In reading
his stories, critics had suggested one relationship between character development and landscape: an American landscape would have suited exemplary accounts of adolescent growth. Such a configuration places emphasis on the individual character, with the setting a secondary concern;
Bowles, however, considered his choice of setting to dictate the form of
his prose. He wrote to one editor explaining that "places have always
been more important to me than people. That is to say, people give the
landscape scale: the landscape is not a background for them"[43] Bowles's
settings, then, dictated the rest of the work; characters were contingent
upon their setting and ultimately only present to reinforce the location
of the story. The meaning of Bowles's stories was, therefore, predicated
upon their context, with the characters "generally presented as integral

parts of situations, along with the landscape," so that, in Bowles's view, "it's not very fruitful to try to consider them in another light" (*Conversations* 92) From a compositional perspective, Bowles organized the stories around their location, with the other elements of the story emerging in relation to their setting. In terms of a story's effect, moreover, Bowles felt that "the motivation of characters in fiction like mine should be a secondary consideration," as he thought "of characters as if they were props in the general scene of any given work"—individual characters were simply extensions of the setting (*Conversations* 91). Bowles explained to one interviewer that, in his stories, "the characters, the landscape," and "the climatic conditions" were "one" with "the formal structure of the story"; his work was organized around achieving a coherence that resisted the separation out, and explication of, the individual elements. Indeed, Bowles felt that his "characters are made of the same material as the rest of the work" and that "since they are activated by the other elements of the synthetic cosmos, their own motivations are relatively unimportant" (*Conversations* 91).

The formal coherence of Bowles's stories thus not only offered a model of fiction structurally divergent from the ideals of expansive novelistic fiction but challenged the philosophical perspective that underpinned it. By presenting a world where characters were a product of their environment rather than free agents whose physical journeys corresponded to intellectual and spiritual growth, Bowles offered an alternative perspective on human identity. Such an overtly oppositional standpoint necessarily undermined the political narratives of postwar America, which were predicated upon the equation of individual and national identity. Indeed, as he confided in Herzog, Bowles intended his texts to have a destabilizing effect on his readers, as "the surest way to win is through conspiracy: not by expressing oneself openly. Sometimes, you win at a decisive moment, by doing everything by surprise."[11] But for what kind of victory was Bowles aiming? On the most basic level, he considered it the responsibility of the writer to critique contemporary society. Although he acknowledged that "human behavior is contingent upon the particular culture that informs it," he strongly believed that writers should "reject, at this moment in history, the mass society" (*Conversations* 58, 48). In fact, the success of any given text could be measured by the extent to which it provoked its reader to reconsider society. Bowles articulated this most clearly when he declared that "if a writer can incite anyone to question and ultimately to reject the present structure of any facet of society, he's performed a function" (*Conversations* 96).

At the same time, Bowles's literary style was explicitly indebted to Poe—a heritage reflected in Bowles's emphasis on the "natural" logic of his stories. While critics have questioned the sometimes fantastic plots of his stories, Bowles himself explained that "it has always seemed to me that my characters act naturally, given the circumstances" (*Conversations* 91). He considered his characters' behavior to be essentially "foreseeable" and explained that within his stories, "characters set in motion a mechanism of which they become a victim" (*Conversations* 91). The initial premise of Bowles's stories, therefore, dictated the way the plots would develop; he considered the ensuing action to be a natural consequence of the initial set-up. As his precise generic classification of his stories suggests, moreover, the "mechanism" of the story was tied to the genre in which he was working—"generally the mechanism [is] operative at the very beginning" (*Conversations* 91). Linked to his choice of genre was his selection of location. As I have argued, Bowles understood his stories as much through their settings as their structure, and the location of his stories exercised an equally strong power over the development of the tales. Bowles considered that "the transportation of characters" to the "exotic" settings on which he insistently focused acted "as a catalyst or detonator, without which there'd be no action" (*Conversations* 91). The context that Bowles established for his stories, then, guided their production to an almost total degree; the choice of genre determined the nature of the story. Indeed, Bowles felt that every element in his texts was designed to reinforce the central motif, so that "the characters, the landscape, the climatic conditions, the human situation, the formal structure of the story or the novel, all these elements are one" (*Conversations* 91)

In diverging from and resisting narrative models oriented around freedom, Bowles actively rejected the ideology that such "open" fiction represented. Indeed, he argued explicitly that his "characters don't attain any kind of freedom" and that instead, freedom was an illusion; people are inherently "bound by physical laws, bound by your body, bound by your mind" (*Conversations* 94). Although the individual always had the option to achieve freedom through death—Bowles explained that "the cage door's always open"—he believed that people implicitly "want freedom inside the cage" (*Conversations* 94). By working within a form characterized by closure and compression, and by intentionally emphasizing those qualities, Bowles could contest the novel on a formal level and at the same time undermine the larger social implications that were being attributed to the novelistic form; ultimately, he sought to contest the narratives of democratic freedom that governed the intellectual discourse of midcentury America.

"My Work Has Nothing to Do with Surrealism": Bowles, Surrealism, and Music

As a polyglot composer, photographer, and translator, Bowles left a broad impression on the artistic world of mid-twentieth-century America beyond his published novels and short stories. The combination of his peculiar style—strikingly precise, vividly violent—and the magazines with which he initially found literary success, saw him still classified "as late as the 70s" as one of a select group of "American Surrealists."[45] Indeed, Bowles had a close relationship with many of the leading figures within the surrealist movement, both in Paris and in exile in New York, and was an important contributor to Charles Henri Ford's surrealist magazine *View* (1940–47). But while the popular association of Bowles's prose with surrealism may have endured, Bowles himself went on to renounce any intellectual relationship, proclaiming that his fiction had "nothing to do with Surrealism" (*Conversation* 137). Bowles's encounters with surrealism, however, profoundly influenced his use of the short story as a countercultural form, and the critiques leveled at his work gesture toward some of the underlying cultural biases against surrealism in midcentury America. Bowles has generally been seen as presenting a vision that is removed from the contingencies of real life, and violent in a way that served no social purpose. By considering his prose within the framework of surrealism, we can recuperate these disjunctive elements as part of an aesthetic that followed the surrealist guru André Breton in challenging what they both understood as the deformed rationality of the Western mind.

Bowles himself repeatedly cited Breton's work on automatic writing, which he read in translation in the pages of Eugene Jolas's Parisian magazine *transition*, as a crucial intervention in his own development as a writer. At the same time, however, Bowles made a point of distancing himself from the surrealist leader and was never a member of the closely organized group. Contrary to assertions by other critics, Bowles never actually met Breton, actively avoiding him even when the two were working on the same issue of *View* during Breton's wartime exile in New York. Instead, Bowles maintained long-term, personal relations with two of the most prominent surrealist painters, Max Ernst and Salvador Dali, with whom he collaborated in various ways during the 1940s. On leaving high school, Bowles had initially anticipated a career as a painter, enrolling in the School of Design and Liberal Arts in Manhattan; during his time in Paris during the 1930s, Bowles wrote back unceasingly to friends in America about the art scene, showing an acute awareness of the development of surrealist painting. He wrote to one friend that he was "especially fond of Klee's work," and that the "[de] Chirico is superlative! Fortunately there is a bench directly in front of it, and one can regard it by the minute in comfort."[46] Bowles felt comfortable making value judgments about the quality of the art he saw and showed a clear preference for artists associated with surrealism, arguing that "the 'new' good [artists] are surely a very decided 'few.' Miró, Roux, Klee, Picabia, Tanguy, Chirico."[47] He was attuned, moreover, to the way that the art world was developing, writing of Max Ernst's work in 1931, that: "He must be mad. certainly the farther he goes, the farther from land he seems to get. have you followed him at all? ten years ago his things were understandable. now they are the maddest maddest one can find anywhere anywhere."[48] For Bowles, the "madness" and incomprehensibility of Ernst's work was one of its strengths, and it drew him to seek out the artist in person. Although he encountered surrealism through Breton, he was nonetheless predisposed to engage with it in less dogmatic way, which was inflected by the visual arts.

So it is not as if surrealism were an alien imposition on Bowles's artistic career. Indeed, from a young age, Bowles had consciously composed works within a specifically surrealist mode of production, and his earliest literary efforts were oriented along specifically surrealist lines. In an unpublished letter to the critic Neil Campbell in 1981, Bowles reflected back on his career, concluding he had "never written anything save in the shadow, at least, of the Surrealist tradition."[49] In the spring of 1928, before Bowles was eighteen, his poem "Spire Song" was published in *transition*. He had tailored this "long Surrealist effort" deliberately toward the aesthetic priorities of the magazine, and his success inspired two trips to Paris, where he would meet Gertrude Stein and later be propelled toward Tangiers, his future home in exile.[50] While the next decade was dedicated to Bowles's musical career as a composer, mentored by Aaron Copland, when he returned to literature in the 1940s, his work appeared in the even more explicitly surrealist publication, Ford's New York–based magazine *View*. With an article entitled "The Jazz Ear," Bowles made his entry into "one of the most important avant-garde magazines of the 1940s."[51] He would later recall how "ideologically *View*'s policy adhered fairly strictly to the tenets of *The Surrealist Manifesto*," a stance that suited his perspective, and he quickly found a place as one of two "master linguists who would become *View*'s chief translators."[52] Bowles also collaborated in cross-disciplinary projects with Ernst and Dali. A longtime admirer of Ernst's collage novels, Bowles composed the score for a film on Ernst's masterpiece, *Une semaine de bonte*, which they later reworked for the segment that Ernst directed in Hans Richter's 1948 film *Dreams That Money Can Buy*. In return, Ernst produced the cover artwork for a recording of Bowles's music issued by Peggy Guggenheim's "Art of this Century" imprint. Bowles also collaborated with Dali on the ballet *Colloque sentimentale*, composing a score based on poems of Paul Verlaine, and advised him on his illustrations for a 1934 edition of Lautréamont's *Les chants de Maldoror*. Bowles had thus planted himself at the heart of wartime surrealism, among both exiled progenitors and local disciples, and his finely honed ear for the nuances of surrealism's fundamental aesthetics allowed him to flourish.

Even after he stopped working on material for an explicitly surrealist forum, moreover, Bowles's method of composition continued to rely upon the method of automatic writing, which had "liberated his style" and continued to govern his artistic output.[53] Bowles characterized his life as one that was largely "unthought," suggesting that he had naturally "never been a thinking person" and that his life went by "without [his] conscious knowledge."[54] The moment, during his teens, of discovering Breton's theories on automatic writing proved a pivotal one, for automatism allowed him to communicate through writing in a way that accounted for his own experience of the world: he could "write without being conscious of what [he] was doing," just as he lived in an "unthought" way.[55] He relished the freedom to be able to "make [his prose] grammatically correct and even to have a certain style without the slightest idea of what [he] was writing," to the point where he did not even feel personal responsibility for what he had written. He protested that "I don't feel that I wrote these books. I feel as though they had been written by my arm, by my brain, my organism, but that they're not necessarily mine."[56]

Bowles's decision to change career, from composer to author, was instigated in part by the publication in *View* in 1943 of some of his childhood writings: a diary-narrative written from the age of nine, beginning at the end of 1919, the entries of which were framed as a surrealist text by the editors of *View*.[57] Described by Ford in the volume's contents page as "the *chef d'ouevre* of the primitive style," Bowles's work was recuperated, ahistorically, as a protosurrealist "document."[58] *Bluey*'s four and a half months of daily entries concern the unfolding relationships of the heroine, Bluey, with the men Dolok Parasol and Henry Altman, her transition to America (to the mythical city of "Wen Kroy," New York's inverted image), and her negotiation of its social customs and mores. In the editors' eyes, its suitability for publication in the pages of *View* was unquestionable—Ford wrote that it was "far more persuasive than the writing of many adults." From its focus on cataloguing seemingly trivial details, its emphasis on the monstrous and disturbing, to its use of the staccato form of diary entries to enhance the discordant juxtaposition of Bluey's experiences with each other, it could readily be produced as evidence of the kind of unconscious connection-making toward which surrealism strove.

In many ways *Bluey* foreshadowed Bowles's later achievements in short fiction, offering a prototype for the unconscious-driven narratives that juxtaposed the alien against the civilized that became his greatest literary legacy. Its publication in *View*, however, positioned it as a kind of protosurrealist work instead that invited comparisons to the *First Manifesto*, in which Breton's mock-encyclopedia entry declared surrealism to be "based on the belief in the superior reality of certain forms of previously neglected associations, in the omnipotence of dream, in the disinterested play of thought."[59] In this formulation, surrealism sought to cultivate "a new *awareness*" of the world around the artist that would reveal a higher level of reality.[60] This process was, as is well known, anchored in the generative powers of the unconscious. *Bluey* references the unconscious, in part through the characters' peculiar habit of fainting every few days, initially with due cause—"Bluey was worse. Doctor says she has Pneumonia. She faints"; "Bluey has a blowout. Dolok dies. Bluey faints"; but increasingly, for no reason at all—"Bluey gets a maid. Lina Minner. Bluey faints."[61] Moreover, the text develops a disturbing theme of madness and violence, also echoing the surrealists' pursuit of extreme psychic states. From the incipient conflict between Bluey and Henry—"Bluey has a fight with Henry. Bluey yells" and "Bluey hits Henry. Henry hits Bluey and gives her a black eye"—the text shifts its focus to the unfortunate Dolok Parasol's parents, who quickly succumb to sickness and insanity.[62] After "Dolok Parasol's mother dies of grief for loss of Dolok," and his sister "weeps and weeps" for two days straight before contracting influenza, Mr. Parasol "gets influenza," "goes crazy," and "almost dies." Perhaps the most disturbing aspect of Bowles's text is the way his characters seem to crave their madness. Localized again in the Parasol family, Dolok's sister Bessie, already sick with influenza, "has Chrisis"; her father, the following day, "wishes he would have chrisis." Recalling the portmanteau words of the surrealists' spiritual ancestor Lewis Carroll or their famous games of "Exquisite Corpses," Bowles blends "crisis" with both "chrysalis," suggesting a kind of rebirth—following her chrisis, Bessie gets "better"—and Christ, suggesting a messianic sacrifice. Indeed, Mr. Parasol gets his wish for "chrisis" and subsequently dies. Bowles's naïve wordplay, reframed within the context of an issue of *View* organized around the theme of Narcissus, thus suggests the dual possibility of a madness that heals and destroys, just as surrealism promised both a death to rational thinking and a subsequent aesthetic "rebirth."

The claustrophobic sense of madness and dislocation in the text is emphasized by Bowles's use of juxtaposition. The cornerstone of surrealist thought, the use of juxtaposition to form "previously neglected associations," is the central process for generating meaning in surrealist writing.[63] Focused around clipped and selective diary entries, the structure of *Bluey* is comprised of a series of seemingly unrelated events that are brought together in a disturbing union: "Dolok gets worse. Bluey gets a Pierce Arrow Automobile"; "Greatest storm in world's history. Bluey knocks Henry down."[64] Through their inclusion together in that day's entry, the events take on a powerfully suggestive, although never explicit, relationship. The text's obsession with inane measurements, reflected in Bluey's compulsion to reweigh herself, recording even the fractional increase from 95 to 95½ pounds, or the cataloguing of temperature and snowfall, becomes part of this broader strategy that makes connections between the mundane and the mysterious. We feel compelled to infer a relationship between the storm and Bluey's violence toward her lover, just as we build a connection when we read, on February 21: "It starts snowing again. 34 degrees. Bluey wants a child.[65] *Bluey*, compressed, violent, and disjunctive, thwarts expectations of a rational, sequential narrative, offering a surreal network of connections and a radically disoriented perspective. Insofar as it differed drastically from the conventions of Western cultural production, it could be readily reappropriated as an example of "primitive" writing by the editors of *View* and thus co-opted into a wider narrative that set the "primitive" or "outsider" in opposition to the "civilized."

Three years later, in 1946, the same year that he published his short story "The Echo" in *Harper's Bazaar*, Bowles took part in a series of personality tests that were published in *Life* magazine, as "one of four successful young New Yorkers," where he was explicitly identified as "composer Paul Bowles."[66] Quite apart from the fascinating conclusion, based on Bowles's responses to a Rorschach test, that he was "amazingly complex and individualistic," with "little in common with 'ordinary' people," the article is useful because it indicates what a high profile Bowles had achieved as a composer at the point at which he turned to producing fiction. Over the last decade, there has been a gradually widening interest in the intersection between music and literature; while an often neglected relationship, there is now a body of scholarship that focuses on what has traditionally been a secondary concern compared to the relationship between literature and the visual arts. In general, this research tends to consider the links between the two forms from two distinct perspectives. The first is to think about the way that music, as an aesthetic model, has influenced writers formally and stylistically. The second is to take a wider view, to consider how the two forms of production have responded to similar cultural changes or have negotiated similar terrain. The case of Bowles is unusual; he stands apart as someone who achieved critical and commercial success in both fields. Considering the relationship between his work as a composer and as a writer offers insight not only into Bowles's own artistic practice but on the connections between American music and literature more widely.

The period over which Bowles worked primarily as a composer, indeed the modernist period more generally, is now being recognized as a highly charged time of exchange between music and writing. In broad terms, the innovations that occurred in music—which critics often mark with the first performance of Igor Stravinsky's *Le sacre du printemps* in 1913—provide fascinating analogies to the developments in literature.[67] Writers themselves were keen to draw on such comparisons, and several prominent authors deliberately adopted a "musical aesthetic" in their work. Naturally, the way individual authors chose to apply aspects of music to their work varied a great deal, as did their actual understanding of the elements they were theoretically appropriating. Music provided quite distinct inspiration for writers as diverse as Virginia Woolf, James Joyce, T. S. Elliot, Ezra Pound, and Gertrude Stein, all of whom approached the appropriation of music with different sets of knowledge and with different aims in doing so. But it can be safely said, at least, that modernist writers turned to music primarily as a model of *formal* innovation, where the changes that occurred in classical music over the early twentieth century, particularly in terms of rhythmic structure and tonality, were used as a template for potential literary experimentation in structure and form. Another sign of the fertility of crossover between the two forms in this period is the prominence of collaborations between high-profile authors and composers, generally in the context of opera. Pound, for example, worked with the American composer and sometime friend of Bowles, George Antheil, in attempting to reconfigure his literary concept of vorticism for an operatic format. Perhaps most famously, two of Bowles's mentors (in separate capacities) collaborated on a sensational opera staged in New York in 1934: Gertrude Stein and Virgil Thomson's

Four Saints in Three Acts. Bowles was very much caught up in this atmosphere of cross-pollination; he wrote back enthusiastically to the absent
Stein about the reception of *Four Saints* and engaged himself in several
such collaborations in the capacity of composer.

As his *Life* profile suggests, Bowles stands out not only in the modernist period but more generally as one of a very small number of artists who
had successful and distinct careers as both a classical composer and as
an author. Where his literary career was marked by its divergence from
America, both in the settings it developed and the values to which it
subscribed, however, his music was characterized to a large degree by the
extent to which it conformed to the developing American musical idiom.
In 1945, Peggy Glanville-Hicks described him as "one of the most interesting of the younger American composers," and her assessment that his
music was "essentially American" has continued to govern the (rather
limited) discussion of this aspect of his life.[68] From the perspective of influence, the American character of Bowles's composition can be attributed
to the man under whom he served his musical apprenticeship and through
whom he gained access to a circle of composers that included Thomson
and Leonard Bernstein: Aaron Copland. When Bowles met Copland
in 1930, he immediately recognized in the composer ten years his senior
"the energy and talent for which he would later become famous."[69] In
fact, by 1945, *Music Quarterly* was able to assert that "few composers of
our time . . . have developed a style so strongly and individually" as had
Copland. Copland's own early training in Europe influenced the sound
of Bowles's music—early listeners noted echoes of Erik Satie and Stravinsky, suggesting his music had "a distinctly French accent."[70] Much more
significantly, however, Copland used both American folk motifs and jazz
qualities, which were carried through in the music of his pupil, as Bowles
developed a style that worked within a distinctly American idiom. By the
time he had established himself as a figure "well known in contemporary musical circles," his style sharply reflected the musical influence of
Copland, Bernstein, and Thomson, to the point where Glanville-Hicks felt
she could not "discuss Paul Bowles in particular without making constant
reference to American composers in general."[71] But equally, as Glanville-
Hicks herself stressed, Bowles's music was characterized by his "highly individual technique," which she attributed to his "having learned in action

the basic laws of composition without implanting in his style mannerisms and dogmas of other personalities."[72] While Copland played a significant role in the development of Bowles's musical sensibilities, Bowles remained "essentially a self-taught musician" who continued to feel insecurities about gaps in his knowledge of musical theory and praxis.[73]

Whatever reservations he may have had about his abilities, Bowles nonetheless felt comfortable enough to take on first a series of articles for the journal *Modern Music*, then a regular position as music columnist for the *New York Herald Tribune*. These would be Bowles's first forays into writing since his early success with *transition*, and they were marked by both the variety of subject matter and the intellectual framework within which they considered music. *Modern Music* was "among the most important music journals of its day" and offered both a critical and an "insider's view" of the American music scene from 1924 to 1946.[74] The *New York Herald Tribune*, too, stood out for "the quality of its news coverage, the literacy of its writing and the affluence of its readership."[75] Bowles made use of this critical voice to promote the music he considered most important—especially folk music from Latin America and North Africa and jazz, on which he wrote regular columns—but also to reflect intellectually on music and aesthetics in a way in which he was reluctant to engage with literature. At the same time as he was composing his own pieces, he was producing a "body of writing that can stand alongside Virgil Thomson's as the most valuable of its era in New York"; Bowles's visibility in American cultural life during the 1940s was a product of the clear and reflective voice he developed through his musical criticism.[76]

Although a distinctly "American" quality in Bowles's music emerged through the influence of Copland, Bowles drew his broader model of musical construction from a specifically European avant-garde, reflecting the equal importance of Thomson on the development of Bowles's aesthetic. Thomson himself deeply admired Bowles's compositions, and, in a review of his music for a production of *Twelfth Night*, argued that Bowles was, at the age of "thirty-four . . . America's most original and skillful composer of chamber music"; he traced Bowles's musical lineage, moreover, back to his own musical predecessor, Erik Satie. Indeed, he suggested that Satie was one of the two composers Bowles's work "most resembled."[77] The term "surrealism" famously originated in a review of Satie's work, and it was from him that Thomson had adopted a surrealist musical praxis. It was, therefore, as a model of surreal musical soundscapes that Thomson's work proved to be one of the most important contributions to Bowles's incipient musical aesthetics.

The other composer from whom Bowles drew clear inspiration was Stravinsky, and as Jonathan Scheffer emphasizes, Bowles emulated the minimalism that characterized aspects of both Satie's and Stravinsky's style. Scheffer locates Bowles's musical references within a strictly de-limited framework: he "employs a vividly specific vocabulary, leaving a narrow but incisive impression."[78] In fact, Bowles pursued this particular aspect of European modernism further than either of his mentors, with the minimalism of his piano pieces "predat[ing] the works of minimalists such as Steve Reich and John Adams by two decades."[79] From Stravinsky, too, Bowles borrowed the striking discordance that had propelled the earlier composer to fame. Throughout much of his music, Bowles was, in Scheffer's words, "toying with discord" and consciously rebelling against the conventional narrative of art music, with his pieces "lacking . . . reso-lution" and characterized by "a relentless off-balance quality."[80] However, while Stravinsky clearly left a lasting impression on Bowles—to the extent that he considered him his favorite composer—he had no liking for his later, "serial inflected pieces"; he thought that the composer's "twelve-tone music" sounded as though "someone had rewritten some Schoen-berg to sound like Stravinsky."[81] Not only does this reflect the prejudices of Bowles's circle of composers, but more specifically it was a symptom of Bowles's departure from what he considered to be the artificial con-ventions and structures of both American and European music. Instead, Bowles was interested in the possibility "of making music which would be expressive, and yet not in the oratorical way European art-music is expressive."[82] He thought of serialized compositions in particular as fol-lowing a staid and inorganic structure and believed that "conversational inflections, even the ones of imaginary conversational remarks inside the head, should replace what seemed to [him] the incredibly formal idiom of delivery" which was taken for granted as "the psychological basis for forming melodic logic."[83] Bowles approached music, then, with a technique that adopted evidently surrealist aesthetics, drawing on an assembly-logic and patterns of juxtaposition. His attitude toward the conventional structures of music, moreover, approximated the icono-clasm of a European avant-garde sensibility, undercutting the formal "psychological basis" of Western music with a surrealistic opposition to rational authority.

This attitude toward how music should be structured ultimately stemmed from Bowles's idiosyncratic conception of what music ought to achieve. His understanding of the power of music suggests why he had been drawn both to a career as a composer and to a European—in particular, surrealist—model of aesthetics; he explained, in a 1944 article outlining his own perspective on music, that his "first interest in music came from a purely hypnotic reaction that musical sounds always had on [him]." This effect was not necessarily produced, however, by what Bowles called "music itself," which he suggested always "showed direction, had some sort of climax and worst of all had a predictable end." Instead, what captivated him were "the musical sounds" that he could produce with everyday objects. Already, Bowles was defining a musical aesthetic in contrast to traditional standards of structure and form and, in this sense, his early definition of the function of music was also tied up with the idea of himself as actor—whether creating sounds by "spinning a large musical top or by sliding a metal object up and down the strings of a German Zither . . . or the creaking of a rusty door hinge." For Bowles, "these sounds seemed . . . the culmination of beauty." [84] Not only was Bowles constructing a model of aesthetic beauty in terms of discordant sounds, but he was placing emphasis on his own role as creator. More-over, the experience of listening to what the young Bowles understood to be music was a transcendent one. Rather than elevating him to a higher state of consciousness, however, his auto-hypnotic sonic experiments gave him the sense of emptiness and disjunction. He certainly figured them as a deliberate method for accessing his own subconscious, as they "always put [him] promptly into a non-thinking state which lasted as long as [he] repeated the sounds." [85] Even as an adult, Bowles still thought these "basic infantile criteria" that he used to assess music as an auto-hypnotic tool "still seemed perfectly valid," as they operated on him "with as much force as ever."

Understanding Bowles's aural aesthetics is intrinsic when approach-ing *The Delicate Prey* as countercultural; most of the short stories in this volume were written while Bowles's primary career was still that of composer. Indeed, within *The Delicate Prey*, his compositional aesthetics are manifested, on a very straightforward level, in the way that his stories register sound. Like the spirit of the Atlájala in Bowles's Borges-inspired story "The Circular Valley," his short stories are "conscious of each gradation in sound and light and smell" and attentive to the process of change and degradation that sounds undergo—the "slow, constant disintegration" that transforms the soundscape around them (*DP* 124). Indeed, it is no coincidence that, through the Atlájala, Bowles emphasizes the decay and discord of sound. Not only do his musical compositions draw on a Stravinskian model of discordance, but within his stories, the most prominent feature of the sounds he describes is their dissonance. In some cases, this means registering the noises that throw the characters off balance or disturb their rhythm. These can be as small as the "thin wail of mosquito wings" (75), or as all-consuming as the monstrous "sound of the nocturnal insects" in the heart of the rainforest, which is "unbearably loud—an endless, savage scream above the noise of the wind . . . a million scraping sounds in the air" (8). Instead of drawing attention to harmonious sounds, as we might expect a composer or someone with an ear for musicality to do, Bowles instead prioritizes sounds that are disturbing and unsettling.

This is especially the case with the music that features in his stories, which is universally represented as scratched, broken, or out of context. When the American missionary Pastor Dowe is forced to play his old phonograph to a native tribe in Central America, he is immediately disturbed by the "hopping rhythmical pattern" (35) of the music it plays; he is surprised, moreover, when his "audience was delighted, even though the sound was abominably scratchy" (54). The language Bowles uses to register the music—"hopping" and "abominably scratchy"—works to create a sense of the sound as viscerally discordant, and the reactions of the listeners reinforce this sense of being knocked off balance by the noise. In "Under the Sky," Bowles takes this discordance to its logical extreme, where the few notes of music that can be heard in the street are almost totally subsumed by static: all that can be heard is "a great crackling and hissing that covered the sound of the marimbas," and only "occasionally a few loud notes of band music rose above the chaos" (84).

Noise, and music in particular, is characterized in *The Delicate Prey* not by its beauty but by its chaotic irregularity. Invoking music, then, serves to help destabilize the production of meaning. Directing the reader away from the indexical meaning of words, it can help suggest an understanding of language as sound rather than word.

The complementary sense of fragmentation evident in Bowles's short fiction evinces the extent to which Bowles's musical training informed his literary compositions. The formal characteristics of his short stories developed out of the practices he honed as a musical composer; he structured his texts around the same qualities he prized on a purely auditory level. This crossover is equally a product, however, of the techniques Bowles maintained when writing. The surrealistic "automatic writing" practice to which he subscribed is commensurate to his method for composing music—detaching himself from the process of creation. K. Robert Schwarz notes that "Bowles's description of his compositional method implies not so much a haphazard approach to form as a cultivatedly subconscious one," and he even suggests that this approach guided the form of music he produced: "Bowles would discover that in music such a surrealist approach would work far better in free-associative, self-generated structures than in the rigorous forms inherited from the Classical masters."[86] In terms of both aesthetic priorities and means of production, Bowles's musical career provided a blueprint for his development of a model of short fiction organized around compression and reiterative motifs, which opposed traditional literary narrative progression.

Bowles as Minor Literature

To read Bowles's fiction as minor literature is to shift the critical dialogue around his work dramatically. During his own lifetime, Bowles noted with a touch of bitterness the extent to which critics had focused on *The Sheltering Sky*, and although there is now a wider body of scholarship that considers Bowles's writing from a number of perspectives, his work has still been primarily understood within a traditional critical matrix. Given the critical bias toward the novel, which is as present in contemporary scholarship as it was in midcentury criticism, attention has been focused largely on Bowles's work within the form of the novel and has tended to

try to recuperate him within a philosophical discourse centered on concepts of freedom and the individual. When his works prove too resistant
to such a framework, they tend to be—as with readings of *The Delicate
Prey*—positioned outside an American context altogether, consigned to
the realm of the exotic. Considering his short fiction as countercultural,
however, necessitates a specific attention to the American context of
his writing; rather than divorced from a nationalist discourse, it instead
formed part of an alternative, satellite tradition. This position was cultivated through the two major transnational artistic traditions that Bowles
integrated into his work: surrealism and music. Understanding Bowles's
conceptualization and use of these overlapping fields emphasizes his efforts to frame his writing within a destabilizing register, which he hoped
would challenge contemporary assumptions about the form and purpose
of the aesthetic, particularly as it related to Bowles's twin bugbears:
freedom and civilization.

The dedication in *The Delicate Prey* reads "for my mother, who first
read me the stories of Poe." And throughout the anthology, the shadow of
Poe can be felt, not simply in a gothic sense of the macabre that haunts
its violence or even in the orientalist flourishes of some of the North
African stories, but in the insistently closed, complete feeling that each
story possesses. Wayne Pounds suggests that "it is in the stark, reiterated
design of Bowles's early fiction that his heritage from Poe seems especially
direct and striking."[87] This description resonates equally strongly with
both Bowles's own phrase "patterns of words" and Poe's famous "Philosophy of Composition," in which he advocates the short story for its
compression and ability to create the "vastly important artistic element,
totality, or unity, of effect."[88] Within *The Delicate Prey*, this tendency
emerges in the effect of "totality" that each story possesses; Bowles's
emphasis on patterning his fiction translates into a kind of story that
feels autonomous and complete. This completion does not necessarily
equate with resolution—in fact, as often as not it is manifested in the
opposite. The dreamlike tale of "By the Water" follows the young Arab,
Amar, as he decides it "is time to visit a neighboring city" (*DP* 266), where
he escapes a subterranean bathhouse and its crablike proprietor, Lazrag.
It concludes with him, startled by "an enormous crab," falling into the
ocean where he "lay still . . . the soft water washing over him," as his small

companion repeatedly tells him, "I saved you, Amar" (276). Throughout the story, Bowles offers no suggestion as to why Amar makes his journey or even why this moment is one that should be chosen for a story—the story concludes even less resolved than when it began. This lack of development, which contemporary critics considered as stagnation, is an essential part of how Bowles creates the patterned effect of his prose.

Indeed, Bowles embedded elements of the story's conclusion in its beginning and crafted the tale so that it loops back on itself, forming a circular whole that concludes where it began. "By the Water" leads Amar from a city that is being slowly emerged in water, where "the melting snow dripped from the balconies" and there were "few spots . . . where the snow was ever cleared away" (266), to a beach that seems to engulf his surroundings in the same way. Bringing the story back to an iteration of where it began—different, but ultimately the same—Bowles closes off the structure of his story, fixing it with a completedness that actively contradicts the kind of openness that his critics were advocating. The structure closes off growth and frustrates character development. But Amar's situation is complicated by his descent into the bathhouse, which mirrors his city even more starkly—almost completely submerged, the grotto repeats the motif of dripping, with "gray icicles" (270) hanging down from its ceiling. Effectively, Bowles is establishing a pattern for Amar's life, defined by water attempting to immerse him—shaping the reiterative pattern that, for Pound, called to mind the fiction of Poe. This patterning suggests an alternative model of experience to that which a liberal model would presume: in Bowles's stories, the actions of individuals are governed by something larger, which patterns the decisions that they make. Rather than directed outward, toward new opportunities, the characters' lives fold back on themselves, returning to where they began, without making any progress. There is no possibility that Amar could have reached anywhere other than the place from which he began.

While not all of the stories in *The Delicate Prey* follow such a clear pattern, they do generally share the same quality of inevitability. This is especially pronounced in the distance between the narration and the events of the stories; in many of his stories, Bowles's prose is clinically detached, rendering the events from a perspective that seems disinterested, uninvested, and removed from what occurs. Critics operating within a similar framework to Trilling's "liberal imagination," concerned with a prose that was inflected with a sophisticated perspective, considered a detached approach to fiction—such as that which Bowles's stories display—naïve. But there is an elegance and a clarity to the way that Bowles narrates his stories, and Lasdun draws attention to the "calm logic with which they unfold"; Bowles describes the action with an authority that suggests not a lack of perspective but one that has a greater understanding of what is occurring than an involved viewpoint could possess.[89] This authority, as Lasdun notes, is often expressed through the way the stories begin: opening "with the impersonal simplicity of folk tales." When the story "The Delicate Prey" opens with the statement that "There were three Filala who sold leather in Tabelbala" (*DP* 277), the authority of the narrator—removed, and drawing our attention to the scene as if pointing out an interesting episode in a history book or beginning a fairy tale—gives the story that follows a sense of impersonality and inevitability. The characters, relayed to us in such detached terms, take on a general, almost archetypal quality, just as "the Professor" (290) of "A Distant Episode," with his "dark glasses" (291) and "two small overnight bags full of maps, sun lotions and medicines" (290), needs no further description than the contents of his luggage; we are clearly intended to treat them, and what occurs to them, in a similarly detached fashion.

This presentation, deliberately distancing the reader from the characters and reducing them to types, underscores the inevitability of the action of the stories and emphasizes the lack of freedom the characters actually have, just as the characters of a fable are inherently set on a specific course, based on their particular type. Fiedler, in particular, suggested that Bowles removed his narration to this distance in order to communicate an allegorical message—that he was perhaps only able to endow his stories with meaning through allegory. But it seems a very strained process to try to draw an allegorical meaning out of the abuse (and eventual insanity) suffered by the professor of "A Distant Episode" or to suggest that the violence of "The Delicate Prey" offered a parable from which we were intended to draw a specific message. If anything, Bowles seems to frustrate his readers' ability to superimpose such a reading on his stories. The blunt brutality of "the pain of the brutal yanking [and] the sharp knife" (301), as nomadic tribesmen remove the professor's tongue, like the castration of one of the young Filala in "The Delicate Prey," seems designed to emphasize that these violent actions have no meaning; they resist any attempt to reduce them to a moral conclusion. So, by distancing his narration from the events of his stories and creating suggestions of a fable-like narrative, Bowles not only heightens the inevitability of their action but also highlights the futility of imposing meaning on what occurs. We could even consider his stories as a challenge to the very concept of literary meaning, as understood by liberal criticism.

Even outside the more explicitly fable-oriented stories, Bowles has a tendency to present his characters in a way that conforms to a certain type. The lack of peculiarity—of "real" touches, which would render them individuals that the reader could "believe in"—made the characters an obvious target for criticism, which argued that Bowles's characters needed to be better developed. But Hassan, noting Bowles's "inability to conceive and develop characters dramatically," suggested that Bowles actually turned this "main weakness" to his advantage.[90] Through his "tight control" of his characterization, Bowles accentuates the inevitable structure of his stories and builds the suggestion that the characters are being impelled by something outside them. Even a character like Aileen, the protagonist of the story "The Echo," who is not located within anything resembling a fable, seems not in control of her own actions. Moving through the story "in the midst of [a] deep dream" (*DP* 156), she seems hardly conscious of making decisions; what little agency she does have is stolen by some external power, so that at night "she would lie transfixed for long periods" (153). The honeymooning couple of "Call at Corazón" exhibit the same sense of being directed by something outside them. Initially registering as acting "carelessly" and "without thinking" (66), their loss of agency sees the wife sleeping with a man "in the crew's quarters" (76) of the boat they are on, and the husband leave her behind on the boat, not thinking, but aware only of "his heart beating violently" (77). Bowles actively draws his readers' attention to this loss of agency, with his characters even acknowledging their own loss of agency; in "The Delicate Prey," it occurs to professor "that he ought to ask himself why he was doing this irrational thing, but he was intelligent enough to know that since he was doing it, it was not so important to probe for explanations at that moment" (298). While conscious that they are not in control of their actions, the characters in *The Delicate Prey* are unable to take charge—instead, they continue on the courses on which they have been set. This poses a serious question to both the reader and the critics with whom Bowles's work seems to be implicitly engaging: do people really possess the freedom and autonomy that a liberal, democratic view would suggest? The lack of control that his characters display challenges the basic assumptions of the agenda underpinning the direction of mid-century criticism, suggesting that individuals may have only a limited capacity for freedom and that, far from unfettered, they are subject to external pressures that control their lives and actions in a fashion they are powerless to resist.

On a broader level, the destabilizing momentum of his short fictions comes from his ability to reconcile aesthetic models drawn from surrealism and music within the form of the short story. Bowles was drawn to surrealism through a personal fascination with the subconscious, and long before he became personally involved with any of the activities of the movement, he had begun using automatic writing as a process for guiding his composition; surrealism offered, at least initially, a technique for literary production. Increasingly, however, Bowles turned to surrealism as a source of aesthetic inspiration and, as I have argued, used his short fiction as a way of mediating an aestheticized form of surrealism to an American audience. On the one hand, Bowles recuperated the dream aesthetics of surrealist work within a deliberately patterned structure. He was preoccupied with hypnotic and somnambulic experiences, and he worked to shape his texts into simulacra of dream experiences, in contrast to the surrealist model of presenting comparatively unstructured "dream images." On the other hand, he also drew on surrealism's fascination with the "primitive" in order to develop his own model for presenting alternative perspectives within his fiction. Through his work in *View* in particular—translating a range of texts, from works by writers like Borges, to sensational murder cases from Mexico, to Mayan sacred stories—Bowles shaped what was, again, a consciously aestheticized version of a "primitive" or non-Western perspective. In both cases, the kinds of aesthetic patterns that Bowles developed out of his involvement with surrealism were complemented by elements he drew directly from his work as a composer. However he may have figured the relationship between the mental processes involved in composing literary and musical works, Bowles actively recuperated aspects of his distinctive musical aesthetic within his written works. The kind of music that Bowles prioritized was characterized at once by its abstraction and by its echoing of motifs from folk music and jazz. The strategies that he developed for rendering these elements of his music within his short stories overlapped with, and in some cases were inseparable from, the way that he adapted particular aspects of surrealism to fit the short story.

More than any other quality of his writing, however, it was Bowles's formal developments within the genre of the short story that secured his reputation, especially among other authors. Throughout his life, Bowles returned to an insistent preoccupation with the patterning and structure of his texts, and this general concern with precision—quite aside from any specific types of patterns—owes a considerable debt to his training and practice as a composer. On a practical level, Bowles composed his stories in a peculiarly musical way. In spite of his protestations that his work was innocent of authorial control, he judged his own works' success based on how well structured they were. He admitted, moreover, in several interviews that he conceived of form in a musical way, constructing his texts as if they were pieces of music, with the appropriate awareness of development, repetition, and syncopation. Indeed, the apparent contradiction between his two accounts of his writing process—automatism on the one hand, following a surrealist model, and highly patterned precision on the other—can only be reconciled by understanding the influence of his work as a composer. Bowles developed his compressed, fragmented, and reiterative model of the short story, therefore, through an application of musical structure to aesthetic practices he drew from the work of the surrealists. This model was equally influenced, however, by Bowles's wider social considerations. Although certain of Bowles's interview responses may suggest that he was writing in a critical vacuum, he was in fact very conscious of the trends in American literature—both in the literary works themselves and in their criticism. In fact, the Bowlesian short story was directed by the oppositional stance it took toward the qualities that contemporary critics valorized as essentially American. Bowles's insistence on claustrophobic narratives was intended as a direct challenge to his readers' and critics' expectations of open, expansive texts.

If we understand his use of form within his short fiction, therefore, as interrogating the concepts of scale and representation, this naturally opens up wider questions about American literary culture in the immediate postwar period and into the second half of the twentieth century. To begin with, the criticism that the *Delicate Prey* elicited suggests the extent to which nationalistic sentiment guided cultural criticism; critics' encouragement to Bowles to "return to his native scene" and write about life in contemporary America reflects a broader preoccupation with the relationship between cultural production and society. The striking similarities between the specifically *formal* criticisms of the stories, moreover, indicate the extent to which a kind of liberal consensus governed American criticism at the time. In retrospect, the qualities most often used to describe America in the 1950s are those of conformity and consensus; the major literature of Cold War America reinforced the social values that, on an international scale, were marshaled to delineate American democracy and Soviet totalitarianism as cultural dichotomies. Bowles yoked the alternative perspectives of his short fiction to a formal structure that questioned the model of experience assumed by this narrative, with the explicit intention of unsettling his readers' cultural expectations.

chapter five

Eudora Welty and the Photographic Capture

What links McCarthy, Williams, and Bowles together? Beyond their public friendships and rivalries, these authors all engaged in an intellectual contest with the prevailing political climate of midcentury America, which each characterized as constraining and enforcing conformity. They all recognized, moreover, that these political narratives—localized in the motifs of freedom, democracy, and growth—inflected literary criticism and contributed to a limitation of personal and artistic expression. This can be seen as early as McCarthy's first reviews for the *Nation* and rings clearest in Williams's charge that America no longer held itself open to scrutiny from within. Their use of the short story form, focused as it was around compression and containment, was guided by the insurrectionary energy of Williams's protest: rather than critiquing American cultural values from without, they used a form that was diametrically opposed to expected narratives of growth and development, as a way of highlighting the constraining energy of midcentury politics. Although, traditionally, studies of countercultural literature have privileged novels and poetry that articulate an expansive sense of freedom, aligned with political narratives of permissiveness and progress, these writers instead used the short story to develop a model of countercultural writing centered on compression, closure, and containment. All three were subordinate to the heteronormative mainstream in the United States, through gender, sexuality, exile, and religious background, and as such, they positioned themselves obliquely in relation to the American canon. Their interest in the short story, therefore, manifested as a corollary and counternarrative to the sprawling, picaresque tropes of authors like Ralph Ellison or Saul Bellow.

Given that their conceptualization of form ran so against the grain of contemporary criticism, however, it is not surprising that their cultivation of such a compressed and confrontational kind of story was met with caustic reviews. Indeed, the criteria against which *One Arm, The Delicate*

Prey, and *The Company She Keeps* were so negatively judged speak to the pervasiveness of political ideology in cultural criticism. The failure of these authors to produce stories that showed growth and development was linked insistently to the social benefit that could be derived from such stories. As specifically *American* writers, they were being held responsible for developing a national culture in line with a partisan ideology. The violent, sexual, and often illicit action of their stories, in conjunction with characters whose attitudes ran from the merely irresponsible and solipsistic, to the amoral or outright depraved, were all the more untenable for critics because of the narrative structures in which they were contained. But, ultimately, the insistent inward turn of their minor aesthetics provoked such peculiar outrage because in each case critics could see the beauty of their literary style and the potential for it to be applied to narratives they construed as socially beneficial. In their rueful, hand-wringing condemnations, critics from Leslie Fiedler to Richard Chase drew attention to the stylistic beauty of these works. In doing so, they subconsciously reinforced one of the central critiques that underpinned McCarthy's, Bowles's, and Williams's use of form: that social structures were so successful in containing identity because they appeared appealing.

Eudora Welty concludes this narrative because, although her use of the short story was oriented around the same compressed and patterned aesthetics, her works received a glowing critical reception—to the point where she was actively encouraged to avoid the more developed narratives of the novel. Today, her name is synonymous with a certain kind of closely patterned short story. Her work is often characterized by its carefully measured use of perspective, and throughout her career, she played on the naturally restricted structure of the form to create works that derived their power from their use of minor detail and foreshortened focus. Unlike McCarthy, Bowles, or Williams, for whom the short story offered a minor key, in contrast or addition to other modes of artistic expression, Welty chose to develop the form as the signature part of her literary style. By 1950, when Bowles's first collection was published, Welty had three volumes of short stories to her name, each widely celebrated: *A Curtain of Green, The Wide Net,* and *The Golden Apples.*[1] She stands out among midcentury writers, moreover, for being consistently praised for her use of the short story form—to the point where her first novel, *The*

Robber Bridegroom, was openly criticized for departing from her earlier model of controlled and compressed fiction. In a particularly telling review, Lionel Trilling emphasized the "impossibility or the impropriety" of Welty's shift from short fiction to the novel—despite his erstwhile endorsement of the novel as the ideal American literary form.[2] Noting that, although they had "expressed great admiration for its prose," other critics had mostly "been disappointed" by Welty's turn to the novel, Trilling concluded by singling out his own chief concern with the work: that "Miss Welty is being playful."[3] Rather than tying her work to identifiable social conditions or suggesting a clear message, the novel was instead "very exasperating" in is "inevitably coy mystification."

Not only do Trilling's remarks suggest a clear cultural demarcation between short fiction and novels in terms of tone, but they also highlight one of the ways Welty herself problematized the classification of her work. Her first volume of stories, *A Curtain of Green,* featured an introduction by Katherine Anne Porter, one of the leading short story writers of the 1930s and 1940s, whose endorsement aided the work's commercial and critical success. In some ways, however, this acted as a mixed blessing; the association with Porter's name tied Welty to a particular classification as a writer working within the genre of Southern Gothic. It was with such expectations in mind that Trilling found himself "disappointed" by Welty's novel—rather than a haunting or brutally honest picture of the South, the "lore of the American frontier" was instead refracted through "elements of European fairy tales." And in spite of the increasingly sophisticated works being published on Welty, this initial framework continues to govern the way that her works are read. In contrast to the other writers in this study, Welty is striking for the lack of overt political motivation in her use of the short story form. Indeed, despite the best efforts of critics and interviewers, she insistently resisted efforts to superimpose any specific social narrative onto her fiction, instead explaining her writing in relation to her photography: "I took the pictures of our poverty because that was reality, and I was recording it. The photographs speak for themselves. The same thing is true of my stories; I didn't announce my view editorially. I tried to *show* it."[4] Although she admitted that, for example, recording "the mass" of poverty stricken southerners "did constitute a plea on their behalf to the public," she framed this in terms of authorial retreat, where the plea came from "their existing plight being so evident" rather than any explicit commentary from her. It was within the same photographic terms that critics framed their discussion of Welty's fiction, characterizing her stories as distanced, detached, and impersonal. The critical success of her writing raises several issues that are at the heart of the short story's countercultural role in midcentury America. Why was Welty praised for her short fiction when it was organized around the same principles of patterned behavior and contained structure as other collections that were heavily critiqued? Why was she encouraged to *avoid* the novel form—by an author who was endorsing her collection, no less—when this was being championed as a literary structure analogous to the dominant political narrative of growth and freedom? Exploring Welty's use of containment (and its critical reception) helps answer these questions and clarify the broader position of short fiction in the period. It also suggests underlying reasons for the form's changing status over the second half of the twentieth century.

Welty's Critical Reception

While Porter's endorsement of *A Curtain of Green* did not harm the work's publicity, she was not the only major writer to lend her name in support of the collection. In a review for the *New Republic* entitled "Full-Length Portrait," the celebrated novelist and short story writer Kay Boyle pronounced that, through this debut volume, the reader was "brought face to face with one of the most gifted and interesting short-story writers of our time."[5] This sentiment was almost unanimously echoed by the book's first reviewers, with critics keen to draw parallels between Welty and other major female writers. Rose Feld, writing in the *New York Herald Tribune,* suggested that it was "not strange" for Porter to "be attracted to the tales" in Welty's collection, given that "they have a great kinship to her own fine work, possessing a quality of mood which surrounds and gives meaning to the incident."[6] Ultimately, however, Feld's judgment was more reserved than Boyle's: although some of Welty's stories indicated that she may "eventually . . . belong" with writers like Katherine Mansfield and Virginia Woolf, "the greater number of them," she wrote, "are interesting as examples of the work of an artist who is still in process of perfecting a technique which will sustain incident as well as mood." Tellingly, Feld repeats the words "mood" and "incident" in a way that suggests that the aesthetic beauty of Welty's style is not necessarily sustained with adequate narrative development. This critique—refiguring the same divergence between plot and style that governed the reception of other short story writers—is relatively unusual when it comes to *A Curtain of Green*. Instead, the general response by critics was admiration for the balance of each story, which tended to be framed with respect to Welty's detached, impartial mode of observation. It is in this vein that Marianne Hauser, in a review for the *New York Times Book Review*, praised the "simple, natural acceptance of everything, of beauty and ugliness, insanity, cruelty and gentle faith which helps the author create her characters with such clear sureness," linking the works' aesthetic cohesion to the impartiality of their author.[7] Her conclusion—that "few contemporary books have ever impressed me quite as deeply as this book of stories"—is indicative of the distinction between Welty and writers like Bowles or Williams. Where their short fiction was criticized for failing to provide clear moral guidelines for its readers, Welty's was praised for its "simple" clarity.

Part of critics' willingness to accept Welty's removed, detail-oriented style came from their ability to place it within a distinctive genre: the Southern Gothic. While an association with Porter certainly helped cement such readings, Welty's emphasis on abnormality, isolation, and violence would surely have led to similar readings in and of itself. Indeed, Louise Bogan explicitly framed her reading of Welty's stories with her observation of "the definite Gothic quality which characterizes so much of the work of writers from the American South," as part of an article for the *Nation* appropriately titled "The Gothic South." Bogan differentiated Welty's "gothic" from that of other writers, including Poe and Faulkner, on the basis of her peculiarly detached perspective; she had "instinctively chosen another method which opens and widens the field and makes it more amenable to detached observation." While this might suggest a commensurate broadening of geographic scope, moving the gothic beyond a simply southern concern, Bogan forecloses such possibilities, underlining her view that Welty's "method" was, ultimately, "only suitable for her Southern characters on their own ground."[8] It is this troubling logic that allowed Welty's subversive stories to be so easily reconciled against the broader critical demands for social realism and progressive narratives of growth. Writing from the perspective of a progressive urban North, critics could reduce the implications of her fiction to an imaginary gothic South, limiting them to a romantic register that could be appreciated outside of any social context. When Feld identified the collection as gothic, therefore, she did so in a way that emphasized its dislocation from reality: the stories "carry a mood of incipient madness," and "in all of them, the characters, twisted for various reasons away from the path of normal experience, make dreadful adjustments to life." These themes, which would be considered "pornographic" when deployed by a writer like Bowles or Williams, were able to be subsumed within a recognizable, regionalized genre—so that, although in some places Welty showed "too great a preoccupation with the abnormal and grotesque," this observation merely prompted for Feld the afterthought that "some day someone might explore this tendency of Southern writers."[9] At the same time as validating her stylistic choices, therefore, the reductive tendency to read *A Curtain of Green* as an exemplar of the Southern Gothic simultaneously invalidated any social critique her work may have offered.

Even when they did not explicitly read her short fiction in such narrowly geographic terms, the way that critics praised Welty's use of form nonetheless reinforced a reading of her work as purely aesthetic, and detached from social concerns. This assumption seems to underpin the insistent desire to compare her work to other "women writers," such as Mansfield or Porter and was articulated more openly in the few reviews that did suggest her style could find application beyond the South. Hauser, for example, was happy to concede that "there is nothing particularly regional about" Welty's stories, and that they "could in a way happen anywhere"; such an acknowledgment, however, was tied to the contention that "Miss Welty's writing is not intellectual primarily." In other words, her work could be admired as a kind of naïve art form—a reading that Hauser develops further in her review: "Many of the stories are dark, weird and often unspeakably sad in mood, yet there is no trace of personal frustration in them, neither harshness nor sentimental resignation; but an alert, constant awareness of life as a whole, and that profound, intuitive understanding of life which enables the artist to accept it." While attentive to the rich detail and sensitive style that characterizes Welty's stories, Hauser fails to register the ironic or critical inflection that is so apparent in these works. Instead, she reveals an important qualification to the general critical hostility toward the short story: as long as a writer (whether due to geography, genre, or gender) was seen as unable to contribute intelligently toward social and intellectual progress, their fiction was no longer judged on the same social criteria and could instead be appreciated as purely aesthetic work. Indeed, this reading aligns *A Curtain of Green* more with poetry than fiction, and Hauser concludes that "her art is spontaneous, and of that poetic quality which values the necessity of form by instinct." From this perspective, then, the idea that Welty's short stories were closer to poetry than prose implies not so much a lack of narrative as a shared preoccupation with form over content. The "almost surrealistic note," or "intimate fusion of dream and reality" that Hauser observes, therefore, does not reflect any Marxist politics or insurrectionary ways of viewing the world, but simply connotes an aesthetically oriented practice of writing, free from social concerns.[10]

This misreading seems to reflect what Porter's introduction prefigured and Trilling's critique of *The Robber Bridegroom* would seem to confirm: as a writer without a social perspective, Welty was precluded from writing longer fiction. Many of her first reviewers, whether openly or subtly, agreed with this judgment, choosing to emphasize the stasis of her narratives, the contained focus of her writing, and its necessarily limited scope. Their central analogue was the painting or photograph: beautiful, rich in detail and "mood," but static. For Hauser, this was self-evident, where to "point out that they are right in form seems to me quite as superfluous as to state that a tree is right in form."[11] In similar terms, when Feld noted that "beyond the incident or series of incidents around which Miss Welty builds her tales, lies the pressure of atmosphere which gives significance to her characters and her facts," it was to reinforce that her style was best suited for short, imagistic pieces. Because her stories "carry the intimacy and intensity of narrow-range observation," a novelistic piece would be necessarily out of her literary register.[12] Not all of Welty's readers, however, took such a standpoint. Although Boyle identified a few "weaknesses" in Welty's writing—the "first one" was "her tendency to carry objectivity so far that at times her characters are seen from such a distance and at such an angle that they lose all human

proportions"—overall, she did not seem to agree that her style was unsuited for a novel. While she agreed that "her short stories are (and here
is my second critical note) not unlike paintings in that they are absolutely
halted as they stand," Boyle did not see this as inherently restricting her
from longer pieces. Indeed, she concludes that she could "foresee no
way of failure for her written or unwritten novel."[13] Focusing instead on
Welty's obsession with a precise visual register, whereby she "adds small
detail to small detail: the fillings in people's teeth, the bright mail-order
shirts of little boys, the bottles of Ne-Hi, the pictures of Nelson Eddy hung
up like icons," Bogan reached the same conclusion as Boyle. In her eyes,
Welty "needs only the slenderest unifying device" in order to "produce
one [novel] whenever she wishes."[14] That this possibility was not an issue
for critics—at least, as long as it remained—speaks to the suspension
of political concerns when it came to either genre fiction (such as the
Southern Gothic) or works that could be recognized as purely aesthetic.
Regardless of its length, such writing was able to sit outside the expectation for socially constructive and progressive narratives.

Indeed, when Welty followed *A Curtain of Green* with her first novel,
The Robber Bridegroom, several critics who had predicted that she would
fail at a novel admitted their error in judgment. Rather more cheerfully
than some, Hauser conceded that "here Miss Welty has fooled us all de-
lightfully," suggesting that Welty's compressed style was equally suited for
this kind of longer narrative. Noting that "instead of following the design
that the critics had laid out for her," Welty "took a big jump, left psychol-
ogy, common sense, and the short-story writer's good-will far behind to
tell a most wonderful fairy tale," Hauser's review still focuses on the same
stylistic qualities as in her short fiction. She quotes one passage "because
it conveys the intenseness of this strange, fanciful tale" and emphasizes
that "Welty's style is concise, yet rich like the sound of an organ." She even
goes so far as to acknowledge that a layer of complexity might lie beneath
the static surface of Welty's novel; she observes that the fairy-tale style
has been adapted "with her tongue in her check," before concluding that
Welty "presents her characters on purpose as simply as if she described
them for children, weaving her intellectual and poetic interpretations
around them like multicolored ornaments."[15] The qualities that reviews of
The Robber Bridegroom insistently return to, however, indicate that Welty's

perceived success was still tied to her work's restriction to a limited genre of fiction, with an attendant emphasis on coherence and form over content. While, for Hauser, Welty's work may be a "modern fairy tale," with "irony and humor, outright nonsense, deep wisdom and surrealistic extravaganzas," it is ultimately an aesthetic object, characterized by "a poetic unity" achieved "through the power of a pure, exquisite style." Even Trilling was not entirely unconvinced by Welty's work—he was prepared to credit it as a coherent whole, save that its prose was in places "a little too childishly wide; it is a little too conscious of doing something daring and difficult."[16] This judgment signals the limitation inherent in critics' praise of Welty. While her work could be admired and praised, this critical acceptance was contingent on a limited scope and a lack of intellectual ambitions.

Rather than by her novel, these limitations were tested instead by Welty's second anthology of short stories. If her first, *A Curtain of Green*, had proven that the short story could thrive in midcentury America when restricted to specific generic conditions, then *The Wide Net* made visible the boundaries of these conditions. Overall, critics were divided over whether the book was successful or not; the issues over which they were split spoke to the implicit conventions of an acceptable short story. Robert Molloy, one of the reviewers in favor of the collection, validated the work for prioritizing the same static, visualistic qualities of her earlier fiction. Identifying Welty as "a photographer before she decided to devote her time wholly to writing fiction," Molloy notes that "the pictorial values in her work are strong, clear and sharp; the background is sometimes subdued, sometimes intensified, at the artist's will."[17] In similar terms, Eugene Armfield's review emphasized Welty's detached perspective and her ability to lift her observations of "real life" to a poetic pitch. From such a perspective, the quality of the stories was uniform, in that they all returned to the same aesthetic principles; a poor story, like "The Purple Hat," was "merely the unsuccessful application of the very methods by which Miss Welty achieves her finest stories." As with her earlier work, this produced stories that succeeded as discrete aesthetic objects, through which ran "the twin strains of fantasy and actuality; when the two are perfectly blended—as they most often are in this book—the stories afford a very genuine pleasure in the reading." Tellingly, the poetic or fantastic qualities of her prose—now no longer simply attributed to a Southern

Gothic register—were accepted insofar as they were blended with a kind of realism. For Armfield, one of Welty's strongest points was "the fineness of her descriptive writing, her evocations of a gleaming fish, a bird, a battered house, a sunlit field filled with butterflies"; the success of these depictions, however, was tied to their connection to reality, so that the "people are disarmingly 'ordinary' and the events have an air of casualness."[18] In strikingly similar terms, Leo Lerman noted that Welty was "interested in people—their lives, their destinies, the irony attendant upon their comings and goings," and that her success in depicting the fantastic was due to writing "of the unusual in terms of the usual."[19]

Those readers who saw the work as a failure tended to focus on precisely this skill. In their eyes, however, Welty had strayed too far from the "usual" into writing that was dangerous because of its subversion of reality. *Time* magazine's review, titled "Sense and Sensibility," voiced this in the most extreme terms, pronouncing that "these eight stories about the South present as perplexing and exasperating a mixture of good and bad as U.S. writing can show." For the unnamed reviewer, even those stories that were "good" still failed as fiction because they were divorced from ordinary life. Using a particularly surreal image, the reviewer notes that although "Chekhov was a master of the art of writing 'mood' stories," his "moods were always rooted deep in the fertility of human souls," whereas the "flashing, strange stories of Miss Welty's are about as human as a fish."[20] Taking up the Dali-esque imagery of *Time*, Diana Trilling lambasted Welty in the *Nation* for exactly this disjunction from reality. She noted that while in her earlier stories, Welty certainly "liked to move toward the mythical, and she had a heart for decay and an eye for the Gothic in detail," at least in *A Curtain of Green*, "when she saw horror, it could be the clear day-to-day horror of actual life." The failure of *The Wide Net* was that this horror was now disconnected from reality and instead characterized by an overly aesthetic "ballet quality" that reminded her "of the painter Dali." Why was the use of the aesthetic problematic, when in earlier works it had been accepted as part of the artful short fiction her readers readily praised? Trilling's review offers a clarification: in this volume, Welty had "developed her technical virtuosity to the point where it outweighs the uses to which it is put, and her vision of horror to the point of nightmare."[21] In other words, not only were her skills being applied to works divorced from reality but, in the process, they were perverting their own beauty by a kind of parodic hyperinflation.

In his review for the *New Republic,* Isaac Rosenfeld came to a similar conclusion. Reflecting on *A Curtain of Green,* he declared that although it "showed a taste for the mildly fantastic, an eye, more than an ear, for an objective poetry of mood and the symbols of mood, and a considerable ease and variety," it was her ability to hold "these styles impersonally and loosely, unsure of her ultimate intentions, sure only of her talent, which she employed with an artiness that gave her gropings an air of finality." While Rosenfeld certainly took issue with *The Wide Net*'s departure from the "ordinary" into a realm that was too fantastic, like Trilling his chief qualm was that in the process, her style had become overly exaggerated. While he did not want to suggest that "a departure from naturalism is necessarily a loss," what Welty's work had rejected was "a clear, engaging quality of immediate presence and appeal, sacrificed to an esthetic of presentation."[22] Why was this accentuated aestheticism so problematic for midcentury critics? In general terms, the nationalistic narratives of growth and development inflected the direction of criticism, and as I have contended, the general hostility toward short fiction was partly a product of its closed form and necessarily contained narratives. In the case of Welty's more acceptable genre of writing, (apparently) devoted solely to an aesthetic closure and devoid of social commentary, the danger was that, taken to an extreme, this style could devolve into a stagnant decadence. It is with this perspective in mind that both Diana and Lionel Trilling organize their critiques around her respective works' self-conscious stylistic overreaching, the former describing *The Wide Net* as "the *reductio ad absurdum*" of her earlier style, which had "no place in such a serious and greatly endowed writer."[23] Rosenfeld summarized this prevailing attitude, declaring that, in *The Wide Net,* "art passes into a desperate, dead-end estheticism," just as "writers become the creatures of their own activity, losing not so much of naturalism as of nature."[24]

Containment and Introspection

In this sense, the negative critical response to *The Wide Net* can be understood as a concerted effort to contain Welty's descriptive language and picturesque style within a particular literary genre. What we might term a "picturesque short story"—or perhaps, more appropriately to Welty, a "photographic short story"—was acceptable to critics so long as it was contained within a framework that they recognized as broadly realist. This reflects the emphasis on cultural containment that was endemic to the midcentury United States and tied closely to the state's emergence as the leading global superpower during a period of intense nationalism and ideological extremism. Oriented around a nuclear family, with traditional gender roles and an insistently middle-class identity, the typical conceptualization of midcentury America has a strong grounding in reality. Allan Nadel summarizes it as "a period, as many prominent studies indicated, when 'conformity' became a positive value in and of itself."[25] This was not a spontaneous reorganization of society but a move that was directed to a large extent by narratives deployed by the government, whereby "the virtue of conformity . . . became a form of public knowledge through the pervasive performances of and allusions to the containment narrative." As I have argued, this containment narrative was encouraged by cultural critics and driven by America's ideological opposition to the external threats of fascism and then communism. While the term originally referred to "U.S. foreign policy from 1948 until at least the mid-1960s," where America would attempt to "contain" the progress of the Soviet Union from a distance rather than engage directly with them, the cultural program of containment had already been mobilized during the Second World War—as the responses to Mary McCarthy's first volume of stories clearly indicate.[26]

As an international and domestic strategy, containment was fundamentally concerned with limiting and patterning—as much with regard to its own subjects as any foreign power. America's branding of itself as global defender of freedom was part of a broader deployment of narratives around which American citizens could orient themselves and were sometimes forced to be oriented. The anticommunist agenda of the House Un-American Activities Committee, for example, provides an example of the way that official organs of the state ensured that the general populace conformed to a "democratic" ideal. In very specific ways, this policy of containment affected Bowles, McCarthy, and Welty, who were all suspected of communist ties after the war, having voiced public or private sympathies for Marxism during the 1940s; Bowles was even, at one stage, prevented from entering the United States on this basis and harassed in Morocco by the CIA. But it also exerted its influence on them in less direct, or obvious, ways. Nadel makes very clear that "containment was perhaps one of the most powerfully deployed national narratives in recorded history," and the extent to which it shaped the opinions and ambitions of critics and authors alike was of equal magnitude.[27] In terms of criticism, narratives of containment informed the valorizing of the novel and led to a broad (and largely unbroken) emphasis on individual growth through experience. These ultimately political priorities underpinned the often violently antagonist responses that McCarthy, Williams, and Bowles drew for cultivating an antithetical style of fiction. As sensitive readers and critics in their own right, each of these authors themselves recognized the role that such normalizing, nationalistic narratives were having on limiting cultural expression—whether literary, theatrical, musical, filmic, or otherwise visual—and adopted a style of writing that emphasized the force of containment on individual identity, through both content and form.

While the use of containment in Welty's fiction is hard to ignore, part of her success in using the short story came from the way that she was able to work *within* critical expectations, developing two distinctive registers of containment. That critics considered these to conform to their expectations of the best contemporary fiction, moreover, is attested to by the level of praise that *A Curtain of Green* accrued and by the way that readers like the Trillings criticized her later works on the basis that it no longer observed the same level of restraint. One quality of Welty's prose on which critics focused intently was its close attention to visual detail, with many emphasizing her early ambitions as a photographer. In fact, Welty had found surprising success in this field while living in New York during the 1930s—albeit in a way that tellingly foreshadowed the reception of her first volume of stories. After visiting the "Photographic Galleries" run by Lugene Opticians, her photographs of the South were unexpectedly accepted for a one-woman exhibition, and as Welty discovered in the program for the exhibition, "the reason he [Lugene] showed them was that they had been printed in Mississippi under 'primitive conditions.'"[28] This sense of her photography as documentary was reinforced both by her own conceptualization of the work, where images of poverty, for example, were meant to speak for themselves, and by one avenue she unsuccessfully pursued: assistant to Berenice Abbott. Abbott, a contemporary and friend of Man Ray who had developed her craft as photographer in Paris during the 1920s, was then head of a Federal Art Project entitled "Changing New York" seeking to document the shifting architecture of the city. Although Welty did not get the position of assistant, the connection to Abbott's project is enticing, in that it suggests a key aspect to the visual register of her stories. While many critics happily equated the pictorialist qualities of her prose with narrative stasis—often stressing that her stories were more successful when they were *not* focused on action or plot—in doing so, they simplified the correspondences between her photography and fiction. Rather than being preoccupied with stasis per se, in both her fiction and photography Welty was concerned with what she termed the "snapshot" quality of her work, organized around capturing a specific moment that contained an implied narrative. In a temporal sense, her writing played with containment not in a limiting sense but in an expansive one.

In his classic study of Welty's use of form, *Eudora Welty's Achievement of Order*, Michael Kreyling observed that, particularly in *A Curtain of Green*, Welty cultivated "the shock of the abnormal, the morbid, the grotesque, and also the reflection after this exposure, in which some heightened sense of reality is attained."[29] His use of photographic language here is deliberate, as he argues that Welty's use of the short story form is indebted to her practice as photographer. But where Kreyling seems to understand their effect in terms of Roland Barthes's *studium* and *punctum,* Welty herself subscribed to a point of view that more closely resembled Henri Cartier-Bresson's concept of the *instant décisif.* Barthes explained that "a photograph's *punctum* is that accident which pricks me (but also bruises me, is poignant to me)"; he clarified that although the word, in Latin, is used "to designate this wound, this prick, this mark made by a pointed instrument," it is one that "also refers to the notion of punctuation," given that the kind of images that he is "speaking of are in effect punctuated, sometimes even speckled with these sensitive points."[30] At its core, this perspective on photography understands it as a static form, where its effect on the reader is as a kind of revelation—an impression that, in Kreyling's terms, the reader then develops internally. Welty's conceptualization of photography differs, however, from Kreyling's account, in that she understood photographs to contain their own narrative movement rather than this being interpolated by the reader on viewing. When asked by Reynolds Price to explain her reasoning in describing her first volume of pictures as snapshots, she responded: "Well, they were snapshots. It refers to the way they were taken, which gave meaning to the book. They were taken spontaneously—to catch something as I came upon it, something that spoke of the life going on around me. A snapshot's now or never.[31] Welty's description suggests that she saw an inherent narrative within her images; she implies that, by capturing the right moment, her photographs could contain both movement and event within an apparently static construction. In this sense, it echoes the language of the influential French photographer Cartier-Bresson, who described in his important 1952 essay "The Decisive Moment" that, "of all the means of expression, photography is the only one that fixes forever the precise and transitory instant" and "deal[s] in things which are continually vanishing."[32] From this perspective, although the finished photograph was necessarily static, by capturing the "instant," the photographer could capture movement, transience, and narrative. Nor was this limited to Welty's photographic practice. Interviewers often pressed her to account for the relationship between her two modes of artistic expression (their questions often prompting a particular kind of connection); Welty, however, tended to refute any overtly intellectual connection between her photography and prose. She did maintain, however, that photography had taught her "about the practice of perception and about technique," where, in both "writing and photography, you were trying to portray what you saw, and truthfully. Portray life, living people, as you saw them." This, in itself, mirrors the kind of language she used to describe her snapshot aesthetic. But in elaborating on what it meant to "portray life," she explicitly connected the formal qualities of short fiction and photography, through their shared interest in narrative containment. For Welty, the magic of a camera was that it "could catch the fleeting moment, which is what a short story, in all its depth, tries to do. If it's sensitive enough, it catches the transient moment."[33]

In a collection of brief, "fleeting" stories, "A Piece of News" stands out as one of the most transient tales in *A Curtain of Green*. Only a few pages long, it shows the reader a series of three tableaux, all within the Fisher household: Ruby Fisher reads a newspaper, lies down, and then shows the paper to her husband, Clyde, over dinner. Within each image, there is scarcely any movement; it is a noteworthy break in stillness when, toward the end of the story, Clyde "spanked" Ruby "good-humoredly across her backside" (16). Welty uses these seemingly static images, however, to create a rich sense of narrative impulse and possibility. In part, this comes through her observation of small details, which suggest personal histories to the characters beyond the events of the narrative. As Ruby reads the newspaper, her appearance prompts the third-person narrator to observe that she "must have been lonesome and slow all her life, the way things would take her by surprise" (12). Equally, quirks and nuances in Ruby's bearing and speech convey more than just tone. Recognizing her name in an article about a woman shot in the leg by her husband, she says to herself, "that's me," speaking, the narrator notes, "softly, with deference, very formally" (13). The behavior and personality that this implies suggest something habitual or patterned, and Welty yokes this to a prose that favors the imperfect over the perfect tense. This offers her a way of suggesting to her reader details that are ongoing, transient, or in motion and that are suspended outside of a linear progression of events, so that, for instance, "at moments when the fire stirred and tumbled in the grate, she would tremble, and her hand would start out as if in impatience or despair" (12). This also allows her to weave in events that have already taken place, outside of the moment of the story, such as the observation that "when Clyde would make her blue, she would go out onto the road" (14). Without being fixed as specific points in time, these allusions take on the quality of being "present" within the tableau itself, happening simultaneously, rather than external to it, and earlier in time.

Another way of understanding the contained narrative of these apparently static stories, then, would be to consider their action as suspended—as in an image of a girl leaping in the air. Without needing to show a sequence of images, the viewer could read into such a photograph the upward spring, the descent; perhaps a slight hint of a twist in her fabric might imply a turn. With prose, Welty is able to go beyond such obvious suspension, however, by containing actions within a scene through subtle use of tense and mood. Alongside the habitual actions, or repeated tone and demeanor, "A Piece of News" uses the subjunctive to create a possible parallel narrative. Although she had, herself, not been shot, reading the article suggests to Ruby an alternative narrative for herself, and the reader watches her as "she stood waiting as if she half thought that would bring him in, a gun levelled in his hand" (13). Rather than developing the plot in a linear way, Welty instead concentrates its narrative potential within a fixed moment, so that although "it was as though Clyde might really have killed Ruby," this possibility does not exist as a separate event. Instead, the narrator transitions into an imaginary scenario—"at once she was imagining herself dying"—but rather than a discrete action this again represents an ongoing state, which does not remove us from the "snapshot" of Ruby so much as suggest a virtual, internal experience. The subjunctive suspension of the phrases in this experience again refuse closure or distinctness but instead coexist within the image of Ruby standing in her cottage: "He would say"; "She would say"; "Then she would die; her life would stop right there. . . . Clyde would have to buy her a dress to bury her in" (14). Even when Welty develops her stories around less obviously static scenarios, she uses this same strategy of containment to at once limit the narrative to a particular moment, which gives it the appearance of stasis, and at the same time build suspended motion into descriptions and scenes that are otherwise still.

If critics misread her narrative structure as documentary, however, then they were perhaps more accurate in understanding her fiction as localized around a particular region and its people. The emphasis placed by both contemporaries and subsequent critics on her works' relationship to the South has led to productive readings; although her first critics tended to overstate her lack of engagement with social issues, more recent scholarship has unpacked her stories' often densely coded critique of entrenched attitudes regarding race and gender. Nonetheless, even exemplary recent criticism has tended to either overstate the importance of Welty's detached narrative voice or read it simply in terms of the tropes and figures of the Southern Gothic. Just as initial critiques saw the strength of her prose as lying in its deliberately distanced, unbiased narrator, so later scholarship has tended to see the same absence of commentary as drawing the reader into an implied dialogue on social issues of the South. As Naoko Fuwa Thornton has argued, contemporary criticism now understands Welty's "ultimate purpose" to be "a critical exposé of contemporary social realities."[34] Either perspective relies on an understanding of Welty's narrative voices and personae as objective observers, commenting on a world into which they have a privileged access. Such a narrative style would be characterized by a static relationship between an observer and their surroundings. For Welty, however, such ostensibly external accounts of places and events were tied to a subjective, internal experience. Rather than freely and openly observed by a removed outsider, the descriptions of her worlds reflect the internal conditions of her narrators, reflecting back fears, prejudices, and ideals and containing the landscape within a necessarily limited perspective. In this sense, the idea that her stories are geographically restricted to the South is misleading; the external landscape, to a large extent, is subordinate to an internal one.

Critics' obsessive focus on tying Welty to the specific geography of the South—when her peer Tennessee Williams was excused the same fate, despite having cultivated his persona as a southerner in much more public fashion—was motivated in part by the perception that her life was itself static. Despite her successful foray into New York and later international travels, the common view of Welty was a domestic, even domesticated one. Indeed, this was an important aspect to her critical acceptance; her writing could be understood as a feminine craft, pursued intimately, privately, and within the home, unaffected by the external world. From this point of view, the slightly patronizing praise that her initial readers granted her is more explicable, as are the insistent comparisons to a world of female writers. One of the most interesting of these comparisons came in Boyle's review of *A Curtain of Green,* when she proclaimed that Welty's authorial skill constituted "a singularly uncorrupt equipment in much the same way that Emily Dickinson's was."[35] For a modern eye, this analogy seems curiously inapt; Dickinson's poetry is recognized as complex, worldly, sophisticated, and often dark—scarcely "uncorrupted." As Christopher Benfy notes, moreover, that this attitude also characterized her initial (posthumous) reception, when the first volumes of her poetry appeared "during the 1890s," when "many readers viewed her as an avant-garde writer" and her "innovations and transgressions in subject and style were the occasion for either censure or celebration."[36] During the early and mid-twentieth century, however, an alternative perspective of Dickinson emerged, which figured her work in insistently domestic terms. In this conservative recasting, Dickinson represented a pure, clean, agrarian past; she "was a heroic voice raised against industrialism and all it stood for."[37] It is into such a tradition that Boyle transposes Welty, rehabilitating her use of containment within an acceptably homely narrative.

At the same time as drawing attention to Welty's lack of social engagement, however, Boyle perhaps unintentionally drew attention to a promising connection between the two writers: their focus on interiority. Noting their shared disinterest in courting publicity—Boyle believed that Welty, like Dickinson, "instinctively mistrusted the outer paraphernalia of literary contacts and activity"—she suggested that both writers, "each in her own way, sought and found in silence an inner and almost mystical tongue."[38] Although neither Welty nor Dickinson benefits from the classification of "domesticated author," the idea that both cultivated a heightened, even obscure style of prose, connected to interiority and absence, does provide a useful way of engaging with Welty's poetics of containment. Wendy Barker has considered Dickinson's frustrations with the trite, prosaic language of her everyday, recognizing that, "metaphorically," she "was enclosed, all but engulfed by what she thought of as 'prose.'"[39] Her strategy for negotiating such containment was to focus on the small possibilities contained in unexpected combinations of words and images; what Boyle understood as her "mystical tongue" was part of a broader poetic strategy that relied on a paradoxically enclosing and expansive movement. Given Welty's own interest in compression, contrast, and the relationship between internal and external landscapes, it is worth looking more closely at the internal mechanics of Dickinson's poetry.

Alerting the reader immediately to the limitations of language's ability to contain ideas, Dickinson begins a particularly striking poem with the declaration that "It was not Death, for I stood up, / And all the Dead, lie down—."[40] This contrast, between an implied feeling (that she might be dead) and an external observation (that she was standing up), establishes the pattern that this poem follows: contrasting external observations in order to access, obliquely, an interior experience. Her language is insistently specific, oriented around physical impressions registered in close sensory detail. She recognizes that the nebulous "it" at the center of the poem, an internal experience that she cannot define, is "not Frost," because on her "flesh" she "felt Siroccos—crawl— / Nor Fire," as just her "Marble feet / Could keep a Chancel, cool." On the one hand, the repeated process of defining a thing by what it is not reminds the reader of how incapable words are of containing experience. But on the other, it also emphasizes our dependence on language to make sense of our experiences—Dickinson *must* use such contrasts if she is to capture what it is that she has felt. Rather than try to account for her thoughts in a purely detached, intellectual register, she instead projects her inner experiences outward, using the physical world to make sense of her mental landscape. This poem turns on a moment of synesthesia, in which Dickinson collapses this distinction between sensory and intellectual perception:

> And yet, it tasted like them all,
> The Figures I have seen
> Set orderly, for Burial,
> Reminded me, of mine— (248–49)

Here, the visual register becomes a taste, so that the moment of intellectual recognition or acknowledgment is understood in combined, even confused sensory terms. After the moment of recognition, she is able to elaborate on her experience in more positive terms, although these terms now reflect her awareness that, ultimately, her internal state is itself characterized by containment. Rather than free from the limitations of physical binaries, she feels as if her "life were shaven, / And fitted to a frame, / And could not breathe without a key," so that she concludes "'twas like Midnight, some—" (249). The only way that Dickinson can make sense of her own internal feelings of containment, then, is by projecting them out onto an objectively registered external landscape, which, qualified by "some," nevertheless refuses closure and finality.

Given her insistence on specificity in language and description, however, it is easy to see how earlier readers could understand Dickinson as a regional, even provincial author. Part of this critical narrative, which understands her specificity not as intellectual but domestic, relies on details of her biography, particularly the popular observation that she left her hometown of Amherst on only three occasions. Dickinson herself was well aware that her specific geography inflected her perspective, and many of her poems openly address her sense of containment within a local geographic sphere. She admits, for example, that "The Robin's my Criterion for Tune" because of her personal context—"Because I grow—where Robins do—" (131). Her aesthetic judgment and sensory perception are keenly inflected by the space in which she developed, and this poem develops the observation that she sees "New Englandly" (132). In the process, however, she broadens this observation to encompass human experience at large; everyone is bound by the same specificity of place, so that she can conclude that "The Queen, discerns like me—/ Provincially—." Rather than considering her own provinciality as inherently limiting, therefore, Dickinson instead elevates it as a strategy for expanding her perspective, by linking it to a broader experience of locality on a global scale. Indeed, critics are increasingly recognizing the tension between different geographic scales inherent in her work, which relies on a similar dynamic to the pull between internal and external senses in poems like "It was not Death." This is what Paul Giles has termed Dickinson's "global antipodality." Arguing that conservative attempts to make sense of her *only* within a specific geography "are fundamentally forms of domestication that would seek conceptually to circumscribe the poet within an excessively limited intellectual setting," Giles proposes that Dickinson, instead, "appropriates various scientific theories of her era to reorient her work within a more antipodean framework" and thus situate it "self-consciously between the local and the global."[41] In spatial terms, this is realized particularly in the way that Dickinson's registers a sense of close internal containment in terms that expand it outward to a global scale. The claustrophobic enclosure of her sense that "I saw no Way—The Heavens were stitched—/ I felt the Columns close—," is thus extended out, to the point where the speaker "touched the Universe—," reaching the boundaries of the atmosphere. In the same way that her projection of internal experiences outward onto objects and external sensations tends to reverse, however, this hemispheric expansion contracts—"back it slid"—so that the speaker becomes "A Speck upon a Ball—," emphasizing the minuscule scale of the speaker against the world, tied to a tiny locality, but also the smallness of the world as set against the universe. While the provincial perspective, for Dickinson, encompasses her perspective on the globe, at the same time she recognizes that the earth is itself simply a tiny cosmic plaything.

From her position in the South, Welty was certainly aware of the same inherent pull of geographic specificity that Dickinson registered. As recent critics have shown, rather than rendering her work naïve, her writing is instead occupied with her regional perspective in a way that is far from blind to social concerns. Peter Schmidt has recently noted the irony that "the writer who in the 1940s through the 1960s was often accused of having too great a concern for formal patterning and too little concern for social and political issues now . . . seems to have a radically innovative conception of both artistry and ideology"; through the authorial detachment that critics initially perceived as purely aesthetic, she in fact enacted a critique of prevailing attitudes toward race and gender.[42] My interest here is not in Welty's social engagement per se—a subject on which there is much fine scholarship—but instead on the way that she linked her sense of geographic specificity to an internal landscape and used her characters' containment within the local as a way to engage with broader human experiences, which are always filtered through both place and an inherently limited perspective. In following this line, I am taking my cue from Welty herself, who saw the social obligation of the writer of fiction as, at its core, opposed to open criticism of politics and culture.

In 1965, ostensibly in response to an article she had read suggesting Faulkner offered only a marginal perspective on the South, Welty wrote a long essay for *Atlantic Monthly* titled "Must the Novelist Crusade?" Although it begins as a defense of Faulkner's ability to speak for the South, the essay is mostly devoted to a much larger question: the social responsibility of the author. Written toward the end of her career, at a point where she could certainly comment on her own practice longitudinally, it is best understood as an account of the relationship she understood her work to have to her own culture and context. As the title suggests, her argument is developed largely through a contrast between "the novelist and the crusader"; while "both have their own place—in the novel and the editorial respectively," Welty believed that the act of "writing fiction places the novelist and the crusader on opposite sides."[43] By the "crusader," Welty did not simply imply a journalistic author but, rather, any writer whose prose was directed by a desire to enact social change. While neither Bowles nor Williams, at first glance, would seem to fit under this umbrella, within Welty's schema they would find themselves allied with McCarthy in a camp of writers focused on social critique, given their professed aims of interrogating contemporary American politics and culture. Such a perspective would seem to affirm critics' initial reading of Welty, as detached from worldly concerns. Rather than completely detached, however, she argued that her fiction was profoundly concerned with "morality as shown through human relationships," which constituted "the whole heart of fiction, and the serious writer has never lived who dealt with anything else" (105).

For some, this has seemed too fine a distinction to draw; how can a writer meditate on morality without becoming involved in the exigencies of political and cultural debate? It is in circumventing this elision that Welty's own literary strategies, as she conceptualized them in this article, most resemble Dickinson's poetics of space and identity. Instead of inflecting her prose with subjective commentary, Welty instead saw her role in crafting narrative voice as part of a larger process of objectification. Rather than completely detached, however, this instead relied on creating a relationship between internal and external worlds; for Welty, the aim of writing a "novel is taking life as it already exists, not to report it but to make an object, toward the end that the finished work might contain this life inside it, and offer it to the reader" (104). Inherently a process of containment, like Dickinson's attempts to mediate her own interiority, Welty's obsessive attention to details inscribes interiority onto the physical world. From this perspective, her authorial distance is a strategy for circumventing commentary and instead guiding the reader toward a shared internal experience through the use of external descriptions. Indeed, she suggests that "the ordinary novelist does not argue" but instead "hopes to show, to disclose," because ultimately his "persuasions" aim to allow "his reader to see and hear something for himself" (105). In order to achieve this kind of detachment, the writer naturally needs to be guided by the specificity of her own context—as Welty asks, "When a novelist writes of man's experience, what else is he to draw on but the life around him?"—but this specificity is, as for Dickinson, a means for accessing the global or universal, where "the life around [the writer], on the surface, can be used to show anything, absolutely anything." Explaining that "we write out of ourselves, using ourselves," Welty thus framed her writing as a fundamentally interiorizing process: one that was realized through a close engagement with a particular geographic context but with broad, humanistic goals of creating a shared experience of internal life, relatable across contexts (106). Her deepest aspiration was for her fiction to create a moment of realization, where fiction could "show us how to face our feelings and face our actions and to have new inklings about what they mean"; in this respect, her poetics of containment were predicated on the same principle of internal explorations as those of Dickinson (107).

Conclusion

Language cannot escape containment. As long as writers commit themselves to translating abstract mental and emotional processes to a fixed combination of words on a page or screen, they are bound by rules of language. As an aesthetic practice, containment is more often associated with poetry than prose, particularly beginning with the minimalist modes of the modernist writers William Carlos Williams and Ezra Pound. Here it is in the precise combination of a few evocative words that the poet is able to gesture beyond their immediate syntactical meaning; paradoxically, it is *through* restriction that poetry transcends containment. The insistence of critics to identify Eudora Welty's fiction as *poetic* draws on such a conceptualization of poetry, where her closely framed, detail-oriented prose suspends a realm of virtual possibility, outside of the action of the story itself. While they may not have recognized the mechanisms and strategies that Welty used to achieve this contained expansiveness, their support of her short fiction was not inaccurate. If midcentury criticism demanded narratives that showed growth and development, suggesting a world of possibility, then Welty's short stories, through their very containment, certainly satisfied this need—regardless of whether critics could explain exactly how she did so. This is not to say that Welty was complicit in a culture of containment but rather to illustrate the complex intersection between aesthetic strategies, political convictions, critical pressures, and nationalist narratives that is implicit in discussing containment.

On the broadest level, my aim in this book has been to expand the current understanding of containment, both in its original incarnation, as an ideologically construed, political strategy, and in its pervasive legacy, as the assumptions it has ingrained in Western culture about the relationship between artistic form, politics, and identity. But I have done so from a particularly literary perspective, which is concerned not simply with texts as abstract, decontextualized events but as historically rooted pieces of writing, which are the product of deliberate aesthetic strategies and which were not received by readers in an unfiltered vacuum but mediated through reviews, criticism, advertisements, and underlying cultural norms. One of the most striking aspects of each of the works on which I have focused is how consistently critics responded to them. Their personal aesthetic priorities are shared to an extent that goes beyond coincidence; in general, American critics during the 1940s and 1950s responded to fiction in a way that elided political and literary imperatives. They encouraged writers like McCarthy, Williams, and Bowles to develop extended narratives that showed personal growth, providing readers with a model of identity they could mimic and learn from. Even for a writer like Welty, whose fiction was praised for its brevity and detail, there was still an expectation from critics that her future work would reflect lived, American reality. In privileging texts that subscribed to these priorities and critiquing those that did not, critics reinforced a narrow iteration of national identity that was tied to a reductive characterization of democratic ideology. Not only did this reinforce, to authors and a literate public, a set of prescriptive cultural values, but it also implied a set of conditions that needed be reflected in their own conduct in real life. Literary containment, as manifested in the writing *around* and *within* midcentury fiction, not only reflected the geopolitical narrative of containment but condensed it and delivered it.

Perhaps the more far-reaching outcome of this program of cultural guidance, however, was *not* that it led readers to prioritize certain qualities within fiction. The disruptive aesthetics of postmodernism overturned these cultural expectations across the spectrum of artistic expression in a much broader and more comprehensive way than did the authors discussed in this work. Instead, the expectations that such criticism reinforced about what fiction ought to do—about the purpose of art itself—infiltrated public discourse in a way that has proven pervasive and entrenched. While there is nothing new about debates over whether art must have a social function other than the uplifting experience of the aesthetic, within the Cold War—a context in which literature was seen as tied not just to social conditions but also to an ideological struggle on a global scale—this debate was effectively bypassed. The stereotype of early Cold War America as consensus-driven is even more applicable to literary criticism, where even formerly fervent Marxists now urged writers to bend their craft toward strengthening America's global position, through a domestic inculcation of a very restrictively conceptualized model of freedom. Lionel Trilling's paradigmatic expression of this relationship, where the greatest cultural imperative was "to construct people whose quality of intelligence, derived from literary study or refined by it, would ultimately affect the condition of society in certain good ways," suggests the extent to which cultural expression, especially literature, was understood as the central tool for *forming* culture.[1] So many of the reviews that McCarthy, Williams, and especially Bowles received were characterized by a response of shock or repulsion. For writing in a style that would see someone like Jorge Luis Borges celebrated in the 1960s, in 1950 Bowles was labeled a "pornographer of terror," just as Williams's stories were compared to a private collection of erotica. Beyond the implication that their work was counterproductive to society, these terms implied that there was something intrinsically illicit about their style—producing ethical fiction was essentially mandated.

One difficulty inherent in thinking about writers like McCarthy or Welty as "countercultural" is that the term itself denotes not only a stance toward contemporary culture but also an epoch; the 1960s and 1970s are often understood as "the counterculture age." While the style of midcentury short fiction that I am describing as countercultural sits uncomfortably between modernism and postmodernism, moreover, the short stories of the following decades are generally understood to embrace the ironic, experimental, and deconstructive modes of postmodernism wholeheartedly. Part of my aim in writing this book has been to help define the distinct aesthetics of midcentury short story writers, in contradistinction to the more widely addressed tendencies either side of the 1940s and 1950s. So how do the stories of writers like Donald Barthelme or Joan Didion—the countercultural corollaries of writers like Williams and McCarthy—differ from their midcentury predecessors?

An obvious place to start would be with a writer like Donald Barthelme, whose short fiction has been read as emblematic of a range of postmodern writers from Thomas Pynchon to John Barth, in terms that emphasize its seemingly willful obscurity and formal eclecticism. Indeed, observing that Barthelme is "the most influential postmodernist writer to specialize in the short story," Charles E. May has noted that "many critics have complained that his work is without subject matter, without character, without plot, and without concern for the reader's understanding."[2] These critiques seem to rehearse the charges leveled against earlier writers like Bowles, only amplified in magnitude. From this perspective, Barthelme exemplifies one of the major tendencies in short fiction of the counterculture era: an obsessive magnification of the earlier emphasis on fragmentation and defamiliarization. Such an emphasis necessarily shifts Barthelme's literary critiques away from the specific conditions of contemporary politics and culture and toward a broader focus on the contingency of identity, presenting "men and women as the products of the media and language that surrounds them."[3] Indeed, his approach takes the same metafictional self-consciousness of writers like McCarthy—who deliberately played with the boundaries of generic expectations—and exaggerates it, so that "Barthelme's fiction continually blurs the lines between fiction and an analytical discourse about fiction."[4] Part of the way that Barthelme sustains this formal collapse is through a collage aesthetic that Julian Cowley describes as "an assemblage in print of words and, on occasion, of pictorial images, forming an addition to the world of things."[5] It is in his stories' yoking of such diverse stylistic elements that Barthelme's work is most distinct from the short fiction of the containment era. Characterized by its collage of different voices, styles, and points of view, his stories (and those of many writers like him) eschew the formal compression and contained unity of these earlier authors in favor of a fluctuating instability.

But not all short story writers aspired to the same dislocated heterogeneity as Barthelme. Many writers of the counterculture era embraced the opposite tendency—a pared-back minimalism that accentuated the coherence of earlier short fiction through increasingly short and descriptively bare narratives. This trajectory famously culminated in the work of Raymond Carver, who is sometimes credited with leading a renaissance in the American short story. His stories famously strip back descriptive and contextual detail, leading to a minimalist style some early critics termed "dirty realism." More striking, however, are the stories of Lydia Davis, whose first volume of stories, *The Thirteenth Woman* (1976), established her distinctive style of very short short fiction, often less than a page long. In many ways, her stories develop the kind of photographic aesthetic that Welty used to such effect: as brief moments, operating as a kind of literary snapshot, Davis's stories work so effectively because of their ability to gesture to, or imply, a much larger narrative. What distinguishes her work from stories like Welty's, however, is the extent to which she cultivates this aesthetic. Her stories are so brief, so lacking in action, that they seem more like observations or vignettes than stories. Suggesting that her fiction ought not to be classified as short stories but simply as stories, Davis has admitted that the extreme sparseness of her work places it outside the genre of the short story, which she notes is "a defined traditional form, the sort of thing that Hemingway wrote, or Katherine Mansfield or Chekhov."[6] Such a story was "more developed, with narrated scenes and dialogue and so on," while few of her stories met any of these demands, to the point where Davis considers that "Some you could call poems." While writers like Welty, Williams, and Bowles often accentuated the compression of their stories by limiting their action, they nonetheless adopted the short story in order to align themselves with a specific genre and its traditions. By contrast, postmodern writers like Davis deliberately subverted the expectations of short fiction, creating a new genre—sometimes described as flash fiction—in the process.

While Davis's short fiction represents a particular trend in fiction of the 1960s and 1970s, her usually domestic or suburban subject matter and style hardly match up to the stereotypes of the counterculture era. By contrast, the writer Richard Brautigan—who developed a similar model of flash fiction that dismantled the conventions of the traditional short story—earned his reputation as much for his readily caricatured persona as for his fiction. Long-haired, mustachioed, and heavy-drinking, Brautigan enjoyed a short period of popularity as a symbol of satirical cultural resistance, thanks in large part to the success of his second published novel, *Trout Fishing in America* (1967). Indeed, Patrick O'Donnell has noted Brautigan's brief but significant popular image—although "now nearly forgotten," he had "attain[ed] counter-cultural status in the 1960s and 1970s as a 'hippie' successor to the beats."[7] And while his short fiction shares with Davis's both extreme brevity and lack of contextual information rather than presenting coherent snapshots, the pieces in his 1971 collection *Revenge of the Lawn* are notable for their lack of cohesion and frequent jumps between different images. In spite of this brief, dislocated style, however, his very short fiction can be understood within an established tradition of literary exploration, embracing a stylistic freedom cognate with personal liberty. Christopher Gair has observed Brautigan's "awareness of an American—and in particular, frontier—literary genealogy," suggesting it was "coupled with the formal experimentation that made Brautigan one of the earliest and most adventurous exponents of postmodern writing."[8] In recuperating Brautigan's fiction within a tradition of frontier writing, Gair links his formal experimentation to national narratives that drew parallels between geographic exploration and personal freedom. This is what most distinguishes short fiction like Brautigan's—or Barthelme's, Pynchon's, or Barth's—from that of writers like Bowles and Williams. The earlier writers that I am interested in used short forms as a way to emphasis claustrophobia, constraint, and, ultimately, the individual's lack of freedom. In the postmodern era, however, extreme brevity—like extreme length—became a way to formally articulate personal freedom in a way that unconsciously replicated the logic of postwar criticism.

As a writer whose work was both experimental and closely linked to the traditions of late nineteenth- and early twentieth-century American literature, Brautigan emphasizes the extent to which many postmodern authors drew consciously and conspicuously on the innovations of modernism. Having famously retyped the stories of Hemingway as a sixteen-year-old, "to learn how the sentences worked," Joan Didion is often held up as an illustration of this same trend.[9] Yet surprisingly, given her avowed stylistic debt to Hemingway, bibliographies of Didion's work are generally conspicuous for their lack of short fiction. This is not because Didion has never produced any but rather because she chose, like Williams, to publish them privately in a short, limited run: the 1978 edition *Telling Stories*, published by the Bancroft Library, which collects three stories that Didion wrote in 1964. As with Williams, her short fiction could be understood as a minor form, in contrast to the novel or the essay. For Williams, however, although the short story was a minor form compared to his major dramatic works, it was equally important, providing a stylistic counterpoint and allowing for the expression of ideas unavailable to his plays. By contrast, Didion relegated the short story to such a secondary role because she found that its formal limitations inhibited the kind of prose she wanted to produce. Claiming that "short stories demand a certain awareness of one's own intentions, a certain narrowing of the focus," Didion illustrated her understanding of the form through an incident she disliked on a trip to Honolulu, which had "the aspect of a short story."[10] The episode was like

> one of those "little epiphany" or "window to the world" stories, one of those stories in which the main character glimpses a crisis in a stranger's life—a woman weeping in a tea room, quite often, or an accident seen from the window of a train, "tea rooms" and "trains" still being fixtures of short stories although not of real life—and is moved to see his or her own life in a new light. Again, my dislike was a case of needing room in which to play with what I did not understand. I was not going to Honolulu because I wanted to see life reduced to a short story. I was going to Honolulu because I wanted to see life expanded to a novel, and I still do.

However greatly she admired the way that Hemingway's stories were put together, then, Didion nonetheless aspired toward a more expansive kind of fiction. As she put it, she "wanted not a window on the world but the world itself," or, more simply, "everything in the picture." Implicitly, Didion is affirming the view that the short story is a selective, limiting form of prose that imposes restrictions on its authors.

One of the ironies of Bowles, Williams, and McCarthy cultivating a style oriented around containment and restriction is that they did so in order to encourage formal experimentation. Whether in the form of McCarthy's criticism, Bowles's involvement with the surrealists, or Williams's constant rejection of theatrical convention, all were engaged in a long-term attempt to broaden the possibilities of artistic expression and create a culture within the United States that could accommodate works that were more formally and thematically diverse. This was felt personally as well as intellectually; they each experienced marginalization, officially, publicly, and critically, for failing to conform to an expected model of identity. In order to resist a cultural system that enforced a limited model of literary expression, they turned to a mode of expression that was itself characterized by compression and limitation—both because it contradicted the expectations of critics and because, as an act of magnification, it helped to expose the consequences of containment.

McCarthy's protagonist in the stories of *The Company She Keeps* attempts to resist the hypocritical expectations that her society holds toward her gender identity and sexual promiscuity. But through a patterned and foreclosed narrative structure, McCarthy highlights Meg's inability to escape the containment enacted by the company she keeps. For Williams and Bowles, the force of containment manifests in more visceral and violent actions, where disrupting normative behavior, through anything from a resistance to marriage to homosexual and masochistic desires, leads to rejection, mental breakdown, and often dismemberment. Their use of fragmentation and disruption offered an open challenge to the totalizing effect of expected narratives of growth and freedom. From their perspective, the only strategy available to them in mounting a resistance to literary limitation was to co-opt containment as an insurrectionary aesthetic.

Given their cultivation of a restricted and oppositional mode of short fiction, it would be easy to assume that these authors had clear conceptualizations of what literature *ought* to achieve. While they certainly articulated strong stances on the kind of effects they hoped their own fiction might have on its readers—alongside fears about how it might be misread—they also maintained a broad, often complicated perspective on the role of cultural production in general. Part of the way that they communicated this was through their metafictional incorporation of literature, art, and music within their stories, but paratextually, they also took pains to convey the role they expected of literature, by approaching the question through the role of criticism. In the case of McCarthy, this was almost obligatory, given her own position as a leading critic of theater and literature, not to mention her early column critiquing the major contemporary critics themselves. Her perspective was that criticism was itself a form of literary expression that held a responsibility to literature to be flexible and adaptable enough to reflect new and experimental structures and ideas. Rather than simply commenting on texts and performing a social function, criticism had aesthetic obligations and consequently needed to open itself to unusual and alternative modes of expression. Although he reached the same conclusion—that criticism needed to be open to new modes of expression—Bowles approached the role of the critic from the opposite standpoint. Reflecting the priorities instilled in him by Virgil Thomson at the *New York Herald Tribune,* Bowles argued that criticism should primarily be descriptive, not prescriptive, in order to accommodate different aesthetic forms without prejudging them. With a similar emphasis on avoiding cutting off new forms of expression, Williams proposed a third model of criticism: one oriented around self-reflection. In his eyes, contemporary society was intellectually closed off and too tied to a single narrative to allow alternative viewpoints to exist. His reviews, and letters to friends and editors, emphasize his perspective that critical culture should be opened up to debate and multiplicity, creating a space for different narratives to coexist. All of these points of view cohere, in that they inherently reject a utilitarian understanding of art. They are interested in literature for its diverse, multifaceted potential and see criticism as having the potential to facilitate new perspectives, which can disrupt and break down social narratives rather than perpetuate them.

As with parody, however, one of the pitfalls of an insurrectionary approach, co-opting an aesthetic in order to undermine its associated order of thinking, is that it can readily be understood as a straight manifestation of that aesthetic, replicating the same cultural logic. Without being able to place books like *The Delicate Prey, One Arm,* or *The Company She Keeps* within the context of their conceptualization, as reactions *against* cultural control, a reader could well understand them as conveying a fundamentally nihilistic view of the world. But instead of seeing literature as a tool for molding readers into better citizens, these writers all conceptualized their use of containment as part of an aesthetic that could effect change by allowing the reader to gain new perspectives, enriching their lives emotionally and intellectually rather than practically or morally. Their emphasis on new ways of seeing is attested to by the often obsessive attention to detail that characterizes their "contained" fiction—a quality that provides the most constructive link between Bowles, Williams, McCarthy, and Welty. While Welty may not have had as pronounced a political standpoint on literary aesthetics as these other authors, and while her use of containment was crafted through an expansive, rather than simply confrontational aesthetic, she nonetheless shared their desire to open new ways of seeing and feeling to her readers. In this sense, she helps cast light on the generative implications of their work. However fatalistic writers like Bowles, Williams and McCarthy may have been, they all wrote in an oppositional way in order to do something they saw as positive: to cultivate alternative perspectives, new literary trajectories, and different ways of seeing.

Notes

INTRODUCTION

1. Julio Cortázar, "Some Aspects of the Short Story," *Review of Contemporary Fiction* 19.3 (1999): 26.

2. Robert Lamb, *Art Matters: Hemingway, Craft, and the Creation of the Modern Short Story* (Baton Rouge: Louisiana State University Press, 2010) xii.

CHAPTER ONE

1. Tony Tanner, *City of Words: American Fiction 1950–1970* (London: Jonathan Cape, 1971) 15.
2. Ibid.
3. John Dewey, *Freedom and Culture* (New York: Capricorn, 1963) 4.
4. Malcolm Bradbury, *The Modern American Novel* (Oxford: Oxford UP, 1983) 159.
5. Leslie A. Fiedler, "Style and Anti-Style in the Short Story," *Kenyon Review* 13.1 (1951): 155–56. Hereafter cited parenthetically.
6. Martha Foley, ed., *The Best American Short Stories 1950* (Boston: Houghton Mifflin, 1950); Herschel Brickell, ed., *Prize Stories of 1950: The O. Henry Awards* (Garden City, NY: Doubleday, 1950).
7. Bradbury, *Modern American Novel* 159.
8. Alan Nadel, *Containment Culture: American Narrative, Postmodernism, and the Atomic Age* (Durham: Duke UP, 1995) 4.
9. Harry S. Truman qtd. in Steven Casey, *Selling the Korean War: Propaganda, Politics, and Public Opinion, 1950–1953* (Oxford: Oxford UP, 2008) 69.
10. Louis Hartz, *The Liberal Tradition in America: An Interpretation of American Political Thought since the Revolution* (New York: Harcourt, Brace and World, 1955). There is a substantial body of research on the New York Intellectuals from recent years. See Neil Jumonville, *Critical Crossings: The New York Intellectuals in Postwar America* (Berkeley: U of California P, 2001); Terry A. Cooney, *The Rise of the New York Intellectuals: "Partisan Review" and Its Circle, 1934–1945* (Madison: U of Wisconsin P, 2004); and *The New York Intellectual Reader*, ed. Neil Jumonville (London: Routledge, 2007).
11. Hartz, *The Liberal Tradition* 1.
12. Ibid. 9.
13. Ibid. 13.
14. Alan Nadel, "Postwar America and the Story of Democracy," *National Identities and Post-Americanist Narratives*, ed. Donald Pease (Durham: Duke UP, 1994) 96–97.
15. Ibid. 113.

16. Lionel Trilling, *Beyond Culture* (New York: Harcourt Brace Jovanovich, 1965) 186.

17. Ibid. 221.

18. Geraldine Murphy, "Romancing the Centre: Cold War Politics and Classic American Literature," *Poetics Today* 9.4 (1988): 738.

19. Lionel Trilling, *The Liberal Imagination: Essays on Literature and Society* (London: Penguin, 1970) 221.

20. Dewey, *Freedom and Culture* 24.

21. Trilling, *Liberal Imagination* 221.

22. Trilling, *Beyond Culture* 186.

23. Trilling, *Liberal Imagination* 221.

24. Ibid. 214.

25. William Carlos Williams, *In the American Grain* (New York: New Directions, 1956) 153.

26. Bradbury, *Modern American Novel* 166.

27. Thomas Schaub, *American Fiction in the Cold War* (Madison: U of Wisconsin P, 1991) 25.

28. Bradbury, *Modern American Novel* 163

29. Schaub, *Cold War* 22; Bradbury, *Modern American Novel* 166.

30. Schaub, *Cold War* 33.

31. Ibid. 43.

32. Bradbury, *Modern American Novel* 162.

33. Nolan Miller, "The Short Story as a 'Young Art,'" *Antioch Review* 10.4 (1950): 544.

34. Ibid.

35. Irving Howe, "Tone in the Short Story," *Sewanee Review* 57.1 (1949): 141–42.

36. Edith R. Mirrielees, "Short Stories, 1950," *English Journal* 40.5 (1951): 247, 248.

37. Granville Hicks, "Our Novelists' Shifting Reputations," *English Journal* 40.1 (1951): 3, my emphasis.

38. Robert Daniel, "No Place to Go," *Sewanee Review* 56.3 (1948): 522.

39. Miller, "Young Art," 544.

40. A. L. Balder, "The Structure of the Modern Short Story," *College English* 7.2 (1945): 86.

41. Mirrielees, "Short Stories, 1950" 250.

42. Ihab Hassan, "The Victim: Images of Evil in Recent American Fiction," *College English* 21.3 (1959): 146.

43. Howe, "Tone" 142.

44. Dewey, *Freedom and Culture* 25.

45. Trilling, *Liberal Imagination* 22–23.

46. Schaub, *Cold War* 23.

47. Bradbury, *Modern American Novel* 167.

48. Ibid. 190.

49. Trilling, *Liberal Imagination* 213–14.

50. Truman, *Korean War* 69.

51. Ibid.

52. Dewey, *Freedom and Culture* 130.

53. Ibid. 162.

54. Bradbury, *Modern American Novel* 162

55. Schaub, *Cold War* 26.

56. Nadel, *Containment Culture* 4.

57. Ibid.

58. J. D. Gaddis, *Strategies of Containment: An Appraisal of American National Security Policy during the Cold War* (Oxford: Oxford UP, 2005) 6; Nadel, *Containment Culture* 2.

59. George Kennan qtd. in Gaddis, *Strategies of Containment* 49.

60. Nadel, *Containment Culture* 4.

61. Trilling, *Liberal Imagination* 22.

62. Ibid. 221.

63. Ibid. 26.

64. Schaub, *Cold War* 33.

65. Ibid. 26.

66. Trilling, *Liberal Imagination* 24, 220.

67. Schaub, *Cold War* 32.

68. Ibid. 34.

69. Ibid. 67.

70. Ibid. 51.

71. Ibid.

72. Bradbury, *Modern American Novel* 189.

73. Schaub, *Cold War* 68

74. Tanner, *City of Words* 15.

75. Andrew Levy, *The Culture and Commerce of the American Short Story* (Cambridge: Cambridge UP, 1993) 29.

76. Ibid.

77. Scofield, *American Short Story* 107.

78. Ibid. 183.

79. William H. Peden, "Publishers, Publishing, and the Recent American Short Story," *Studies in Short Fiction* 1.1 (1963): 42.

80. Trilling, *Beyond Culture* 214.

81. Murphy, "Romancing the Centre" 738.

82. Richard Chase, "A Novel Is a Novel," *Kenyon Review* 14.4 (1952): 678–84.

83. Ibid. 679.

84. Ibid.

85. Ibid. 682.

86. Ibid. 683.

87. Ibid.

88. Ralph Ellison, *The Collected Essays of Ralph Ellison,* ed. John F. Callahan (New York: Modern Library, 2003) 160.

89. Lawrence Buell, *The Dream of the Great American Novel* (Cambridge: Harvard UP, 2014) 105.

90. Ibid. 106.

91. Trilling, *Liberal Imagination* 220.

92. Donald Pease, "New Americanist Interventions," *Boundary 2* 17.1 (1990): 6.

93. Ibid. 4, 8.

94. Ibid. 8.

95. Ibid. 9.

96. Ibid. 12.

97. Ibid. 13.

98. Levy, *Culture and Commerce* 2.

99. Peden, "Recent American Short Story" 33.

100. Scofield, *American Short Story* 139.

101. Ernest Hemingway, "The Art of Fiction," *New Critical Approaches to the Short Stories of Ernest Hemingway*, ed. Jackson J. Benson (Durham: Duke UP, 1990) 3.

102. Paul Smith, "Hemingway's Early Manuscripts: The Theory and Practice of Omission," *Journal of Modern Literature* 10.2 (1983): 271.

103. Ibid. 276.

104. William Du Bois, "Books of the Times," *New York Times* 1 May 1953; James Kelly, "The Have-Not-Enoughs," *New York Times* 10 May 1953.

105. Charles Poore, "Books of the Times," *New York Times* 9 Apr. 1953.

106. Eudora Welty, "Threads of Innocence," *New York Times* 5 Apr. 1953.

107. Jean Cocteau, *Opium: The Diary of His Cure*, trans. Margaret Crosland (London: Peter Owen, 1990) 19.

108. Paul Bowles to Susan Sontag, 11 Nov. 1966, Charles E. Young Research Library's Department of Special Collections, UCLA.

109. Frances Kiernan, *Seeing Mary Plain: A Life of Mary McCarthy* (New York: Norton, 2000) 537.

110. Susan Rubin Suleiman, "Culture, Aestheticism and Ethics: Sontag and the 'Idea of Europe,'" *PMLA* 120.3 (2005): 839.

111. Susan Sontag, *Against Interpretation, and Other Essays* (London: Eyre and Spottiswoode, 1967) 5. Hereafter cited parenthetically.

112. Dana Polan, "Translator's Introduction," *Kafka: Towards a Minor Literature* (Minneapolis: University of Minnesota Press, 1986) xxiv.

113. Ibid. xxiii.

114. Giles Deleuze and Félix Guattari, *Kafka: Towards a Minor Literature*, trans. Dana Polan (Minneapolis: University of Minnesota Press, 1986) 18.

115. Ibid. 3.

116. Ibid. 7.

117. Ibid. 26.

118. John Cheever, "The Country Husband," *Collected Stories* (London: Vintage, 2010): 420–46. Hereafter cited parenthetically.

119. Jonathan Franzen, "The Birth of 'The New Yorker Story,'" *The 50s: The Story of a Decade*, ed. Henry Finder (New York: Random House, 2016): 597–600.

120. Ibid. 598.

121. Cortázar, "Some Aspects" 27.

122. Tennessee Williams, "The Human Psyche—Alone: *The Delicate Prey and Other Stories* by Paul Bowles," *Where I Live: Selected Essays*, ed. John S. Bak (New York: New Directions, 2009) 202.

123. Ibid. 203.

CHAPTER TWO

1. Mary McCarthy, "The Art of Fiction," *Paris Review* 27 (1962): 62.

2. Donald Barr, "Failure in Utopia," *New York Times* 14 Aug. 1949; Wendy Martin, "Mary McCarthy," *The Columbia Companion to the Twentieth-Century American Short Story,* ed. Blanche Gelfant (New York: Columbia University Press, 2001) x.

3. McCarthy, "The Art of Fiction" 72.

4. Mary McCarthy, *Memories of a Catholic Girlhood* (New York: Harcourt, Brace and World, 1957) 3, 4. Hereafter cited parenthetically.

5. McCarthy, "The Art of Fiction" 72. Mary McCarthy and Margaret Marshall, "Our Critics, Right or Wrong," *Nation* 23 Oct. 1935: 468–72; McCarthy and Marshall, "Our Critics, Right or Wrong II," *Nation* 6 Nov. 1935: 542–44; McCarthy and Marshall. "Our Critics, Right or Wrong III," *Nation* 20 Nov. 1935: 595–99; McCarthy and Marshall, "Our Critics, Right or Wrong IV," *Nation* 4 Dec. 1935: 653–55; McCarthy and Marshall, "Our Critics, Right or Wrong V," *Nation* 18 Dec. 1935, 717–19. Hereafter cited parenthetically.

6. Mary McCarthy, "I Was There But I Didn't See It Happen," *New Republic* 4 Nov. 1940: 633.

7. Mary McCarthy, "A Pudding of Saints," *New Republic* 2 Aug. 1933: 323.

8. Mary McCarthy, "Coalpit College," *New Republic* 2 May 1934: 343.

9. Mary McCarthy, "A Bolt from the Blue," *New Republic* 4 June 1962: 27. Hereafter cited parenthetically.

10. Norman Mailer, "The Mary McCarthy Case," *New York Review of Books* 17 Oct. 1963: 1. Hereafter cited parenthetically.

11. A. S. Byatt qtd. in Elizabeth Day, review of *The Group*, by Mary McCarthy, *Guardian* 29 Nov. 2009.

12. Charles Poore, "Mary McCarthy's Lives of the Vassari," *New York Times* 29 Aug. 1963.

13. Richard Sullivan, "Mary McCarthy Gives Some Vassar Alumnae 'F' as Human Beings," *Chicago Tribune* 15 Sept. 1963.

14. Edmund Fuller, "Eight Women Go Forth," *Wall Street Journal* 28 Aug. 1963.

15. Arthur Mizener, "Out of Vassar and on the Town," *New York Times* 25 Aug. 1963.

16. Tom Fitzpatrick, "Scanning the Paperbacks," *Chicago Tribune* 6 Oct. 1963.

17. Fuller, "Eight Women."

18. Mizener, "Out of Vassar."

19. John Chamberlain, "Books of the Times," *New York Times* 16 May 1942.

20. Edith Walton, "The Company She Keeps," *New York Times* 24 May 1942

21. Malcolm Cowley, "Bad Company," *New Republic* 25 May 1942: 737.

22. Chamberlain, "Books of the Times."

23. Walton, "Company She Keeps."

24. Chamberlain, "Books of the Times."

25. Cowley, "Bad Company" 737.

26. Chamberlain, "Books of the Times."

27. "Two Short Story Authors Show Special Talent," *Chicago Daily Tribune* 10 June 1942.

28. Chamberlain, "Books of the Times."

29. Walton, "Company She Keeps."

30. Orville Prescott, "Books of the Times," *New York Times* 29 Jan. 1943.

31. Martin, "Mary McCarthy" x; Jane Housham, "The Company She Keeps," *Guardian* 8 Nov. 2011, Web.

32. McCarthy, "The Art of Fiction" 58–94, 65.

33. McCarthy, *The Company She Keeps* (New York: Harcourt Brace, 1942). Hereafter cited parenthetically.

34. McCarthy, "The Art of Fiction" 65.

35. John Crowley, "Mary McCarthy's *The Company She Keeps*," *Explicator* 51.2 (1993): 111–15.

36. Dewey, *Freedom and Culture* 4.

37. Paul Giles, *American Catholic Arts and Fictions: Culture, Ideology, Aesthetics* (Cambridge: Cambridge UP, 2008) 457.

CHAPTER THREE

1. John Lahr, *Mad Pilgrimage of the Flesh* (London: Bloomsbury Circus, 2014) xiii.

2. David Savran, *Communists, Cowboys, and Queers: The Politics of Masculinity in the Work of Arthur Miller and Tennessee Williams* (Minneapolis: U of Minnesota P, 1992) ix.

3. Dennis Vannatta, *Tennessee Williams: A Study of the Short Fiction* (New York: Twayne, 1988) ix.

4. Savran, *Communists, Cowboys* 111.

5. Ibid.

6. Tennessee Williams, *The Selected Letters of Tennessee Williams: Volume 1: 1920–1945*, ed. Albert J. Devlin and Nancy M. Tischler (New York: New Directions, 2000) 211.

7. Tennessee Williams, *The Selected Letters of Tennessee Williams: Volume 2: 1945–1957*, ed. Albert J. Devlin and Nancy M. Tischler (New York: New Directions, 2004) 26–27.

8. Ibid. 67.

9. Ibid. 212.

10. Savran, *Communists, Cowboys* 113.

11. Williams, *Letters: Volume 2* 139.

12. Ibid. 563.

13. Joseph Wood Krutch, review of *A Streetcar Named Desire*, by Tennessee Williams, *Nation* 20 Dec. 1947: 686.

14. Mary McCarthy, "Oh, Sweet Mystery of Life," *Partisan Review* 15.3 (Mar. 1948): 360, 359.

15. Ibid. 358.

16. Ibid. 359

17. Ibid. 358.

18. Robert Roth, "Tennessee Williams in Search of a Form," *Chicago Review* 9.2 (1955): 86.

19. Ibid. 87.

20. James Kelly, "Madness and Decay," *New York Times* 2 Jan. 1955.

21. McCarthy, "Sweet Mystery" 359.

22. Elizabeth Hardwick, "Much Outcry; Little Outcome," *Partisan Review* 15.3 (Mar. 1948): 376.

23. Ibid.

24. Leslie Fiedler, "Poetry Chronicle," *Partisan Review* 15.3 (Mar. 1948): 381.

25. Clement Greenberg, "The Decline of Cubism," *Partisan Review* 15.3 (Mar. 1948): 366.

26. Ibid. 369

27. Jean-Paul Sartre, "For Whom Does One Write?" *Partisan Review* 15.3 (Mar. 1948): 318–19.

28. Ibid. 314.

29. Ibid. 315.

30. Williams, *Letters: Volume 1* 509.

31. Williams, "The Human Psyche—Alone," 19.

32. Chris Baldick and Jane Desmarais, introduction to *Decadence: An Anthology*, ed. Baldick and Desmarais (Manchester: Manchester UP, 2012) 1.

33. Williams, "The Human Psyche—Alone" 202.

34. Ibid. 203

35. Evan Brier, "Constructing the Postwar Art Novel: Paul Bowles, James Laughlin, and the Making of *The Sheltering Sky*," *PMLA* 121.1 (2006): 193.

36. Paul Bowles qtd. in Gena Dagel Caponi, *Conversations with Paul Bowles* (Jackson: UP of Mississippi, 1993) 36.

37. Tennessee Williams, *Memoirs* (New York: Doubleday, 1973), 159. See also Bowles's account in *Conversations with Paul Bowles* 36–37.

38. John Bak, *Tennessee Williams: A Literary Life* (New York: Palgrave Macmillan, 2013) 133.

39. Tennessee Williams, "An Allegory of Man and His Sahara," *New York Times* 4 Dec. 1949.

40. Paul Bowles, *In Touch: The Letters of Paul Bowles*, ed. Jeffrey Miller (New York: Farrar, Straus and Giroux, 1995) 228.

41. Paul Bowles, interview by Jeffrey Bailey, "The Art of Fiction LXVII: Paul Bowles," *Paris Review* 81 (1981): 75.

42. Bowles, *In Touch* 228.

43. Charles Bernheimer, *Decadent Subjects: The Idea of Decadence in Art, Literature, Philosophy, and Culture of the Fin de Siècle in Europe*, ed. T. Jefferson Kline and Naomi Schor (Baltimore: Johns Hopkins UP, 2002) 2.

44. Tennessee Williams, *Conversations with Tennessee Williams*, ed. Albert J. Devlin (Jackson: UP of Mississippi, 1986) 253.

45. Henry Miller, *The Time of Assassins: A Study of Rimbaud by Henry Miller* (New York: New Directions, 1956) vii.

46. Ibid. x.

47. Tennessee William, *One Arm and Other Stories* (New York: New Directions, 1948) 78. Hereafter cited parenthetically.

48. Williams, *Memoirs* 159.

49. Bowles, *Conversations* 58, 48.

50. Ibid. 96.

51. Nathan Tipton, "What's Eating Anthony Burns? Dismembering the Bodies That Matter in Tennessee Williams's 'Desire and the Black Masseur," *Southern Literary Journal* 63.1 (2010): 40.

52. Kelly, "Madness and Decay."

53. Williams, *Letters: Volume 2* 139.

54. Ben Brantley, "Hustler on the Streets, Missing Both a Limb and a Capacity to Feel," *New York Times* 9 June 2011.

55. Roth, "Tennessee Williams in Search of a Form" 86.

CHAPTER FOUR

1. Jean-Paul Sartre, *No Exit*, trans. Paul Bowles (New York: Samuel French 1958).

2. Driss ben Hamed Charhadi, *A Life Full of Holes*, trans. Paul Bowles (New York: Grove, 1964).

3. Paul Bowles, *The Delicate Prey and Other Stories* (New York: Random House, 1950). Hereafter cited parenthetically as *DP*.

4. Bowles, *In Touch* 219.

5. Bowles, interview by Bailey, "The Art of Fiction LXVII" 75.

6. Paul Bowles, *The Sheltering Sky* (New York: New Directions, 1949). Hereafter cited parenthetically.

7. Fanny Butcher, "A Brilliant First Novel That Lives," *Chicago Daily Tribune* 18 Dec. 1949.

8. Raj Chandarlapaty, *The Beat Generation and Counterculture: Paul Bowles, William S. Burroughs, Jack Kerouac* (New York: Peter Lang, 2009); Rob Wilson, "Masters of Adaptation: Paul Bowles, the Beats, and 'Fellaheen Orientalism,'" *Cultural Politics* 8.4 (2012): 193–206.

9. Bowles, "Windows on the Past," *Holiday* Jan. 1955: 35.

10. Bowles, *Conversations with Paul Bowles*, 94, 213. Hereafter cited parenthetically.

11. Paul Theroux, introduction to *The Sheltering Sky*, by Paul Bowles (London: Penguin, 2009) v.

12. The question of what constitutes "civilization" and Bowles's position toward it are challenging and deserve fuller attention. I analyze this within the particular context of surrealism later in this chapter.

13. James Lasdun, introduction to *Paul Bowles: Collected Stories* (London: Penguin, 2009) x.

14. Joyce Carol Oates, "Aspects of Self: A Bowles Collage," *Twentieth Century Literature* 32.3–4 (1986): 281.

15. Brian T. Edwards, *Morocco Bound: Disorienting America's Maghreb, from Casablanca to the Marrakech Express* (Durham: Duke UP, 2005) 83.

16. David Dempsey, "Cross Section," *New York Times* 15 Jan. 1950.

17. "Best Books I Read This Year," *New York Times* 4 Dec. 1949.

18. Williams, "An Allegory of Man and His Sahara" 21.

19. Cyril Connolly, "On Englishmen Who Write American," *New York Times* 18 Dec. 1949.

20. Williams, "Allegory" 21.

21. Paul Bowles qtd. in *What Good Are Intellectuals? 44 Writers Share Their Thoughts*, ed. Bernard Henry Lévy (New York: Algora, 2000) 6.

22. Paul Bowles and Phillip Ramey, "A Talk with Paul Bowles," www.paulbowles.org/talk .html.

23. In an interview by Daniel Halpern, Bowles emphasized that "of the published volumes, I like *The Delicate Prey* the most" (*Conversations* 99).

24. Brier, "Postwar Art Novel" 195.

25. Thomas Barbour, "Little Magazines in Paris," *Hudson Review* 4 (1951): 281.

26. Charles Jackson, "On the Seamier Side," *New York Times* 3 Dec. 1950.

27. Ibid.

28. Prescott, "Books of the Times" 21.

29. Barbour, "Little Magazines" 280.

30. Jackson, "Seamier Side."

31. Ibid.

32. Ibid.

33. Ibid.

34. Barbour, "Little Magazines" 280.

35. Prescott, "Books of the Times" 21.

36. Butcher, "Brilliant First Novel."

37. Jackson, "Seamier Side."

38. Ibid.; Barbour, "Little Magazines" 280.

39. Rear cover of *The Delicate Prey*, by Paul Bowles, Modern Classics ed. (London: Penguin, 2011). This edition included "The Delicate Prey," "A Distant Episode," and "The Circular Ruins."

40. Jackson, "Seamier Side."

41. Williams, "Allegory" 38.

42. Barbour, "Little Magazines" 280.

43. Bowles, *In Touch* 440.

44. Bowles, *What Good Are Intellectuals?* 28.

45. Catrina Neiman, introduction to *View: Parade of the Avant-Garde*, ed. Neiman (New York: Thunder's Mouth, 1991) xiii.

46. Bowles, *In Touch* 46, 47.

47. Ibid. 47.

48. Ibid. 70.

49. Paul Bowles to Neil Campbell, 29 July 1981, Harry Ransom Center, Texas.

50. Bowles qtd. in Virginia Spencer Carr, *Paul Bowles: A Life* (New York: Scribner, 2004) 46.

51. Bowles, foreword to *View: Parade of the Avant-Garde* xi.

52. Ibid., xi; Neiman, introduction to *View: Parade of the Avant-Garde* xii.

53. Neiman, introduction to *View: Parade of the Avant-Garde* xiii.

54. Bowles, interview by Bailey, "The Art of Fiction LXVII" 75.

55. Ibid. 76.

56. Ibid. 79.

57. Paul Bowles, "Bluey," *View* 3.3 (1943): 81–82.

58. Charles Henri Ford, "Contents," *View* 3.3 (1943). 71.

59. André Breton, *Manifestoes of Surrealism*, trans. Richard Seaver and Helen R. Lane (Ann Arbor: U of Michigan P, 1969) 26.

60. Ibid. 160.

61. Bowles, "Bluey" 81, 82.

62. Ibid. 82.

63. Breton, *Manifestoes* 26.

64. Bowles, "Bluey" 81, 82.

65. Ibid. 82.

66. "Personality Tests: Ink Blots Are Used to Learn How People's Minds Work," *Life* 7 Oct. 1946: 55.

67. For more on Stravinsky as an emblem for modernism, see Modris Eksteins, *Rites of Spring: The Great War and the Birth of the Modern Age* (Toronto: Lester and Orpen Dennys, 1989).

68. Peggy Glanville-Hicks, "Paul Bowles: American Composer," *Music and Letters* 26.4 (1945): 88.

69. Anne Foltz, "Paul Bowles," *Review of Contemporary Literature* 20.2 (2002): 84.

70. Arthur V. Berger, "The Music of Aaron Copland," *Musical Quarterly* 31.4 (1945): 420; Bob Gilmore, "Review of Paul Bowles on Music," *Music and Letters* 86.2 (2005): 318.

71. Glanville-Hicks, "American Composer" 88–89.

72. Ibid.

73. Foltz, "Paul Bowles" 81.

74. Tim Mangan, introduction to *Paul Bowles on Music*, ed. Mangan and Irene Herrmann (Berkeley: U of California P, 2003) ix.

75. Ibid. x.

76. Gilmore, "Review" 318.

77. Virgil Thomson, "Music: Two B's," *Paul Bowles: Music*, ed. Claudia Swann and Jonathan Scheffer (New York: Eos, 1995) 80, 81.

78. Jonathan Scheffer, introduction to *Paul Bowles: Music* 2.

79. Gena Dagel Caponi. "A Nomad in New York, 1933–1947," *Paul Bowles: Music* 75.

80. Scheffer, introduction to *Paul Bowles: Music* 2.

81. Bowles and Ramey, "Meet Prokofiev" 17.

82. Paul Bowles, "Bowles on Bowles," *Paul Bowles: Music* 6.

83. Ibid. 6, 7.

84. Ibid. 5.

85. Ibid. 6.

86. K. Robert Schwarz, "There Are Those Who Refuse to See Bowles as Anything More Than a Dilettante," *Paul Bowles: Music* 47.

87. Wayne Pounds, *Paul Bowles: The Inner Geography* (New York: Peter Lang, 1985) 424.

88. Edgar Allan Poe, "The Philosophy of Composition," *Edgar Allan Poe: Essays and Reviews*, ed. G. R. Thompson (New York: Library of America, 1984) 13.

89. Lasdun, introduction to *Paul Bowles: Collected Stories* v.

90. Hassan, "Review" 219.

CHAPTER FIVE

1. Eudora Welty, *A Curtain of Green* (New York: Doubleday, 1941), hereafter cited parenthetically; *The Wide Net* (New York: Harcourt, Brace, 1943); *The Golden Apples* (New York: Harcourt Brace, 1949).

2. Lionel Trilling, "An American Fairy Tale," *Nation* 19 Dec. 1942: 686.

3. Ibid. 687.

4. Eudora Welty, interview by Reynolds Price, *Eudora Welty: Photographs* (Jackson: UP of Mississippi, 1989) xvii.

5. Kay Boyle, "Full-Length Portrait," *New Republic* 24 Nov. 1941: 707.

6. Rose Feld, review of *A Curtain of Green* by Eudora Welty, *New York Herald Tribune* 16 Nov. 1941.

7. Marianne Hauser, "*A Curtain of Green* and Other New Works of Fiction," *New York Times Book Review* 1 Nov. 1941.

8. Louise Bogan, "The Gothic South," *Nation* 6 Dec. 1941: 572.

9. Feld, review.

10. Hauser, "*Curtain.*"

11. Ibid.

12. Feld, review.

13. Boyle, "Full-Length Portrait" 707.

14. Bogan, "Gothic South" 572.

15. Hauser, "*Curtain.*"

16. Trilling, "American Fairy Tale" 686.

17. Robert Molloy, "Elusive Tales from the Pen of a Newcomer," *New York Sun* 24 Sept. 1943.

18. Eugene Armfield, "Short Stories by Eudora Welty," *New York Times Book Review* 26 Sept. 1943.

19. Leo Lerman, "Daughter of the Mississippi," *New York Herald Tribune* 26 Sept. 1943.

20. "Sense and Sensibility," *Time* 27 Sept. 1943: 100.

21. Diana Trilling, "Fiction in Review," *Nation* 2 Oct. 1943: 386.

22. Isaac Rosenfeld, "Consolations of Poetry," *New Republic* 18 Oct. 1943: 525.

23. D. Trilling, "Fiction in Review" 386.

24. Rosenfeld, "Consolations of Poetry" 525.

25. Nadel, *Containment Culture*, 4.

26. Gaddis, *Strategies of Containment* 6; Nadel, *Containment Culture* 2.

27. Nadel, *Containment Culture* 4.

28. Eudora Welty, "Eudora Welty and Photography: An Interview," *Eudora Welty: Photographs,* ed. Reynolds Price (Jackson: UP of Mississippi, 1989) xiii.

29. Michael Kreyling, *Eudora Welty's Achievement of Order* (Baton Rouge: Louisiana State UP, 1980) 5.

30. Roland Barthes, *Camera Lucida: Reflections on Photography,* trans. Richard Howard (New York: Hill and Wang, 2010) 26–27.

31. Welty, "Welty and Photography" xiii.

32. Henri Cartier-Bresson, "Introduction to *The Decisive Moment,*" *Photographers on Photography,* ed. N. Lyons (Englewood Cliffs, NJ: Prentice-Hall, 1966) 44.

33. Welty, "Welty and Photography" xv.

34. Naoko Fuwa Thornton, *Strange Felicity: Eudora Welty's Subtexts on Fiction and Society* (Westport, CA: Praeger, 2003) 4.

35. Boyle, "Portrait" 707.

36. Christopher Benfy, "Emily Dickinson and the American South," *The Cambridge Companion to Emily Dickinson,* ed. Wendy Martin (Cambridge: Cambridge UP, 2002) 30.

37. Ibid. 78.

38. Boyle, "Portrait" 707.

39. Wendy Barker, "Emily Dickinson and Poetic Strategy," *The Cambridge Companion to Emily Dickinson* 77.

40. Emily Dickinson, *Complete Poems of Emily Dickinson,* ed. Thomas Johnson (Boston: Little, Brown, 1997) 248. Hereafter cited parenthetically.

41. Paul Giles, "'The Earth Reversed Her Hemispheres': Dickinson's Global Antipodality," *Emily Dickinson Journal* 20.1 (2011): 1, 8.

42. Peter Schmidt, *The Heart of the Story: Eudora Welty's Short Fiction* (Jackson: UP of Mississippi, 1991) xv.

43. Eudora Welty, "Must the Novelist Crusade?" *Atlantic Monthly* Oct. 1965: 104. Hereafter cited parenthetically.

CONCLUSION

1. Lionel Trilling, *Beyond Culture* (New York: Harcourt Brace Jovanovich, 1965) 186.

2. Charles E. May, *The Short Story: The Reality of Artifice* (New York: Twayne, 1995) 87.

3. Ibid. 88.

4. Ibid. 89

5. Julian Cowley, "'weeping map intense activity din': Reading Donald Barthelme," *University of Toronto Quarterly* 60.2 (1990): 292.

6. Lydia Davis, "Art of Fiction 227," *Paris Review* 212 (Spring 2015): 175.

7. Patrick O'Donnell, *The American Novel Now: Reading Contemporary American Fiction since 1980* (Oxford: Wiley, 2010) 15.

8. Christopher Gair, "'Perhaps the Words Remember Me': Richard Brautigan's Very Short Stories," *Western American Literature* 47.1 (2012): 5.

9. Joan Didion, "Art of Fiction 71," *Paris Review* 74 (Fall/Winter 1978): 146.

10. Joan Didion, interview by Maria Popova, *brainpickings* 19 Feb. 2014, www.brainpickings. org/2014/02/19/joan-didion-telling-stories/.

Bibliography

Armfield, Eugene. "Short Stories by Eudora Welty." *New York Times Book Review* 26 Sept. 1943: BR3.

Bak, John. *Tennessee Williams: A Literary Life.* New York: Palgrave Macmillan, 2013.

Balder, A. L. "The Structure of the Modern Short Story." *College English* 7.2 (1945): 86–92.

Baldick, Chris, and Jane Desmarais, eds. *Decadence: An Anthology.* Manchester: Manchester UP, 2012.

Barbour, Thomas. "Little Magazines in Paris." *Hudson Review* 4 (1951): 278–83.

Barker, Wendy. "Emily Dickinson and Poetic Strategy." *The Cambridge Companion to Emily Dickinson.* Ed. Wendy Martin. Cambridge: Cambridge UP, 2002. 77–90.

Barr, Donald. "Failure in Utopia." *New York Times* 14 Aug. 1949.

Barthes, Roland. *Camera Lucida: Reflections on Photography.* Trans. Richard Howard. New York: Hill and Wang, 2010.

Benfy, Christopher. "Emily Dickinson and the American South." *The Cambridge Companion to Emily Dickinson.* Ed. Wendy Martin. Cambridge: Cambridge UP, 2002. 30–50.

Benson, Jackson J., ed. *New Critical Approaches to the Short Stories of Ernest Hemingway.* Durham: Duke UP, 1990.

Berger, Arthur V. "The Music of Aaron Copland." *Musical Quarterly* 31.4 (1945): 420–47.

Bernheimer, Charles. *Decadent Subjects: The Idea of Decadence in Art, Literature, Philosophy, and Culture of the Fin de Siècle in Europe.* Ed. T. Jefferson Kline and Naomi Schor. Baltimore, Johns Hopkins UP, 2002.

Bogan, Louise. "The Gothic South." *Nation* 6 Dec. 1941: 572.

Bowles, Paul. "The Art of Fiction LXVII." *Paris Review* 81 (1981): 62–89.

———. "Bowles on Bowles." *Paul Bowles, Music.* Ed. Claudia Swan and Jonathan Scheffer. New York: Eos Music, 1995. 5–8.

———. *The Delicate Prey.* New York: Random House, 1950.

———. *In Touch: The Letters of Paul Bowles.* Ed. Jeffrey Miller. New York: Farrar, Straus and Giroux, 1995.

———. *The Sheltering Sky.* New York: New Directions, 1949.

Boyle, Kay. "Full-Length Portrait." *New Republic* 24 Nov. 1941: 707.

Bradbury, Malcolm. *The Modern American Novel.* Oxford: Oxford UP, 1983.

Brantley, Ben. "Hustler on the Streets, Missing Both a Limb and a Capacity to Feel." *New York Times* 9 June 2011.

Breton, André. *Manifestoes of* Surrealism. Trans. Richard Seaver and Helen R. Lane. Ann Arbor: U of Michigan P, 1969.

Brickell, Herschel, ed. *Prize Stories of 1950: The O. Henry Awards.* Garden City, NY: Doubleday, 1950.

Brier, Evan. "Constructing the Postwar Art Novel: Paul Bowles, James Laughlin, and the Making of *The Sheltering Sky.*" *PMLA* 121.1 (2006): 186–99.

Buell, Lawrence. *The Dream of the Great American Novel.* Cambridge: Harvard UP, 2014.

Butcher, Fanny. "A Brilliant First Novel That Lives." *Chicago Daily Tribune* 18 Dec. 1949.

Caponi, Gena Dagel. *Conversations with Paul Bowles.* Jackson: UP of Mississippi, 1993.

Carr, Virginia Spencer. *Paul Bowles: A Life.* New York: Scribner, 2004.

Cartier-Bresson, Henri. Introduction to *The Decisive Moment: Photographers on Photography.* Ed. N Lyons. Englewood Cliffs, NJ: Prentice-Hall, 1966. 44–45.

Casey, Steven. *Selling the Korean War: Propaganda, Politics, and Public Opinion, 1950–1953.* Oxford: Oxford UP, 2008.

Chamberlain, John. "Books of the Times." *New York Times* 16 May 1942.

Chandarlapaty, Raj. *The Beat Generation and Counterculture: Paul Bowles, William S. Burroughs, Jack Kerouac.* New York: Peter Lang, 2001.

Charhadi, Driss ben Hamed. *A Life Full of Holes.* Trans. Paul Bowles. New York: Grove, 1964.

Chase, Richard. "A Novel Is a Novel." *Kenyon Review* 14.4 (1952): 678–84.

Cheever, John. *Collected Stories.* London: Vintage, 2010.

Cocteau, Jean. *Opium: The Diary of His Cure.* Trans. Margaret Crosland. London: Peter Owen, 1990.

Cooney, Terry A. *The Rise of the New York Intellectuals: Partisan Review and Its Circle, 1934–1945.* Madison: U of Wisconsin P, 2004.

Connolly, Cyril. "On Englishmen Who Write American." *New York Times* 18 Dec. 1949.

Cortázar, Julio. "Some Aspects of the Short Story." *Review of Contemporary Fiction* 19.3 (1999): 25–33.

Cowley, Julian. "'weeping map intense activity din': Reading Donald Barthelme." *University of Toronto Quarterly* 60.2 (1990): 292–304.

Cowley, Malcolm. "Bad Company." *New Republic* 25 May 1942.

Crowley, John. "Mary McCarthy's *The Company She Keeps.*" *Explicator* 51.2 (1993): 111–15.

Daniel, Robert. "No Place to Go." *Sewanee Review* 56.3 (1948): 522–30.

Davis, Lydia. "Art of Fiction 227." *Paris Review* 212 (Spring 2015): 168–95.

Deleuze, Giles, and Félix Guattari. *Kafka: Towards a Minor Literature.* Trans. Dana Polan. Minneapolis: U of Minnesota P, 1986.

Dempsey, David. "Cross Section." *New York Times* 15 Jan. 1950.

Dewey, John. *Freedom and Culture.* New York: Capricorn, 1963.

Dickinson, Emily. *Complete Poems of Emily Dickinson.* Ed. Thomas Johnson. Boston: Little, Brown, 1997.

Didion, Joan. "Art of Fiction 71." *Paris Review* 74 (Fall/Winter 1978): 142–63.

Du Bois, William. "Books of the Times." *New York Times* 1 May 1953.

Edwards, Brian T. *Morocco Bound: Disorienting America's Maghreb, from Casablanca to the Marrakech Express.* Durham: Duke UP, 2005.

Eksteins, Modris. *Rites of Spring: The Great War and the Birth of the Modern Age.* Toronto: Lester and Orpen Dennys, 1989.

Ellison, Ralph. *The Collected Essays of Ralph Ellison.* Ed. John F. Callahan. New York: Modern Library, 2003.

Feld, Rose. Review of *A Curtain of Green* by Eudora Welty. *New York Herald Tribune* 16 Nov. 1941.

Fiedler, Leslie. "Poetry Chronicle." *Partisan Review* 15.3 (March 1948): 381.

———. "Style and Anti-Style in the Short Story." *Kenyon Review* 13.1 (1951): 155–56, 158, 168, 170–72.

Fitzpatrick, Tom. "Scanning the Paperbacks." *Chicago Tribune* 6 Oct. 1963.

Foley, Martha, ed. *The Best American Short Stories 1950.* Boston: Houghton Mifflin, 1950.

Foltz, Anne. "Paul Bowles." *Review of Contemporary Literature* 20.2 (2002): 81–120.

Franzen, Jonathan. "The Birth of 'The New Yorker Story.'" *The 50s: The Story of a Decade.* Ed. Henry Finder. New York: Random House, 2016. 597–600.

Fuller, Edmund. "Eight Women Go Forth." *Wall Street Journal* 28 Aug. 1963.

Gaddis, J. D. *Strategies of Containment: An Appraisal of American National Security Policy during the Cold War.* Oxford: Oxford UP, 2005.

Gair, Christopher. "'Perhaps the Words Remember Me': Richard Brautigan's Very Short Stories." *Western American Literature* 47.1 (2012): 5–21.

Giles, Paul. *American Catholic Arts and Fictions: Culture, Ideology, Aesthetics.* Cambridge: Cambridge UP, 2008.

———. "'The Earth Reversed Her Hemispheres': Dickinson's Global Antipodality." *Emily Dickinson Journal* 20.1 (2011): 1–21.

Gilmore, Bob. "Review of Paul Bowles on Music." *Music and Letters* 86.2 (2005): 318.

Glanville-Hicks, Peggy. "Paul Bowles: American Composer." *Music and Letters* 26.4 (1945): 88–96.

Greenberg, Clement. "The Decline of Cubism." *Partisan Review* 15.3 (March 1948): 366–69.

Hardwick, Elizabeth. "Much Outcry; Little Outcome." *Partisan Review* 15.3 (March 1948): 376.

Hartz, Louis. *The Liberal Tradition in America: An Interpretation of American Political Thought since the Revolution.* New York: Harcourt, Brace and World, 1955.

Hassan, Ihab. "The Victim: Images of Evil in Recent American Fiction." *College English* 21.3 (1959): 140–46.

Hauser, Marianne. "*A Curtain of Green* and Other New Works of Fiction." *New York Times Book Review* 1 Nov. 1941: BR6.

Hicks, Granville. "Our Novelists' Shifting Reputations." *English Journal* 40.1 (1951): 1–7.

Housham, Jane. "The Company She Keeps." *Guardian* 8 Nov. 2011.

Howe, Irving. "Tone in the Short Story." *Sewanee Review* 57.1 (1949): 141–52.

Jackson, Charles. "On the Seamier Side." *New York Times* 3 Dec. 1950.

Jumonville, Neil. *Critical Crossings: The New York Intellectuals in Postwar America.* Berkeley: U of California P, 2001.

Kelly, James. "The Have-Not-Enoughs." *New York Times* 10 May 1953.

———. "Madness and Decay." *New York Times* 2 Jan. 1955.

Kreyling, Michael. *Eudora Welty's Achievement of Order.* Baton Rouge: Louisiana State UP, 1980.

Krutsch, Joseph Wood. Review of *A Streetcar Named Desire* by Tennessee Williams. *Nation* 20 Dec. 1947: 686–87.

Lahr, John. *Mad Pilgrimage of the Flesh.* London: Bloomsbury Circus, 2014.

Lamb, Robert. *Art Matters: Hemingway, Craft, and the Creation of the Modern Short Story.* Baton Rouge: Louisiana State UP, 2010.

Lerman, Leo. "Daughter of the Mississippi." *New York Herald Tribune* 26 Sept. 1943.

Levy, Andrew. *The Culture and Commerce of the American Short Story.* Cambridge: Cambridge UP, 1993.

McCarthy, Mary. "The Art of Fiction 27." *Paris Review* 27 (1962): 58–94.

———. "A Bolt from the Blue." *New Republic* 4 June 1962: 21–27.

———. "Coalpit College." *New Republic* 2 May 1934: 343.

———. *The Company She Keeps.* New York: Harcourt, Brace and World, 1942.

———. *The Group.* New York: Harcourt, Brace and World, 1963.

———. "I Was There but I Didn't See It Happen." *New Republic* 4 Nov. 1940: 633–35.

———. *Memories of a Catholic Girlhood.* New York: Harcourt, Brace and World, 1957.

———. "Oh, Sweet Mystery of Life." *Partisan Review* 15.3 (March 1948): 358–60.

———. "Pudding of Saints." *New Republic* 2 Aug. 1933: 523.

McGurl, Mark. *The Program Era: Postwar Fiction and the Rise of Creative Writing.* Cambridge: Harvard UP, 2011.

Mailer, Norman. "The Mary McCarthy Case." *New York Review of Books* 17 Oct. 1963: 1–3.

Martin, Wendy. "Mary McCarthy." *The Columbia Companion to the Twentieth-Century American Short Story*. Ed. Blanche Gelfant. New York: Columbia UP, 2001.

May, Charles E. *The Short Story: The Reality of Artifice*. New York: Twayne, 1995.

Miller, Henry. *The Time of Assassins: A Study of Rimbaud*. New York: New Directions, 1956.

Miller, Nolan. "The Short Story as a 'Young Art.'" *Antioch Review* 10.4 (1950): 543–46.

Mirrielees, Edith R. "Short Stories, 1950." *English Journal* 40.5 (1951): 247–54.

Mizener, Arthur. "Out of Vassar and on the Town." *New York Times* 25 Aug. 1963.

Molloy, Robert. "Elusive Tales from the Pen of a Newcomer." *New York Sun* 24 Sept. 1943.

Murphy, Geraldine. "Romancing the Centre: Cold War Politics and Classic American Literature." *Poetics Today* 9.4 (1988): 737–47.

Nadel, Alan. *Containment Culture: American Narrative, Postmodernism, and the Atomic Age*. Durham: Duke UP, 1995.

———. "Postwar America and the Story of *Democracy*." *National Identities and Post-Americanist Narratives*. Ed. Donald Pease. Durham: Duke UP, 1994.

Neiman, Catrina, ed. *View: Parade of the Avant-Garde*. Ed. Neiman. New York: Thunder's Mouth, 1991.

Oates, Joyce Carol. "Aspects of Self: A Bowles Collage." *Twentieth Century Literature* 32, nos. 3–4 (1986): 281.

O'Donnell, Patrick. *The American Novel Now: Reading Contemporary American Fiction since 1980*. Oxford: Wiley, 2010.

Pease, Donald. "New Americanist Interventions." *Boundary 2* 17.1 (1990): 1–37.

Peden, William H. "Publishers, Publishing, and the Recent American Short Story." *Studies in Short Fiction* 1.1 (1963): 33–44.

Poe, Edgar Allan. "The Philosophy of Composition." *Edgar Allan Poe: Essays and Reviews*. Ed. G. R. Thompson. New York: Library of America, 1984. 13–15.

Poore, Charles. "Books of the Times." *New York Times* 9 Apr. 1953.

———. "Mary McCarthy's Lives of the Vassari." *New York Times* 29 Aug. 1963.

Pounds, Wayne. *Paul Bowles: The Inner Geography*. New York: Peter Lang, 1985.

Prescott, Orville. "Books of the Times." *New York Times* 29 Jan. 1943.

Rosenfeld, Isaac. "Consolations of Poetry." *New Republic* 18 Oct. 1943: 525.

Roth, Robert. "Tennessee Williams in Search of a Form." *Chicago Review* 9.2 (1955): 86–94.

Sartre, Jean Paul. "For Whom Does One Write?" *Partisan Review* 15.3 (March 1948): 314–19.

———. *No Exit.* Trans. Paul Bowles. New York: Samuel French 1958.

Savran, David. *Communists, Cowboys, and Queers: The Politics of Masculinity in the Work of Arthur Miller and Tennessee Williams.* Minneapolis: U of Minnesota P, 1992.

Schaub, Thomas. *American Fiction in the Cold War.* Madison: U of Wisconsin P, 1991.

Schmidt, Peter. *The Heart of the Story: Eudora Welty's Short Fiction.* Jackson: UP of Mississippi, 1991.

Smith, Paul. "Hemingway's Early Manuscripts: The Theory and Practice of Omission." *Journal of Modern Literature* 10.2 (1983): 268–88.

Suleiman, Susan Rubin. "Culture, Aestheticism and Ethics: Sontag and the 'Idea of Europe.'" *PMLA* 120. 3 (2005): 839–42.

Sullivan, Richard. "Mary McCarthy Gives Some Vassar Alumnae 'F' as Human Beings." *Chicago Tribune* 15 Sept. 1963.

Tanner, Tony. *City of Words: American Fiction 1950–1970.* London: Jonathan Cape, 1971.

Thornton, Naoka Fuwa. *Strange Felicity: Eudora Welty's Subtexts on Fiction and Society.* Westport, CA: Praeger, 2003.

Thomson, Virgil. "Music: Two B's." *Paul Bowles: Music.* Ed. Claudia Swann and Jonathan Scheffer. New York: Eos, 1995. 80–81.

Tipton, Nathan. "What's Eating Anthony Burns? Dismembering the Bodies That Matter in Tennessee Williams's 'Desire and the Black Masseur.'" *Southern Literary Journal* 63.1 (2010): 39–58.

Trilling, Diana. "Fiction in Review." *Nation* 2 Oct. 1943: 386–87.

Trilling, Lionel. "An American Fairy Tale." *Nation* 19 Dec. 1942: 686–87.

———. *Beyond Culture.* New York: Harcourt Brace Jovanovich, 1965.

———. *The Liberal Imagination: Essays on Literature and Society.* London: Penguin, 1970.

Vannatta, Dennis. *Tennessee Williams: A Study of the Short Fiction.* New York: Twayne, 1988.

Walton, Edith. "The Company She Keeps." *New York Times* 24 May 1942.

Welty, Eudora. *A Curtain of Green.* New York: Doubleday, 1941.

———. *Eudora Welty: Photographs.* Jackson: UP of Mississippi, 1989.

———. *The Golden Apples.* New York: Harcourt, Brace and World, 1949.

———. "Must the Novelist Crusade?" *Atlantic Monthly* Oct. 1965: 104–8.

———. "Threads of Innocence." *New York Times* 5 Apr. 1953.

———. *The Wide Net.* New York: Harcourt, Brace and World, 1943.

Williams, Tennessee. "An Allegory of Man and His Sahara." *New York Times* 4 Dec. 1949.

———. *Conversations with Tennessee Williams.* Ed. Albert J. Devlin. Jackson: UP of Mississippi, 1986.

————. "The Human Psyche—Alone: *The Delicate Prey and Other Stories* by Paul Bowles." *Where I Live: Selected Essays.* Ed. John S. Bak. New York: New Directions, 2009. 202–3.

————. *Memoirs.* New York: Doubleday, 1973.

————. *One Arm and Other Stories.* New York: New Directions, 1948.

————. *The Selected Letters of Tennessee Williams: Volume 1.* Ed. Albert J. Devlin and Nancy M. Tischler. New York: New Directions, 2000.

————. *The Selected Letters of Tennessee Williams: Volume 2.* Ed. Albert J. Devlin and Nancy M. Tischler. New York: New Directions, 2004.

Williams, William Carlos. *In the American Grain.* New York: New Directions, 1956.

Wilson, Rob. "Masters of Adaptation: Paul Bowles, the Beats, and 'Fellaheen Orientalism.'" *Cultural Politics* 8.4 (2012): 193–206.

Index

Abbott, Berenice, 166
aesthetics, minor, 1, 16, 19, 35–36, 41,
    44–47, 50–52, 100, 145, 154, 183–184
Anderson, Sherwood, 35
Antheil, George, 139
Arendt, Hannah, 54
Arp, Jean, 98

Barth, John, 179, 182
Barthelme, Donald, 179–180, 182
Barthes, Roland, 166
Baudelaire, Charles, 101
Beats, the, 25–27, 122, 181
Bellow, Saul, 7, 30, 153
Bernstein, Leonard, 140
Borges, Jorge Luis, 122, 144, 150, 179
Bowles, Paul, 2, 4–5, 17, 19, 22, 40,
    42–44, 47, 50, 57, 96, 111, 117, 153–154,
    157–158, 164, 175, 178–182, 184, 186;
    and automatic writing, 136, 145,
    150–151, 183; Bluey, 136–138; "By the
    Water," 146–147; "Call at Corazón,"
    149, "Circular Valley, The," 144; as
    composer, 52, 100, 119, 121–123, 136,
    138–143, 145, 150–151; Delicate Prey,
    The, 4, 5, 99–102, 113, 120–123, 125–
    130, 143–150, 152–154; "Delicate Prey,
    The" (story), 102, 112, 148–149; "Dis-
    tant Episode, A," 128, 148–149; "Echo,
    The," 138, 149; Let It Come Down, 31;
    and Morocco, 23, 119–120, 128, 165; as
    music critic, 141, 185; Sheltering Sky,
    The, 4, 100, 102–103, 120, 122–129,
    145; "Spire Song," 135; "Under the Sky,"
    98–99, 144

Boyle, Kaye, 7, 156, 159–160, 170
Brautigan, Richard, 181–182
Breton, André, 133–134, 136
Burroughs, William, 24, 91, 122
Byatt, A. S., 65

Caesar, Julius, 57
Calder, Alexander, 122
canon, American literary, 28, 32–34, 36,
    95–96
Capote, Truman, 97, 103
Carroll, Lewis, 137
Cartier-Bresson, Henri, 166–167
Carver, Raymond, 180
Chase, Richard, 10, 32, 154
Cheever, John, 2, 7, 37–38, 47–50
Chekhov, Anton, 162, 181
Cocteau, Jean, 40–41, 44
Copland, Aaron, 123, 135, 140–141
Cowley, Malcolm, 69, 71
Cold War, the, 1, 8–10, 19–21, 28–30,
    34, 39, 40, 77, 88, 90, 92–95, 118, 124,
    152, 178
Communism, 8–9, 23, 34, 39, 53, 55,
    97–98, 159, 164, 177
containment culture, 22–23, 25–27, 41,
    52, 164, 177, 183–184
Cortázar, Julio, 1, 50, 51

Dali, Salvador, 122, 134–135, 162
Davis, Lydia, 180–181
de Chirico, Giorgio, 134
decadence, 4, 101, 104–108, 114
Deleuze, Giles, and Guattari, Felix, 41,
    44–47, 51–52

democracy, 6, 8–10, 18–21, 23, 28–29,
  32–33, 39
Dewey, John, 6–7, 11, 77
Dickinson, Emily, 170–176
Didion, Joan, 179, 182–183

Eliot, T. S., 124, 139
Ellison, Ralph, 30–33, 39, 44, 153
Ernst, Max, 122, 134–135

Faulkner, William, 7, 16, 124, 157, 174
Fiedler, Leslie, 7, 10–11, 13–15, 17–20,
  27–28, 34, 36, 40, 97–98, 125–130, 154
Ford, Charles Henri, 121, 133, 136
fragmentation, 16, 35–36, 62, 71–73, 79,
  109–117, 145, 180–184
Franzen, Jonathan, 47
freedom (aesthetic), 6, 15–17, 19–20, 25,
  30–32, 39, 122, 132, 156, 182–184
freedom (ideology), 1, 4, 6–11, 18, 20–23,
  26, 33, 41–42, 52, 77–79, 97–98, 119,
  124, 127, 132–133, 153, 164
Frost, Robert, 97

gender, 22, 75, 153
Ginsberg, Allen, 122
Greenberg, Clement, 98–99
Guggenheim, Peggy, 135

Hassan, Ihab, 18, 35, 149
Hardwick, Elizabeth, 97, 103
Hartz, Louis, 8–9
Hellman, Lillian, 54
Hemingway, Ernest, 16, 28, 35–37, 124,
  181–182
Howard, Robert E., 89
Howe, Irving 15, 18, 28

James, Henry, 24
Jane Eyre, 85
Jolas, Eugene, 134
Joyce, James, 35, 139

Kafka, Franz, 41, 44–47, 52
Kaufman, Moisés, 115
Kennan, George, 23
Kerouac, Jack, 24, 44, 52, 122
Klee, Paul, 134

Laughlin, James, 89, 91–92, 99, 103–107,
  114
liberalism, 8–9, 11–13, 19, 22, 30–31,
  34–35, 54, 179
Life Full of Holes, A, 120
Lorca, Frederico García, 122

Mailer, Norman, 64–65, 67–69, 78
Mansfield, Katherine, 15, 156, 158, 181
Marshall, Margaret, 58, 60–61
Matthiessen, F. O., 33–34, 96, 98
McCarthy, Joseph, 93. *See also* McCarthyism
McCarthy, Mary, 2–5, 7, 14, 17, 19, 22,
  42–44, 47, 50, 93, 111, 118, 153–154,
  164–165, 178–180, 186; *Cast a Cold Eye*,
  53–54, 62; *Company She Keeps, The*, 27,
  53–54, 56, 59, 63, 64, 69–79, 81–87,
  95, 113, 154, 164, 184–185; as critic, 53,
  55, 58–64, 77, 94–98, 175, 183–185;
  "Cruel and Barbarous Treatment," 76,
  81–82; "Ghostly Father I Confess," 84–
  87; *Group, The*, 2, 53, 54, 64–69, 70–72,
  78, 80–81, 83–84; *Groves of Academe,
  The*, 54, 64; *How I Grew*, 54; "Man in
  the Brooks Brothers Shirt, The," 73–76;
  Memoirs of a Catholic Girlhood, 54–57,
  79–81, 82–84; *Oasis, The*, 54, 64; and
  religion, 56–57, 75; "Rogue's Gallery,"
  73, 76, 81–84; *Venice Observed*, 66
McCarthyism, 9, 23, 68, 90, 93–94, 108, 118
Miller, Arthur, 88
Miller, Henry, 106–107
Miró, Joan, 98

Nabokov, Vladimir, 2, 63–64
Nation, The, 33, 55, 58, 62, 94, 153, 157, 162

New Criticism, 13, 22–23, 33
New Republic, The, 55, 63, 69, 156, 163
New School of Decadence, 100–101,
103–104. *See also* decadence; Bowles,
Paul; Capote, Truman; Vidal, Gore;
Williams, Tennessee
New York Intellectuals, 8–10, 12–13,
22–23, 27, 30, 187n10. *See also* liberal-
ism, public intellectuals
New Yorker, The, 2, 37–38, 47, 80

Oates, Joyce Carol, 123
omission, theory of, 34, 36–37, 40

Partisan Review, 2, 53, 55, 77, 97–98, 102,
119
photography, 47–51, 155, 165–167
Picasso, Pablo, 98
Poe, Edgar Allan, 28, 35, 43, 120–121, 132,
146, 157
Pollock, Jackson, 98
Porter, Katherine Anne, 155–159
Pound, Ezra, 139, 177
public intellectuals, 3, 42, 55 56, 77 78
Pynchon, Thomas, 179, 182

Rahv, Phillip, 54–55, 77
Ray, Man, 155
realism, 12, 13, 18, 20, 24, 30–31
Rimbaud, Arthur, 99, 101, 105–107, 109

Salinger, J. D., 7, 37–39, 47
Sartre, Jean-Paul, 99, 119
Satie, Erik, 140–141
Schwitters, Kurt, 98
Second World War, the, 6–7, 10, 12, 19,
24, 29, 38, 53, 62, 164
Sex and the City, 72
sexuality, 3, 22, 74, 90–92, 94–97, 106,
153, 184
Shaw, Irwin, 7, 17
Sontag, Susan, 41–44

Stein, Gertrude, 135, 139
Stravinsky, Igor, 139–140, 142
southern gothic, 5, 97, 155, 157–158,
160–162, 169–170
surrealism, 119, 121, 133–138, 141–142,
150–151

Tanner, Tony, 6, 19, 21, 26
Thomson, Virgil, 123, 139–142, 185
Time (magazine), 92, 108, 162
Trilling, Diana, 162–163
Trilling, Lionel, 10–13, 17–19, 24, 27, 30,
33–34, 52, 54, 77, 98, 148, 155, 159, 161,
163, 179
Truman, Harry S., 8, 20–21

Vassar College, 53, 62, 68, 80
Verlaine, Paul, 101, 106, 122, 135
Vidal, Gore, 103
View, 119, 125, 133–138

Welty, Eudora, 2, 5, 19, 22, 44, 47, 50, 57,
154, 177–179, 181; as critic, 39, 174–176,
185; *Curtain of Green, A*, 154 163, 165,
167, 170; *Golden Apples, The*, 154; as
photographer, 52, 155–156, 161, 164–
167; "Piece of News, A," 167–169;
Robber Bridegroom, The, 154–155, 159–
161; *Wide Net, The*, 154, 161–163
Wilde, Oscar, 14, 106
Wilder, Thornton, 59
Williams, Tennessee, 2–5, 19 22, 44, 47,
50, 57, 119, 153–154, 157–158, 165,
170, 175, 178–179, 181–182, 184, 186;
"Angel in the Alcove," 111; *Battle of
Angels*, 89; as critic, 52, 99, 100–103,
107, 124, 185; "Field of Blue Children,
The," 109–110, 112; "Desire and the
Black Masseur," 113–114, 117; *Glass
Menagerie, The*, 89, 90, 93–94, 100;
Hard Candy, 92; *Memoirs*, 112–113;
"Night of the Iguana," 110–112; *One*

Williams, Tennessee (*continued*)
  Arm 3, 5, 89, 91–93, 95, 98, 106–118,
  153, 185; "One Arm" (story), 91, 115–
  118; as playwright, 88–91, 93–95, 100,
  183; "Portrait of a Girl in Glass," 89,
  115; *Streetcar Named Desire, A,* 90, 93–
  96; "Vengeance of Nitocris, The," 89
Williams, William Carlos, 7, 12, 124, 130, 177
Wilson, Edmund, 53, 69
Woolf, Virginia, 139, 156